The Two Doors

of

Life

Which Door Will Your Life Open?

Heaven or Hell

by Curtis D. Johnson

The Two Doors
of
Life

Which Door Will Your Life Open?

Heaven or Hell

by Curtis D. Johnson

LOWBAR
PUBLISHING COMPANY

905 South Douglas Avenue • Nashville, Tennessee 37204
Phone: 615-972-2842
E-mail: Lowbarpublishingcompany@gmail.com
Web site: www.Lowbarbookstore.com

Printed in the United States of America

ISBN: 978-0-9886237-5-0

Lowbar Publishing Company
Nashville, Tennessee 37204
615-972-2842
E-mail: Lowbarpublishingcompany@gmail.com
Web site: www.Lowbarbookstore.com

For additional information, workshop, and seminars, here is how you may
contact the author:

Curtis D. Johnson
Decatur, IL
217-454-7289

Editor: Sharon K. Sims

Graphic and Cover Design Artist: Norah S. Branch

"Scripture used in this work is taken from the King James Version unless
otherwise stated"

This book is dedicated to:

My Parents and Siblings
Thank you for showering me with love and support all of my life.

And to:

My wife, Jane; my daughters, Kellie and Meredith;

My son, Brian; my grandchildren, Kiara, Caidyn, and Miles

You are my life.

And to:

My Heavenly Father

You are the source of my life.

Table of Contents

The Calling of God on My Life

I had been sick with a very bad cold and flu and had missed the previous Sunday service. I'd been to the doctor twice and still I was not getting any better. The chills, fever, sore throat, and long coughing spells were still plaguing me. However, I made up my mind that today I was going to church, no matter what!

I took my shower and was getting dressed, all the while thinking "Lord, am I ever going to get over this cold?" Immediately, I heard (in my spirit) the Lord's response that as long as I did to not do what He had told me to do, I was not going to get better! I answered, "Lord, how am I to know what you want me to do?" He very plainly said, "Preach my Word!" I questioned God and thought, "Lord, how do I know these are Your thoughts and not my thoughts?" I always asked God for a real sign so that I would know that I was called and not someone who just went on their own. God told me, "I gave you a sign when you saw me at Barnes Jewish Hospital standing beside Jane after her surgery. I was walking through the room three times during her stay there. That was your sign." "Yes Lord, I did see that and I will never forget what You allowed me to see."

The sign that I had asked from God was similar to the sign that Gideon asked. Gideon asked for a wet fleece on a dry ground, and then a dry fleece on a wet ground. Judges 6:36-40 says, *"And Gideon said unto God, If thou wilt save Israel by mine hand, as thou has said, Behold I will put a fleece of wool in the floor; and if the dew be on the fleece only, and it be dry upon all the earth beside, then shall I know that thou wilt save Israel by mine hand, as thou hast said. And it was so; for he rose up early on the morrow and thrust the fleece, and wringed the dew out of the fleece, a bowl full of water. And Gideon said unto God, let not thine anger be hot against me, and I will speak but this once: let me prove, I pray thee, but this once with the fleece; let it now be dry only upon the fleece, and upon all the land let there be dew. And God did so that night: for it was dry upon the fleece only, and there was dew on all the ground."*

God did something very unusual for me as a confirmation. The Sunday I was determined to go to church, I went downstairs to share with Jane what had just happened. I began to tell her about my conversation with the Lord, and she interrupted me and said, "What's wrong with your shirt?" I looked down at my gray tee-shirt and saw unusual wet markings like handprints all over the front of it. Jane said, "Why is your tee-shirt wet like that?" I hadn't noticed or felt anything wet on my body and when I checked, my skin was completely dry! Looking at the tee-shirt again, it looked like long finger marks from a big hand were directly over my heart!

I remembered the specific sign that I had asked of the Lord. My body was completely dry, yet the tee-shirt I was wearing was wet only on the exact finger marks over my heart. I believe through faith, that God had indeed called me into the ministry of the Most High God. It is because of this faith that I will now step out and believe that God will confirm and sustain me as I begin my journey.

As I left for church that morning, the sun seemed more radiant than ever before. This was a different day. The clouds covered the sun, which looked like a big eye in the sky looking down at me. I felt God's presence all around me in ways that I could not truly understand. The weather was actually very windy and getting worse. As I approached the church, there were dark clouds in the sky. Later on that day I learned there were several tornados that had passed over our city, Decatur, IL, but had devastated several towns in Illinois including Washington, Peoria, Champaign and Chicago. They even had to stop the Chicago Bears' football game for fear of the tornado passing through the area. There had been so many leaves in my yard, but it appeared as though a big broom had come through and put my leaves in my neighbor's yard, leaving only a small portion for me to rake. He even cleaned my yard for me!

I had a talk with my pastor and shared with him what God had called me to do. My pastor was very attentive to all that I said and told me, "If you think you have been called, it is not up to me to say otherwise. That is between you and God." To God be the Glory!

Curtis D. Johnson

November 18, 2013

The Two Doors of Life

Chapter 1

I was lying on my sofa one evening watching the NBA playoff games. It was in early April, 2010, and for no apparent reason, a strong voice entered my mind. This voice gave me a specific thought that was combined with a strong vision. It was as if SOMEONE was speaking directly into my mind. It was a still small voice, but the voice was as clear as a bell ringing in my ears.

The words were: "In life, there are two doors." Immediately, I began to see a vision of the significance of these two doors. The vision that was manifesting itself within my mind's eye clearly revealed that it is of critical importance that we choose correctly which door of life to enter. This manifestation became my burden, or assignment, to complete.

The two doors of life that God's Spirit spoke into my mind that day were later confirmed for me in Deuteronomy 30:15-19. The book of Deuteronomy is also known as the "second giving of the Mosaic Laws" to God's chosen people before they were to enter into the Promise Land, known as Canaan.

People have two choices in this life:

1) We can choose to obey God and keep His commandments and live a blessed life now and have eternal life when we die; or,

2) We can choose to disobey God and forsake all His commandments and live a life under our own rules. This kind of living leads to eternal damnation.

We better know which direction we are traveling; we must be sure, because our decision after death is final and irreversible.

Let's do a quick review of the two choices that God gave His chosen people back in Deuteronomy. These few scriptures confirm and lay the foundation for the remainder of this book.

In Deuteronomy 30: 15-19, the choice of death and life are set before them.

[15] *"See, I have set before thee this day life and good, and death and evil;* [16] *In that I command thee this day to love the LORD thy God, to walk in His ways, and to keep His commandments and His statutes and His judgments, that thou mayest live and multiply: and the LORD thy God shall bless thee in the land whither thou goest to possess it.* [17] *But if thine heart turn away, so that thou wilt not hear, but shalt be drawn away, and worship other gods, and serve them;* [18] *I denounce unto you this day, that ye shall surely perish, and that ye shall not prolong your days upon the land, whither thou passest over Jordan to go to possess it.* [19] *I call heaven and earth to record this day against you, that I have set before you life and death, blessing and cursing: therefore choose life, that both thou and thy seed may live."*

We'll learn more about the number two later.

The message of the scriptures above is very clear to all who believe the Word of God. If you still choose not to believe, then I pray that you continue to read this book. My prayer is that after you finish this book, you will re-evaluate your life in reference to the Word of God and make a change.

The Bible tells us to repent, confess our sins to God and stop living a sinful life. We need to find a good church home, and devote our life to studying and meditating on the Word. *"If you draw near to him, He will draw near to you."* (James 4:8) But, be careful!

There are many false religions, false teachers, false preachers and churches whose sole purposes are to line their pockets with money and to lead people astray. This is why we are to study God's Word and follow the leading of the Holy Spirit that leads and guides in truth. The Holy Spirit knows the heart and He will not allow anyone to take advantage of you.

Depending upon which door you open, you will be eternally blessed or eternally cursed. Choose carefully which door you enter and which door you choose to live the rest of your life.

We all entered this life the same way - male and female. Our birth into this world, this planet, this dispensation, was recorded in God's Book of Life and authentically confirmed. Additionally, birth records, early baby photographs, family announcements, baby showers, etc., all announced to the world our arrival. We all entered and passed through the matrix of birth into this human stage of existence called life that we now enjoy. When we die, we will exit this life through one of these two doors. Not only are the two doors invisible and impossible to discern with the human eye, they are everlasting and immutable. This means, that the door from which you exit this life will be an eternal door which is closed forever! You will not be given a second chance to exit and re-enter the other door that you failed to choose when you left this world in death - so choose wisely, my friend. Let me say this again, no one can see either door; yet both doors are easy to find if your heart is in the right place.

A few years later the "two doors" was revealed to me as the doors of life and death that we all must go through to reach eternity. The most significant thing to know about either of these two doors is that once you go through them, you cannot return again. If, for example, you went through a particular door and you did not like what you saw, you will not be allowed to go back through that door and get, as golfer's say, a "do over" shot at this life again. Once you have entered and passed through the door, you will find yourself staring into the face of eternity. Therefore, be wise before you reach those two doors of life: choose the way, choose the truth, and choose the light. You need to choose Jesus.

A major question that should be asked is: How do we humans end up at either of the two doors of life? It all depends on the road of life that we have been travelling. This road starts the minute we are born and some of us never change our road of travel. We continue on a path of destruction from birth to the grave.

Still, others during the process of life will one day change and repent of their sinful and wicked ways and switch to the road of righteousness. It is only there where they learn about a Savior, called Jesus. After some time, they will begin to fellowship with the body of Christ (the church) and seriously begin to study the Word of God and learn about Him. They will soon learn that it is through His grace and mercy that we are saved through faith in Him and not by our own works.

In Mathew 7:13-14, Jesus tells His disciples which gate to enter that leads to salvation. He said, *13 "Enter ye in at the strait gate: for wide is the gate, and broad is the way, that leadeth to destruction, and many there be which go in thereat: 14 Because strait is the gate, and narrow is the way, which leadeth unto life, and few there be that find it."*

In other words, Jesus is saying there are two roads in this life. The wide gate or road is full of people. It is crowded and well-traveled every day. The people on this road are self-willed; they feel no need for a Savior. They are sure of themselves. Some are mighty, some are rich and powerful; some are world leaders; and there are some who are very religious and pastor huge church assemblies. What they fail to realize is this road leads to a particular door that opens into eternal separation from God. Proverb 16:25 tells us that *25 "There is a way that seemeth right unto a man, but the end* thereof are the ways of *death".* Following the crowd is not always the best decision to make when it comes to decisions with eternal implications.

Let's not forget about Noah and his family of eight individuals. They were the only survivors when God destroyed the world with a flood. Therefore, doing what may seem right to man could be entirely wrong in reference to the will of God. We are to seek God's will for us and not follow our own ideas and desires.

The narrow gate or small path leads to the door that opens into eternal acceptance and oneness with God. This is the road that is referred to in Mathew 7:14, *"Strait is the gate, and narrow is the way, which leadeth unto life, and few there be that find it."* How do we find this narrow gate? The answer is recorded for us in John 10:9 where Jesus tells us: *"I am the door: by me if any man enter in, he shall be saved, and shall go in and out, and find pasture."*

Jesus also tells us in John 14:6 – *"I am the way, the truth, and the life: no man cometh unto the Father, but by me."* Jesus' words are clear. The way to eternal salvation is through Him. By no other way can a man be saved. Good works alone won't get you there. Money, power, race, church membership, positions in life, etc. - nothing will get you into heaven except the blood of Jesus. You must humbly submit yourself and be born again to make it. Only the truly righteous shall see God.

Two kinds of people are mentioned in the Bible - the believer (sheep) and the nonbeliever (goats). With that as a foundation, let's review what is going to happen to the two kinds of people as revealed to us in the book of St. Mathew 25:31-46 in reference to the coming last day of judgment of all mankind. (Sheep will be to the right and the goats to the left.)

Jesus said:

> 31 *"When the Son of Man shall come in his glory, and all the holy angels with him, then shall he sit upon the throne of his glory: 32 And before him shall be gathered all nations: and he shall separate them one from another, as a shepherd divideth his sheep from the goats: 33 And he shall set the sheep on his right hand, but the goats on the left. 34 Then shall the King say unto them on his right hand, Come, ye blessed of my Father, inherit the kingdom prepared for you from the foundation of the world: 35 For I was an hungred, and ye gave me meat: I was thirsty, and ye gave me drink: I was a stranger, and ye took me in: 36 Naked, and ye clothed me: I was sick, and ye visited me: I was in prison, and ye came unto me. 37 Then shall the righteous answer him, saying, Lord, when saw we thee an hungred, and fed thee? or thirsty, and gave thee drink? 38 When saw we thee a stranger, and took thee in? or naked, and clothed thee? 39 Or when saw we thee sick, or in prison, and came unto thee? 40 And the King shall answer and say unto them, Verily I say unto you, Inasmuch as ye have done it unto one of the least of these my brethren, ye have done it unto me. 41 Then shall he say also unto them on the left hand, Depart from me, ye cursed, into everlasting fire, prepared for the devil and his angels: 42 For I was an hungred, and ye gave me no meat: I was thirsty, and ye gave me no drink: 43 I was a stranger, and ye took me not in: naked, and ye clothed me not: sick, and in prison, and ye visited me not. 44 Then shall they also answer him, saying, Lord, when saw we thee an hungred, or athirst, or a stranger, or*

naked, or sick, or in prison, and did not minister unto thee? ⁴⁵ Then shall he answer them, saying, Verily I say unto you, Inasmuch as ye did it not to one of the least of these, ye did it not to me. ⁴⁶ And these shall go away into everlasting punishment: but the righteous into life eternal.

I do not need to say any more on this. Jesus has already said all there is to say: (Sheep will go to the right – Goats will go to the left.) Which side will your life be on? Review Matthew 7:13-14 to understand the black door. The one door is a very big imposing and authoritatively looking door while the other door is small and of no particular beauty to the eye. They stand directly opposite each other. Like two gladiators from antiquity ready for battle, they face each other. They stand their ground and nothing can or will cause them to deviate from their divinely-sanctioned position in life.

The larger door is a beautifully bold red door with a rich lacquered finish. This door is very shiny and it reminds me of a car that has been washed and waxed to perfection. This door also has a deep ebony black interior and looks elegant and mysterious. It has decorative and mysterious-looking designs (very pleasing to the eyes) around the sides, middle, top and bottom. The door knob on this beautiful door appears to be made of pure gold. Isaiah 53:2 explains more about this door. The smaller door is a very plain looking door. It does not have any outstanding features. The one thing that both doors have in common is life, because they are both living entities. They stand silently facing each other through a generation which includes the creation of man. Yet, ideologically, they are as far apart as the east is from the west.

Behind the beautiful black/red door, you will hear the sounds of merriment, laughter, women and men at play, music, excitement that is very similar to an exciting party in progress. It will sound like the kind of party you might expect to find when the world is celebrating the birth of the New Year. The music is "bumping". The tempo is steady with a strong "funky" baseline. There are people at this party, some we know, and others we do not know. As you listen outside of this door, you can hear the voices of some of your best friends. You can also hear the voices of some of your own family members. Everyone seems to be having a good time laughing, and enjoying each other.

As you open the door for a peek inside, you are hit with the irresistible smell of good food. People from all races and nationalities are at the party and representatives from the world's most powerful and politically correct politicians are there. The rich and famous are there; big name movie stars, and major platinum recording artist "rappers" are there. "Man what a party" you say; "I need to get in there and see what's going on."

That's when you hear the seductive voice of the "sin of unbelief", better known as Satan. The devil knows exactly what to say as he begins to "whisper" into your ears. If you listen carefully you can actually hear the "hisses" like a snake, as he invites you to come on in and join the party. The unknown voice says: "There is no cost to come in, to see what's going on, to look around; and to enjoy what the world has to offer. As a matter of fact," the voice continues, "I've been waiting for you. I've been watching you and I have always wanted to get to know you and to show you my side of life - the fun side."

The sin of unbelief is the main prerequisite and is a non-negotiable contract for living comfortably behind the black/red door. This requirement states that all the inhabitants that enter and choose to live their life behind the black/red door of life must be in agreement with its owner – the devil. His mandate is: Everyone who follows him must also worship him! The Devil's people, his followers, cannot be followers of Jesus Christ, or believe in God. This spiritual truth is confirmed in Genesis 3:15, when God Almighty, not the devil, caused "enmity" to eternally exist between the seed of the serpent and the seed of His people.

The enemy of our soul (the devil) and of God knows that as long as people are un-believers, they will continue to practice the sin of unbelief. This practice will ultimately lead them to their death and destruction. If the devil can keep them believing in the sin of unbelief and they unrepentantly die in their un-belief, they will be his servants forever; and they will be eternally separated from God.

Tragic Examples of the Sin of Unbelief

Chapter 2

Let's meet a few of the people the devil has skillfully maneuvered to trust in him. Remember, there are many, many, more who are being poisoned by his lies. At one time, I was one of the many people whose mind had been corrupted by Satan to the point I no longer desired to see right vs wrong. My life had begun to take a downward spiral into experimentation with drugs, and alcohol. My faith in God was in a range of minuscule at best, to dead and none existent. My lifestyle was beginning to get out of control to the point of self-destruction. I had lost my focus in life and was drowning my troubles with bottles of booze. I was now living a life of self–pleasure, of satisfying the demands of my flesh. I did not want to do those things that were pleasing to God. As sad as it is to say this, I have to admit it as truth. I hope that this admission of truth will save someone else who is struggling with any kind of addiction and drug abuse. **Jesus is the only answer!**

I thank the Lord for coming into my life and saving me from Satan's grasp. The devil knows the sin of unbelief is the primary cause of all the "pure evil" that is present in the world today. I am talking about the kind of evil that allows a full grown man to sexually abuse and kill a seven year old girl. When caught, the man fails to admit his sins and ask for forgiveness then goes on to hang himself in his own jail cell, to avoid facing the responsibility for his own crime. Following are grievous examples of the sin of unbelief.

Ryan Brunn

I am referencing the case of a 20 year old maintenance man - Ryan Brunn of Canton, Georgia. He was facing life in prison for raping, torturing and finally killing his seven year old child/victim that he abducted from a playground near her apartment complex. Her body was later found in a trash bin.

Mr. Brunn was found guilty on December 2, 2011 for the murder and killing of *Jorely Rivera.* He was sentenced to life in prison without the possibility of parole for his crime. However, on January 20, 2012, Mr. Brunn hung himself in his jail cell to avoid facing the punishment of his crime - life imprisonment.

Apparently, Mr. Brunn, like so many other non-believers, had a false sense of security. People like this actually think that they are in control of their destiny. They view their life or death as a slave to them only. In other words, it is their decision if they should live or die. People with this mindset, similar to Mr. Brunn, think that they can do anything they want and if they are caught, they will take their own life and get out of this life free, or more specifically, an out-of-jail card. Wrong! Wrong! Wrong! Just Wrong!

Evidently, Mr. Brunn did not read the Bible. Because, if he had, he would have known that after death comes the judgment. What we do in this life will be judged, your belief will have nothing to do with it. We learn in the book of 2nd Corinthians 5: 8 which states: *"We are confident, I say, and willing rather to be absent from the body, and to be present with the Lord."*

This means that after death the judgment will come. You (your spirit) will be in the presence of God immediately after your death. You will not escape this judgment. I believe that the sin of unbelief is the driving force behind all the atrocities that we see in the world today. This sin, in my opinion, is responsible for all the murders, rapes, robberies, child molestations, racial hatred, mass murders, and the list goes on and on.

The Lord God always confirms His Word. As I was about to leave this distressing topic on child abuse as it relates to unbelief in man, the Holy Spirit directed me to a few more cases. The next case of child abuse is almost identical to the child abuse case previously shared.

This case was reported by television media and in our local newspaper and on the internet. Mr. Jarred Harrell was given life in prison for murder and dumping the body of a seven year old girl in Florida. He admitted in court to kidnapping, raping, murdering and dumping the girl in a trash bin. He took a plea deal to avoid the death penalty.

God's response to child abuse is clear: He says in the book of Matthew 25:40, *"And the King shall answer and say unto them, Verily I say unto you, In as much as ye have done it unto one of the least of these my brethren, ye have done it unto me."* I ask this question: "How demented and demonic of spirit must a person be to commit such an evil, despicable and heartless crime against an innocent child?" Anybody that can do this to a child, or to anyone for that matter, and go on living their life in normal society as though they have done nothing wrong, is beyond the human mind's ability to understand.

I feel if a person is so bold, cruel and unmerciful to children, then let them be given long prison sentences and physically punished for their crimes. Here is what I am proposing: Each state in the U.S. of America takes a position of "zero tolerance" on child abuse. Each state should enact laws that bring to light special punitive and physical punishment laws for all child molesters and child killers.

I would propose a law that, although cruel, might help deter others, and would recommend: Any person that is found guilty of raping and killing an innocent child is sentenced. It is my recommendation that this person also be given a year of daily, physical abuse. For example: In addition to his sentence of life in prison without parole, the authorities should for each day for a year, at exactly the same time every day, tie this person across a barrel hand to feet, and take a thick long paddle, leather strap, cane, or whip, and for the next ten minutes, give him a good paddling. This is done to him as a daily reminder of the cruelty and without-mercy sin that he committed against an innocent child.

This is yet another article that also appeared in our local newspaper on February 4, 2012. This story took place in Los Angeles, California at an inner-city elementary school. This is the school where a teacher, Mark Berndt, was accused of committing lewd acts on twenty-three children.

Mr. Berndt worked for the school for thirty-two years. He is accused of committing lewd acts on 23 children, ages six to ten years old. As of this writing, he remains in jail and his bail is $23 million dollars.

The second teacher is Martin B. Springer, age forty-nine. He was arrested for fondling two girls in his classroom. His bail was set at $2 million dollars. The victims in this case were seven and eight year olds from Miramonte Elementary School.

This case of child abuse was so bad that the Los Angeles School district drastically closed the whole school for two days while they were investigating the inappropriate behavior that was reported. This story made national headlines across the nation. I read that the elementary school, when it reopened, did so with new staff. One hundred twenty staff members were replaced.

In light of the immorality that seems to be running wild - not just in our school system - but in our society and country as a whole, it seems very illogical to me, that we have people who still hold to the position of unbelief – and say that God does not exist. We have teachers who are immoral, teaching and instructing our children. And, we have the nerve to question the existence of a Holy God. If man is so smart, why can't we hire teachers who are not child molesters, and perverts?

The fact is we cannot govern our own lives. Question: What makes some people, and especially unbelievers, so sure that the God of Creation is not real? Why do unbelievers throughout the history of man somehow come to the false conclusion that the statues, commandments, and ordinances of the Holy God do not apply to them; that somehow, because of their unbelief, they are exempt from God's laws. Wow – talk about our human arrogance! "Lord, help, me to open their eyes."

The truth is that all the words that God spoke, starting in Genesis 1:1 and all the way through to the book of Revelation 22:21, still exist and apply literally to all mankind today. It applied to all the generations that preceded us, and it still applies to this new and so-called modern and technically "savvy" face-bookers/twitter generation as well. Oh foolish man, you better wake up, and get in a hurry to change your life.

The sin of unbelief also allows our lawmakers to pass laws that make it legal for same sex marriages to flourish. This law of civil unions is nothing more than the devil in disguise - working through man to try and usurp God's laws of nature. Remember what the Lord Jesus said to us in 1 Peter 5:8 *"Be sober, be vigilant; because your adversary the devil, as a roaring lion, walketh about, seeking whom he may devour."* The devil is a deceiver. He knows that the sin of "sodomy" is an old sin that is against God.

God completely destroyed the cities of Sodom and Gomorrah (Genesis 18: 20-21) and the surrounding communities for this sexually immoral sin. His judgment on homosexual sin is to serve as a reminder to all mankind not to duplicate this sin in following generations. Not only is man now repeating the sexually immoral sins of Sodom and Gomorrah, we are taking it to a new level. We are making laws that mandate same sex unions as an alternative legal lifestyle with all the privileges of holy matrimony that was sanctioned by Almighty God.

God's Word is clear regarding the sacredness of matrimony between a man and a woman, as ordained by God. Anything or any law that seeks to take precedence over the law of God will encounter severe and dreadful consequences. Look at all the proponents for same sex marriage by big name celebrities. The list is endless. You cannot turn on the television without seeing celebrities who flaunt their lifestyle for the whole world to see. Some of them boldly project their lifestyle (same sex marriage) as an alternative to the ordained path of life that was breathed into our human creation by the Almighty God of Creation.

Many laws that were once illegal and considered immoral in this country have now been made legal. It is like the clay telling the potter what is best, or the two year old granddaughter making decisions and dictating to her family what is best for the family. It is like the "grunt" on the battle field telling the general with what military strategies to engage the enemy. Or the patient - who has no medical school training - telling the doctor what to do/ not to do in the upcoming surgery. It is like man telling God, "I know what is best for me; not you." Do not think the Lord God will not deal with such high-minded arrogance, especially when it applies to His Word. Please take note and never forget this: God always honors His Word!_

The devil "hisses" into your ear again. He says, "Life lived behind the black/red door allows you to live your life any way you want. That's our motto here." "Who are you?" you politely ask. The voice replies, "I am the god of this world. What do you say, come on in? It's all here waiting for you just behind my door." The voice is a caring voice that gives the impression of complete trustworthiness and sincerity on the part of the host of this grand party. But what the host of this party conveniently failed to mention is the road of life that leads to this door is like a game similar to the old "pinball machine" with its hidden holes in the floor and sides of the machine.

Remember when this game first came out? You would put a coin in the machine and it would light up and make weird and funny sounds. Then, when you pulled the knob back to launch the steel ball forward , the ball would run into different obstacles and bounce around, back and forth, up and down, east to west, and side to side. Eventually all the balls fell through one particular hole and did not come back. In short, the game was over.

Does the name James Eagan Holmes, from Aurora, Colorado ring a bell? This young man at the young age of twenty-four is considered to be the worst mass killer in American history. I remember at the time of this horrific crime, my family and I were on vacation in Orlando, Florida. We had just returned to our apartment from dinner with friends, when we were shocked to learn of the mass killings of innocent people who were eagerly waiting to see the recently released Batman Movie Trilogy: _"The Dark Night Rises."_ People, who are fans of the batman genre of movie, had packed the movie theater. The movie showing was scheduled to start at midnight.

The movie started on a Friday night July 20, 2012, and no one would hardly think or suggest a need for caution. I am sure none of the movie goers ever suspected their very lives were in danger and about to be dramatically changed forever. Shortly after the movie started, Mr. Holmes entered the theater through an unlocked emergency exit door he had rigged to stay open and wearing what some movie goers say was a military camouflaged suit. He was heavily armed with an AR -15 assault rifle. This weapon is capable of holding 100 rounds of ammunition. He also had Remington 12 gauge shot gun, and a .40 Glock hand gun as a side arm.

Mr. Holmes' personal assault gear included wearing a ballistic helmet, a bullet-proof vest, bullet-proof leggings, gas mask and gloves. He, without mercy, coolly set off multiple smoke bombs (tear gas) inside the packed movie theater, and began his deadly assault to kill innocent people. After all the rapid fire shooting stopped, twelve people were killed and fifty-eight others were left with serious to life threatening injuries.

According to police sources, Mr. Holmes referred to himself as "The Joker" which is a reference to the villain of the movie "The Dark Knight." To add to his desire to fit the character of the Joker or Dark Knight of the movie, Mr. Holmes had his hair completely dyed red to fit the movie image of the Joker.

When Mr. Holmes was arrested, he warned the arresting police officers that his apartment was completely booby-trapped with flammable and explosive material. To add to the mystique surrounding Mr. Holmes, he was not your typical everyday terrorist. He was originally from San Diego, California. He is a Caucasian, and from all I could find on him, he is the product of an educated family. He moved to Aurora, Colorado to pursue his doctorate in the medical field called Neuroscience, which is the study of the nervous system and advances the understanding of human thought, emotion, and behavior. Neuroscientists use tools ranging from computers to special dyes to examine molecules, nerve cells, networks, brain systems, and behavior. From these studies, they learn how the nervous system develops and functions normally and what goes wrong in neurological disorders.

A trained neuroscientist studies questions like: What is the mind? Why do people feel emotions? What are the underlying causes of neurological and psychiatric disorders? These are among the many mysteries being unraveled by neuroscientists.

Could it be that Mr. Holmes found himself involved with questions that he could not answer, and his brain somehow malfunctioned? It would seem to me that on the day that he committed this awful crime spree, he was clearly showing no mercy, and based on what he did, he was emotionless as he killed helpless men, women, and children. This mass murder caused many to take a second look at the Second Amendment, with specific reference to the outlaw or banning of assault weapons.

Ironically, President Barack Obama had previously been quoted as saying that we should look at and review our gun laws with regards to assault weapons. He was bombarded with opposition from the NRA for taking this position. Moreover, the majority of the Republican Party and also a few members of his own Democratic Party opposed him. A few descending democrats joined forces with their republican peers/friends to fight against the President's assault gun proposal. They seemed to lack the intestinal fortitude to do what was right! Therefore, they tucked their collective tails and yielded to the demands of the powerful NRA. That is the perception that many in the news media confirmed.

But my question is: What could cause a 24-year-old doctoral student with no criminal record, to organize, plan, and carry out one of the most vicious mass murders in our U.S. history? I am no psychologist, but my opinion is that people who are truly insane lack the patience and discipline necessary to organize, plan, and strategically implement their deadly illusions. I could be wrong.

My opinion of Mr. Holmes is that he came under the influence of a demonic "evil spirit", a spirit of the devil. In John 10:10, Jesus called Satan a thief. He says, *"The thief ("Satan" - emphasis mine) cometh not, but for to steal, and to kill, and to destroy: I am come that they might have life, and that they might have it more abundantly."*

Therefore, whenever I see mass murders and killings, I know that the devil has made his presence felt in some unsuspecting soul. Man has a hard time trying to make sense out of true evil. True evil is of the devil. It is a spirit that has been present on earth long before we got here and it will be here until the Lord God returns to rule. If you spell the name of "devil" backwards, the word is "lived". Additionally, when you first spell the word "devil" and take away the first letter "D" – the remaining letters spell the word "evil." Make no mistake, the enemy of our soul, the devil, is very real. But we give thanks to God, who has complete control over the evil spirits of this world, spirits who would destroy all of God's creation if it were not for the work of the Holy Spirit of God which holds it back.

The evil spirit of hatred that caused Mr. Holmes, to so coolly and without mercy, kill, murder, and severely injure women, men, and children on that fateful night, is the same spirit of evil hatred that allowed Bobby Frank Cherry, Thomas Blanton, Herman Frank Cash, Roberts Chambliss, all members of the United Klan of America, a Ku Klux Klan racial terrorist group, to plant bombs loaded with dynamite in the basement of the 16th Street Baptist Church in Birmingham, Alabama on September 15, 1963.

When the bombs went off, twenty-two God-fearing innocent people were severely injured, and four young black girls (basically all babies) were killed instantly. Killed in the explosion were: Addie Mae Collins, age fourteen, Cynthia Wesley, age fourteen, Carole Roberts, age fourteen, and Denise McNair, age eleven. On May 24, 2013, President Barack Obama awarded the Congressional Medal of Honor to the families of the victims of the Birmingham, Alabama massacre.

Too many of the minorities living during the turbulent fifties and sixties in America, stood against inhuman treatment and faced down the Jim Crow racist laws and considered the acts that were perpetrated against them as nothing short of cold blooded murder and domestic terrorism. The planting of a bomb in a church and killing innocent black children, is no different than the act committed by two brothers on April 15, 2013. Tamerlan Tsarnaev and his younger brother Dzhokar Tsarnaev were both responsible for planting homemade bombs in the midst of spectators who were gathered to watch the 116th running of the Boston Marathon. This event was first started back in April, 1897 and has gained worldwide fame for professional runners around the world who come to Boston to compete.

These four beautiful black girls were never given the chance to blossom, mature, and live, because of the racial hatred that was prevalent in the land of America in 1963. I believe it is still alive and well in 2013. If anyone is so naïve as to think that racial hatred is a thing of the past, you need only to take a good honest look at the 2012 Presidential election campaign that was waged against President Obama by members of Congress, and some of the rich and powerful racists in the good old USA.

It was that same evil spirit of racial hatred that resulted in the deaths and whole scale slaughter of over six- million Jews by Adolf Hitler. The list of mass killings as a result of evil hatred is endless.

I truly stand on and believe what God's Word says in the book of Galatians 6:7, *"be not deceived; God is not mocked: for whatsoever a man soweth, that shall he also reap. For he that soweth to his flesh shall of the flesh reap corruption; but he that soweth to the Spirit shall of the Spirit reap life everlasting."*

I want to just briefly point out one more case of the evil that lurks deep with the hearts of man, especially, in the hearts of men who do not acknowledge, or who were taught not to fear the Lord. I want to share very briefly about the awful and mind-boggling murder of twenty young children, along with the deaths of six of their teachers, who will forever be remembered infamously as The Sandy Hook Heroes.

In the early morning hours of December 14, 2012, pure evil broke into the Sandy Hook Elementary School in the human form of twenty-four year old man by the name of Adam Lanza. The school is located in the small community of Newtown, Connecticut. Newtown is located 45 miles south west of Hartford, Connecticut and 60 miles north east of New York.

What could cause Mr. Lanza to, without mercy, gun down and take the innocent lives of twenty helpless school children, all under the age of ten? He also killed six adults at the school after he had already killed his own mother as she slept in her bed that fateful morning. It would be totally inhuman not to ask the one question "Why? Why?" What did the kids do to cause Mr. Lanza to just kill them? He committed suicide before the arresting authorities could confront him. Yes, he took the coward's way out.

When I look at the pictures of this young man, he seems to be almost too meek and timid-looking to be considered the second worst mass school shooter in U.S. history. I can't even begin to imagine or to understand how much evil and hatred one must have in his heart to just kill this mother as she slept in her bed. What kind of relationship did they have? There are far too many questions that will probably go unanswered, but the one thing I am sure of is this: Mr. Lanza did not fear the Lord Jesus. To do what he did tells me that he did not know the Lord. The God that we serve is a God of love, not a God who tells someone to massacre innocent people just because you're having a bad day.

We learn from reading John 10:10-11 the following: *"The thief cometh not, but for to steal, and to kill, and to destroy: I am come that they might have life, and that they might have it more abundantly. I am the good shepherd: the good shepherd giveth his life for the sheep".*

■ ■ ■

Whenever we see death on a major scale, it is a sure "trademark" and a purposely left behind calling card of Satan. It is way of telling the world that he is truly the enemy of God and His creation. The taking of innocent lives is demonic and goes as far back as King Herod.

Another horrible evil was of Jimmy Lee Dykes, who is sixty-five years old and was reported in the news of taking hostage a five year old boy and kept him in an underground bunker for more than three days. He had snatched the boy off the school bus after shooting and killing the bus driver.

This is yet another horrifying story of a man possessed with evil. What drives a sixty-five year old man (white or black – or any race, for that matter) - to board a school bus and kill the school bus driver and attempt to take kids off the bus? He had so much evil in his heart that he was so brazen enough to storm a school bus in broad daylight to kidnap a five year old child (he tried to get more children, but they escaped). This deranged man overpowered the child and took him into an underground bunker he had already prepared. If this is not evil and demonic behavior, then what is?

What is the logically sound reason that would explain the behavior of a sixty-five year old man kidnapping a five year old child? What rational justification can our human minds come up with that might explain why this man would kill a school bus driver and take a child from the bus? He did not even know the child. I admit, I am not a psychologist or a psychiatrist, but I think that I am balanced enough to know that this is not normal behavior. This man was either completely insane, or possessed by the devil to commit this horrible crime. This tragic occurrence came to its dramatic conclusion on February 14, 2013. At 3:30 pm, the FBI forced their way into the bunker that Mr. Lee had built underground and secured the release of the five-year-old boy. This episode from start to finish lasted seven days.

Maybe if we knew what kind of life this person had lived prior to his decision of doing what he did we could have a better understanding. I am sure that when this situation is resolved, and as more information surfaces as to the background on Mr. Dykes' life, maybe then we will understand more truly why he did what he did. For example, I wonder if he had a family. I wonder if he had children of his own. I wonder if he had a church home. I wonder if he believed in Jesus Christ as the Lord and Savior of all creation. I wonder if he was an atheist.

Aaron Alexis of Fort Worth, Texas, the **alleged Washington shooter, served as Navy reservist, and may have recently lost his job.** On September 16, 2013, this man went on a killing spree and took the lives of twelve people in the Washington D.C. area. What we think happened is that Mr. Aaron Alexis may have lost his job as a civilian contractor and he plotted his revenge. This is what the media reported.

I, for one, do not know what drives a person to kill twelve people just because they are having a bad day. I do know that God is against the taking of innocent life just so a person can satisfy his self-righteous demands. But when we stop to look at a nation that is turning away from God, I am not surprised. When a nation or any country devalues life, it would appear that morality and humanity are also diminished.

Every day in this country we hear where a child is abducted and killed. We see professional people abusing kids, and not to mention the Catholic priests scandals that have plagued the diocese for many years and are still continuing. Looking back at the history of racism in this country, it is not hard to come to the conclusion after what a co-worker from the state of Arkansas told me. He said the first terrorist that he ever saw wore white hoods on their heads and they beat, raped, robbed, and killed black people during the Jim Crow era of segregation in America.

Anger and the Power of our Words

Chapter 3

It is not surprising that people snap when they see TV images of mass shootings and murder played out on a grand scale. Weak minds are drawn to this type of sensationalism. It is my opinion that the more we talk about this behavior, the more it gives the wrong people ideas. That's the way sin is. The more you think about it, the more the chances are that you will one day complete the act.

I do not mean to sound critical or judgmental of anyone, but my thoughts continue to rage against the situation. For example, I'm thinking, that since the election, and now re–election of President Barack Obama, we've had an over-abundance of strong, self-willed people across this nation doing weird and willful things. In some segments of American society, I've heard people mention or talk about seceding from the union, similar to what they did back during the Civil War days. Some people, (tea party representatives, and various party coalitions from the red states), are so dissatisfied with the current affairs of our government that they are actually thinking of starting their own statehood within America. I don't believe that is ever going to happen!

On the surface, it seems that there are a lot of very unhappy people in America. Could it be hatred for President Barack Obama and the administration that he represents that is the driving force that caused Mr. Dykes to become consumed with rage, and hatred? He was so consumed, that it compelled him to unleash his deep-seated anger on the killing of an unsuspecting bus driver, and brazenly attempting to kidnap children off that school bus. Whatever the underlying reasons are, they do not and cannot justify harming a child.

When it comes to anger, God gives each of us specific warnings. He tells us that we are to control our hearts with all diligence because out of the heart flows the issues of life. As a matter of fact, God also says that a man who hates his brother is a murderer. I, for one, do not ever plan to argue with God again. If he said it in His word to us in the Bible, I will receive and truly accept it and will build my life on it.

There are many passages in scripture that cover anger. Let's discuss what our Lord teaches us in Ephesians 4:25-31. God's Word says: 25"*Wherefore, putting away lying, speak every man truth with his neighbor: for we are members one of another. 26 Be ye angry, and sin not: let not the sun go down upon your wrath: 27Neither give place to the devil. 28 Let him that stole steal no more: but rather let him labour, working with his hands the thing which is good, that he may have to give to him that needeth. 29 Let no corrupt communication proceed out of your mouth, but that which is good to the use of edifying, that it may minister grace unto the hearers. 30 And grieve not the Holy Spirit of God, whereby ye are sealed unto the day of redemption. 31 Let all bitterness, and wrath, and anger, and clamour, and evil speaking, be put away from you, with all malice: 32 And be ye kind one to another, tenderhearted, forgiving one another, even as God for Christ's sake hath forgiven you.*"

God is saying that it is okay to be angry, but we are not to sin. In this life, we all will get angry sometime. However, we must learn to control our anger. Just because I am angry at my wife or my boss at work does not give me the right to go into a school and kill innocent people. Just because I am angry does not give me the right to take another person's life. The taking of innocent life is not of God. "*Let not the sun go down upon your wrath*", is found in Ephesians 4:26. In other words, don't give up space to the devil to enter into your mind. By letting the sun go down on your wrath, means you are thinking evil, you are contemplating things in your heart that you should not be thinking about. You are now allowing the devil to enter into your mind, to take over, and to set you on a course of action that is not of God. The more we think of how we are mistreated and abused, the more we think of retribution and retaliation, then the more anger and malice we will have in our hearts.

The Scripture in verse number 31 of Ephesians goes on to tell us to *"put aside all bitterness, and wrath, and anger, and clamor, and evil speaking."* But note that it says when it comes to malice, "put it far away from you". Malice is the active part of rage; it seeks to do physical actual harm to someone. Malice is the actual laying of the hands on someone's body to hurt them, or even kill them.

To close this short summary on controlling our anger, the Lord says in the book of Ephesians 4:25-32, that the devil will use our anger against us. He does this in stages: 1) the devil sees that a situation has made us angry. Like the stocking of coals in a coal burning stove, the devil tries to stock the coals in the fire to make your anger hotter than it really is, and 2) don't let the sun go down on your wrath. When you do this you give the devil permission to come into your life to resolve your problem. Trust me; you do not want the devil to solve a problem. When the devil helps you solve a problem, you are going to be the loser and the devil is going to be the winner. By going to bed with your anger and giving the devil space in your life, you wake up the next morning with a lot of wrath on the inside of your body. The seeds of wrath are now firmly implanted in your heart and wrath will sprout anger and bitterness.

We all know that words have power. As a result of the bitterness and anger from your heart, you communicate and say things that verbalize your deep-seated thoughts of anger and rage against a person or situation. Evil communication is known as "clamour". You are putting into words how you really feel. This is the last step before malice. 3) Malice is the actual desire fulfilled. It is the culmination of strategy, plans and actions taken in retribution, retaliation, and vengeance, by getting even with someone or something. This stage is the most serious of behaviors of a sinful act of anger.

I have learned that all anger that is not based on Godly indignation is sin. So what am I saying here? I am saying that it doesn't matter what I am angry about if I allow my anger to control me and the result is someone ends up being hurt or killed. This is not of God; this is sin! The sin of pride which says that my rights are violated, the sin that says to me, "How dare you speak to me in that manner? I am better than you. Therefore, since you don't know this, and now I am angry you must die." That sin is of the flesh, not of God.

On the other hand, when I see a situation that I know is wrong, a situation that is based on the Scripture and the Word of God, I have a right to be angry. For example, a young black boy just barely sixteen can be gunned down by a person in the State of Florida just because he thinks that the child is up to something wrong. Under the current laws of Florida, if a person with a gun feels threatened, they have the right to kill an innocent person.

I have the right to get angry when I see our small children killed every day as a result of someone who is having a bad day. Because this man is angry, he goes home and gets his AK47 rifle and walks into a large restaurant or movie theater and just starts shooting people at random. Yes, I have a right to get angry about that! When the leaders of our government think that it is ok to promote same sex marriage, and take the Name of God out of our American school system, yes, I have a right to get angry about that!

It was through pure greed, lying, and cheating that the leading financial institutions of America almost sent this country into bankruptcy and forced the President to take drastic actions to prevent the loss of untold millions. These same rich people, who brag about their Swiss bank accounts and their blind trust, could care less for the real issues facing this nation. Most of them see America like it was back in the 1950's when the white man ran everything and segregation was the rule of the day. I believe many of them now would love to turn back the clock to that time period.

I do not want to sound like a racist, but I am committed to telling the truth. And the truth is: There are a large amount of conservative rich people and many who are as poor as Job's turkey, who will never accept a black man as nothing more than a slave. That is what drives racism - the belief that they are superior to all races of people!

If the spirit of pride was used against Jesus, causing the spiritual leaders of His day to crucify Him, what do you think these same self-righteous non-Jews will do to anybody that gets in their way and upsets their way of life today? You hear words like, "we are going to take back our country". However, they failed to realize, God Almighty rules in the affairs of men. I believe it was God who had a direct hand in the election of President Barack Obama.

Verses 31 and 32 of Ephesians 4 says, "*Let all bitterness, and wrath, and anger, and clamor and evil speaking, be put away from you, with all malice:* [32] And be ye kind one to another, tenderhearted, forgiving one another, even as God for Christ's sake hath forgiven you."

The Small White Door

Chapter 4

Let's return to the other door of eternity; the small white door that leads to Heaven and eternal life.

Behind this door you smell the sweet fragrance of the fruit of the Spirit. The fruit of the spirit is: love, joy, peace, long-suffering, gentleness, goodness, faith, meekness and temperance. You can hear the soft voices of people singing, praying, and worshiping. Immediately after you open this door, you can see steps that incline upward, leading to paradise and to the throne of God.

The steps are the stairway to Heaven. The steps do not have side rails and the steps themselves are very narrow. A person who is not watching where he is walking can fall. However each step is lit by the Word of God. Each person who walks these narrow steps must concentrate and focus on the voice of God's "indwelling spirit" to keep from falling.

In short, the goal of this journey is to focus on God and not the steps. The steps are there to point you in the right direction; but they will not prevent you from falling. The goal at the top of this very long and seemingly endless staircase is the throne of God. Paradise and eternal life await all that are blessed to follow and obey the Word of God.

Life – Part 1

When I close my eyes and allow my mind to meditate on all the positive and unique characteristics of life, and how precious it is, I can almost see parts of God's creation at work. I see life in the warmth of the early morning sun on a clear, cloudless day shining down on God's creation.

Life is like the joy of a first-time father's love. He rushes home after a hard day of work, just so he can hold his newborn baby boy or girl in his arms again and inhale the sweet aroma of new born life. This is most precious.

Life is like that first kiss that tells both the kisser and the one being kissed that this encounter has the potential of going somewhere.

Life reminds me of the Pacific Ocean, in that, when we are born or launched, we are on a journey. During this journey of life, it is similar to crossing a great body of water. Any seaman will tell you that the ocean plays by its own set of rules. Things that were considered normal and solid on land, do not apply to a large body of water. You know that once you set sail, there are going to be days that are going to make or break you. There will be days that you will either sink or stay afloat in the little boat called life. The goal of this life is to safely make it across this vast body of water/life and to reach the other side - Heaven. God Almighty is the distant shore that we are all trying to reach. We have all been given the map that shows us how to safely cross this vast body of water called life.

However, some people will discard their map because of non-belief. Others will have the map, but fail to read its instructions and as a consequence, run aground, or worse, run directly into a major typhoon or hurricane at sea and drown. Still there will be others who will play it safe and never really set out to cross the ocean. These people like things the way they are and do not want to change. They will just cruise up and down the shore line and never face the real challenge of crossing the sea of life. They do not know that the way up is down on your knees praying and being obedient. They need to study the passage of scripture in Luke 17:33. Jesus said, *"Whosoever shall seek to save his life shall lose it; and whosoever shall lose his life shall preserve it."*

To get to the other side, we must be born again, or should I say, born from above. Playing it safe because we have all the things that we think we need in this life is not pleasing to our God. He wants us to develop a relationship with Him and to trust Him. He wants us to not play it safe but launch out and set sail into the deep waters of life and follow Him across the vast sea of life. Jesus is the Captain of my little boat and I trust Him completely. I want to experience all that He has in store for me, and to do that, I must set sail.

I've heard it said: "calm waters do not a good sailor make". In other words, to be considered a good sailor with solid credentials, a sailor must encounter the rough waters of the ocean and its surprises. I would rather follow a lowly combat veteran into battle than a high ranking official who has never been to war. I have also heard it said that he who is a slave to the compass is the master of the ocean. Everyone else must stay within eye sight of the land or run the risk of being lost at sea.

The sea is a funny thing. As long as you can see land you are okay. But if you are not paying attention and drift too far away and lose sight of land, you now have a problem. This is especially true during the dark of night. At sea, when all you can see is water going in every direction, a wrong decision about which direction to go could be your final and last decision. If you make the wrong decision, it could mean going farther out to sea or if you are lucky, heading back to shore.

God Almighty has given to us a book called the Holy Bible as His map to us. This book/map is 100 percent reliable. It has saved many lost souls during their journey across the sea of life. When we study this special book/map, we will notice that it points us in the direction of a Master Navigator – his Name is **Jesus Christ**. Our Master has made this journey across the sea of life many times and He has never lost a crew.

He knows when it is the best time to set sail, and He shows us how to navigate around or through the storms on the sea of life. Our Navigator knows the directions to the distant shore that we seek, the distant land of paradise and a city that sits high on a hill. Some say that within this beautiful city, the streets are paved with gold. Still, others say this city has 12 gates and all of them are made of pearls. I hear it's a beautiful city that is not made with hands. I am told that all who successfully follow our Master Navigator and make it across the sea of life will inherit a mansion in this place called Heaven. "Oh God, teach me to be obedient to my Master Navigator of Life, Jesus Christ. Wherever He leads me, I will follow."

The Lord taught me to know early in my journey, that if I am to be a disciple of Jesus Christ, I must learn discipline. The two words are similar in that they even look like they belong together - Disciple and Discipline. They complement each other in that when it comes to following Jesus, you can't have one without the other. You must have both to be a part of the army of Christ.

To be a good follower of Christ we must study and meditate on His Word. We can pray for wisdom, but we must study to learn spiritual instructions. What good does it do for a soldier to be in the army but never follow instructions? This is also true in the army of God. If you are committed to following Christ, you must study His Word. The enemy we fight against knows the Word better than we do. However, the enemy cannot live it or put it in to practice as a true believer can. The full power of the Word comes only to those through faith in our Master, Jesus Christ. Faith is the key that unlocks the door of the power of God over the life of a believer. The Bible states: *"Without faith, it is impossible to please him."* (Hebrews 11:6)

Note: Genesis: 1:27 - please refer to this scripture as you read the next few paragraphs below:

God alone is the Creative Source, Sustainer and Redeemer of Life. Life was, is, and always will be, His creation. God is the reason for living. He is the source of life. God makes life interesting. If you do not believe me, try living a God-centered life in a world that is anti-God and you will be challenged at every turn by those who are opposed to godly living, and by those who are living their life as they choose, free from a God conscience.

What good is life without God? Think about it. God gives life direction, discipline, purpose, hope, faith, guidance, joy, humbleness, reason, meaning, love for your fellow man, and love for self with purity of thought from a righteous nature. Without God, life is self-glorification, selfishness, unhappiness, meaningless, joyless, sin-centered, lustful, without mercy, world-controlled, mean-spirited, prejudiced, wicked, evil, complex and cluttered with materialism, vanity-centered, and uninteresting. In short, a life that is Godless is a life similar to a life lived in the flesh. This lifestyle is discussed in Galatians 5:19-21.

Life! Do you ever sometimes just stop to wonder about it and contemplate what it really means? Think about it. Wow! Two people meet, male/female, they socialize and they get to know each other and get together and before you know it "bam", a baby boy or girl is born. This little bundle of life is a living and breathing representation of its parents. Given time and opportunity, this little bundle of life will grow up and repeat this process and re-produce its own little bundle of life, and the cycle continues. But is that it?

Consider how life continues from one generation to the next generation because it is not under man's or woman's control. Conversely, it was life that was first breathed into man by God, who established the creation of man, and allowed man to continue to manifest himself at the direct will of God. This is confirmed by the Word of God in Genesis 2:7 *"And the Lord God formed man of the dust of the ground, and breathed into his nostrils the breath of life; and man became a living soul."*

Life's choices are the roads that lead each of us to either of these two doors. It may be hard to realize, but it is true. The journey of temporal life begins when we are born, and eternity begins when we die. All humans will participate in the game of life. No one sits on the side lines because life is constantly evolving.

Some people on this road of life will find the two doors early, and some will find them later in life. But the point is this: all people, rich, poor, regardless of race, color, creed, or national origin will find and open one of these two doors. And when they reach the end of the road they are traveling on, they will have to make a choice as to which door to open and live eternally blessed or eternally damned.

> Hebrews 9:27, *"Just as surely you were born – you will one day die."*

> Job 14:1 *"Man that is born of a woman is of few days, and full of trouble."*

The most precious thing that we can possess, protect, and cherish is our life. Yet, the truth of the matter is, our life does not truly belong to us. It is a gift, a precious gift that is allotted to us for a specific period of time. We take possession of and receive life from our biological parents. Your life is not an accident. Your birth is a blessing from God.

I've Been Where You Are

Chapter 5

I am very well aware, that there are some people who are non-believers of God, Jesus Christ, and The Holy Spirit. There are also people who cringe with hatred at the very mention of God's Name. I pray that God forgives them and that this book will help to open the eyes and hearts to any and all non- believers to the reality and truth of the living God.

This book is written, I feel, with the help of the "Holy Spirit". My purpose for writing this book is to save souls, to plant seeds of spiritual belief, and to reach as many non-believers and people who cringe at the mention of God's Holy Name. It is written for any and all who want to re-evaluate their current life position and for those who are unsure of what to believe. It is my prayer that if they continue reading this short book, they will be encouraged to seek God for themselves and establish a living and working relationship with Him.

This book is not an attempt to get rich or make a lot of money. God teaches us in 1Timothy 6:10 *"for the love of money is the root of all evil: which while some coveted after, they have erred from the faith, and pierced themselves through with many sorrows."* Therefore, I will not allow the love of money to be the guiding force for writing this book. It is my prayer that the divine hand of God, through the Holy Spirit, will lead and guide me in this burden. His grace and mercy is enough for me. Go ahead and laugh if you want, as I am sure some of you will say, yea right! But the truth of the matter is I would rather have Jesus than all the gold the world could ever give me. I will explain why I feel this way later in the book, but you will have to keep reading to find out.

The second thing that I need to make clear is that this book is not about me! Yes, I will share many personal experiences of what God has done for me, what God has allowed me to see, and what God is doing in my life now. However, God Almighty is the goal. He is the light that shines in all my many failures and attempts to walk and compete on this road we humans all call life.

It is by God's mercy and His grace that I am not dead and in my grave, long before I was given this task to complete. Yes, I have a story to tell. And I am not going to hold back! Some of the events, some of the visions, and many of the experiences that I will share with you, I do not completely understand myself.

I cannot tell you why God has allowed me to see different signs and wonders. I can truthfully say that I am in agreement with the old hymn writer William Cower (1731–1800) who wrote, "God moves in mysterious ways, His wonders to perform." God works in mysterious ways, because I never in my wildest dreams thought I would come to know, trust and obey the God of Abraham, Isaac and Jacob, as well as the God of my fathers, as I do to this day. I certainly never thought that I would be writing a book about God. But I am compelled to do just that.

The events and visions that I plan to share with you in this book are not make-believe or fairytale. They happened and are truly real. If you choose not to believe me, I will not get upset, because if I had not seen them with my own eyes, I would have a hard time believing them as well. However, they are real. My testimony is about the "Omnipotence, the Omnipresence, the Omniscience," about an "All powerful and completely Divine," Sovereign God. I am not fabricating or spinning some make-believe or pretend fairytale story.

There are those – who collectively as a group - choose to dabble in the occult. There are Satan worshipers, demon worshipers, atheism worshipers, atheist believers, witchcraft followers, vampire lovers, and spiritualists. People who believe in the dark mysteries of life seem to embrace stories about witches, witchcraft, sorcery, magic potions, flying brooms, fire breathing- dragons and magic rings. They read and research stories about medieval European folklore.

You do not have to look very far to see the types of movies that Hollywood executives are producing. The potential for huge profit is the sole reason that the movie industry is making such chillingly scary movies. Some of the movies are ghoulishly gruesome. They focus on the macabre for a plot and rely on realistically bloodletting scenes that look all too real; this helps to sell their high price tickets for admission. They are producing movies that reflect a growing trend of our youth's interest in such debauchery.

That is not my goal. The things that I am going to share with you are true and are not a figment of my imagination. If you choose not to believe them, as I have previously indicated, it will not be a surprise to me. Most people will probably say that I made them up.

Some of things that I will share with you are personal, meaning, that I haven't talked about them with many people. Some of the things that I will tell you about will be rejected as make-believe; some of you will find them hard to believe. However, those who are filled with the Spirit will discern correctly that I speak the truth and your walk with God will be strengthened and encouraged.

Bless you in advance. But as God is my witness, I speak the truth; the things that I am about to share with you, I am God's witness to you, they did happen. You be the judge.

Events That Changed My Life

Chapter 6

I was born on a Wednesday morning on March 1, 1950, in a small farming community in Ripley, Tennessee. I am the fifth child of a family of eighteen children. My father and mother were both God-fearing people and strong in the Southern Baptist faith. Our family attended Springhill Missionary Baptist Church. Springhill is where I was baptized at an early age, in a pond that was a short distance from our church. The pastor at that time was the Reverend Matthew E. Allen. Pastor Allen was affectionately called by his members "Old Man Allen". He was a big tall man with a very powerful voice.

Reverend Allen and his family lived 50 miles away in Memphis, Tennessee. He was also the pastor of another church that was near Brownsville, Tennessee called Upper Salem Baptist Church. Pastor Allen would minister at our church – Springhill - the 1st and 3rd Sunday of each month. He would also minister the 2nd and 4th Sunday at Upper Salem Baptist Church.

Pastor Allen was a very dynamic preacher and teacher. People used to say that if you listened to any of Pastor Allen's sermons and the Word did not move you, you might already be dead. He was that kind of preacher. Looking back, I will say that he had a preaching genre that was similar to the late, great Baptist minister, the Reverend C.L Franklin, in style and delivery. However, Pastor Allen was not as well-known as Rev. Franklin. He was a preacher chosen by God to preach the Word, and preach the Word he did, with fire and conviction.

The church I attended as a young boy has a long history. It just recently celebrated 139 years at the same location. Pastor Allen's son is now the steward of the flock. "Old Man Allen" is now deceased.

I want to begin with what I call my first and early encounters with God. I promise, that what I am about to share with you is no fabrication. I will recapture things from my childhood and will share my thoughts. The things that God has allowed me to see will never fade from my memory. Some of the experiences that I am going to talk about, most of you will not believe. And that's okay with me, just as long as you know that I am not making things up just to sell a book to make money. I give you my word and make a pledge of truthfulness too - that on the Word of God, I lie not. This book is not a pretend fairytale story or a figment of my imagination. These visions and events all really happened, and it is all true. You just have to decide for yourself if you are going to believe them or not.

Take the time to read in John 1:11-12 what was said about Jesus. John said, *"He came unto his own, and his own received him not. But as many as received him, to them gave the power to become the sons of God, even to them that believe on his name."* God will continue to exist in spite of your acceptance or rejection of Him, and, God will continue to be God all by Himself regardless of whether you believe Him or not. What I am going to share with you is no pretend. I will start at the very beginning with the "hand experience".

The Invisible Hand – Event 1

When I was five or six, we lived on a farm that was owned by a white man whose name was Lawson Elder. Mr. Elder and his family lived in a nice red, brick house, at the top of the hill on his farm. We lived in an old, wood-framed house at the bottom of the hill.

There were several black families that lived on this farm. Besides our family, there was also the Scott, Walker, Sims, and Malone family; as well as a few other white families. I did not know the white families because the adults did not socialize with our parents and they did not allow their kids to play with us. During the middle fifties, a lot of white people were very prejudiced against black people, so black parents taught their kids at an early age not to hang around them. Their fear was that something bad would happen and the black person would get the blame. Sometimes this could end up causing a young black boy or girl to get in serious trouble with the law. Back then, a white person could call the police on you and your words - as to whether or not you did something - meant nothing to the police. Depending on the charge, you could end up in jail, beaten, or even worse, hung on a tree.

White people and black people did not socialize at all. This was the acceptable custom in Ripley, Tennessee in 1955. The white people had their churches, and social gatherings and we had ours. The town of Ripley, Tennessee was, and still is, a small farming community. Most people, white and black, worked the fields planting cotton, corn, or soybeans which were the main crops for the market.

Most of the black families did not own any land. The only work that they could get was called "sharecropping." Looking back on the sharecropping form of living, I see it as another form of slave labor. For example, no matter how long or how hard you worked, you would never get out of debt, and the white land-owner's pockets kept getting fatter and fatter. If the sharecropper made the mistake and voiced any displeasure with the record-keeping, or complained about how he and his family were treated, the response from the white land-owner was usually swift and to the point. "If you feel you are being mistreated Nigger, move. I want you and your family off my land immediately."

Sharecropping is when a white land-owner allowed a family to live on his land in a house. Some of the houses were so dilapidated and run down that they hardly fit the description to be called a house. I am talking paper-thin walls, wood floors with holes in them, windows without screens. The roof was made of aluminum or tin, and usually there was one coal or wood-burning stove in the house. The stove was usually in the kitchen of the house. The land-owner allowed you to farm or a crop of let's say cotton, because most of the black sharecroppers planted cotton.

The black sharecropper would have the expense of buying the cotton seeds and fertilizer on credit. He needed these items to plant and grow; the cotton crop. He would work the land by plowing the fields usually with one or two mules. After the cotton began to grow, he had to go out in the boiling hot Tennessee sun to chop the cotton. The chopping of cotton means to chop around the cotton plants (plant after plant, row after row) to get rid of the unwanted crab grass, that, if left unchecked, would choke or prevent the cotton from growing. This chopping process was done with a hoe. If you had ten acres to chop in a couple days, you would start early that morning at sunrise and chop cotton all day, only stopping for lunch. People would wear old straw hats to protect their heads from the sun and the women folk would have old rags or scarves tied around their heads under their straw hats. You either walked to the fields if the field was close to your house or, if your father had a wagon, you rode in the back of it with someone driving the mules. People would carry their water for the day and food for lunch. They would tie the food high up in a tree to keep the animals from eating it while they worked the fields. When you start chopping the cotton, you might have to walk a half mile or a mile in one direction chopping the cotton. The field might be as large as a mile or two square miles with hundreds of cotton rows to chop.

I don't quite remember all the details because this event is early in my childhood, and I do not remember if both of our parents were in the field or not, but I do know that Lewis, my younger brother, and I were home and getting in serious, life-altering trouble. As I said earlier, we lived in an old shabby farm house with a tin galvanized roof. (You have never slept, until you sleep under a tin roof during an easy rainstorm with the sound of the rain hitting that metal roof. It's the best sleep in the world, far superior to any sleeping pill or machine!)

My little brother and I were upstairs in our parents' bedroom messing around. Their bedroom was about 15 to 20 feet up from the bottom floor and they had these small wooden steps that led up to their room. I remember that Lewis and I went up there, but I can't remember why it was probably because I was curious about their room. I remember my parents had an old single light bulb hanging directly over their bed with a pull switch that turned the light on and off. I was curious as to what made the light bulb come on. I got on top of their bed and while standing, I unscrewed the light bulb and put my finger in the socket. I pulled the switch and turned the power on to see what would happen. The electricity shocked me so bad that if my weight had not pulled me away when I fell from the bed, I probably would not be writing this book today.

Lewis began to cry. He was afraid and I wanted him to stop crying. He would not stop crying so I pushed him down the stairs. He was standing at the top of the steps and I pushed him off the top step. Just before he reached the bottom of the stairs, I saw this hand appear out of nowhere right before Lewis reached the bottom floor.

This hand was larger than a normal man's hand; otherwise, it was identical to a man's hand with five fingers. It was a hand that you could see through, yet, it caught my little brother before he hit the floor. As it caught Lewis, it gently laid him down on the floor and disappeared from under him. I was a child, but instantly, I knew that what I had done to my brother was wrong. I also knew what I had seen. I was too young to fear what I had seen, but I will never forget it. I did not tell anyone about this until many years later. To this day, I can still see that hand appear from nowhere, and disappear after it gently placed my little brother on the floor. I believe that this was the hand of God or His Spirit, or an angel assigned to watch over us and to protect us from evil. I was the one who did a bad thing to my little brother, but God was there to undo what I had done.

I thank you God for watching over my little brother Lewis and me that day. I could have seriously injured Lewis, and I could have electrocuted myself by sticking my finger in that light switch. I cannot tell you why I got the idea to push Lewis off those steps, but I would be lying if I said that it was an accident. It was no accident. I did it on purpose, why I do not know, but I will say, kids left alone sometimes can get into trouble, and usually they are sorry for doing what they should not have done.

The Mysterious Sign of God – Event 2

I remember this event as clearly as if it happened yesterday. This event was a vision that happened on a Sunday - Easter Sunday - to be more specific. On this Sunday, I went outside to sit on our little front porch to sulk because I was angry with my parents. I was upset because they were getting us ready for church again. I did not like going to church, and I wanted to stay home and play with the rest of the kids who lived nearby because some of them did not go to church.

I couldn't understand why we had to go to church every Sunday and sit in an old, hot, building with a bunch of old people, singing and sometimes shouting and falling out on the floor. It did not make any sense to me - a young boy of six or seven years old.

However, I did know that in our house, what my father said was the law. And if you wanted to get mad or upset at any decision that he made, it was wise to make sure that he or my mother did not find out about it. That was why I went outside to pout privately. I was not completely immature. As I was sitting on the front porch being mad at the world, something got my attention up the road, a distance of 75 to 100 feet, no more than that.

I saw something that would mystify me for the rest of my life. The vision that I saw was just a short distance from the Malone's family home. They lived at the top of the small hill to the left of this old rock road. I noticed what looked to be a small twister or as they would say down south a "dirt devil". A dirt devil is a small funnel-like tornado that appears and moves across the land before it spins itself out. They are small harmless representations of tornadoes that usually happen when the weather is hot, windy and dry.

This is how this particular vision started. It started quickly and grew into a stronger more pronounced whirlwind. I use "whirlwind" for lack of a better word because as of this day I do not know what it was. The best way I can describe it is that it looked like a miniature small tornado with very powerful winds centered directly on it. It started quickly and grew in size quickly. I saw the earth directly under this little twister open up into a perfectly round circle of about 6 feet to 10 feet in diameter. And after the earth opened up, every rock, every pebble or speck of dust, dust grains and particles of the rock road that was swirling, rotating around, stopped in a precise location.

I saw what appeared to be a man. I was not sure what it really was. This vision had the body of a man's shape and I could only see the side of the figure. I could see the side of a transparent face and I could make out that this was a side-view figure of a man's face.

The body appeared to be clothed in some kind of gown that was made out of material that reminded me of cheese cloth (an off-white color) that went from his shoulders down to his feet. I could not see his feet. There was a purple band or sash that went from the left shoulder around the body and around the waist. If he had feet, I did not see them because the gown covered everything. His hands were raised up toward Heaven and with the twinkle of an eye he flew out of the ground and went straight up towards

Heaven at a slight angle. It moved so fast, that it was as if "now you see it, now you don't." Like the snap of a finger it was caught up into the heavens. And every pebble, rock, sand, and dirt that was frozen in time reversed itself and went back into its exact position as if nothing had ever happened.

I was never afraid but I knew that what I had just seen was real. Finally, after some time, I went to the position on the road where the vision was revealed. I bent down to pick up a rock from off the road, and when I picked up a small rock, I quickly dropped it because the rock was so hot that it burned my hand. I returned to our house, but I never told my parents about this because I knew they would not believe me and I was not sure if I could really describe it anyway. I will never forget the vision and to this day I still do not know why I saw it or what it meant. I do not think what I saw was an accident because I just happened to be sitting where I was when the vision appeared. I do believe what I saw was a message from God and I was meant to see it. Over the years, I have shared this vision with a few people, but no one can interpret what it means. One day God will reveal the vision and its purpose to me.

A Very Large Bird – Event 3

I am not sure if the following event or incident was a vision or actually a freak occurrence. The one thing that I know for sure is: I know that I saw it and it was real. If this was meant for me to see as a sign from God, I cannot discern what it means. I will just tell you what happened, and what I saw and allow you to draw your own conclusion.

When I was near seven years of age, my mother asked me to take my fathers' lunch to him. He was out in the field plowing the fields and getting the ground ready to plant our crop of cotton. My mother fixed his lunch, and put his lunch in a round molasses bucket, placed the lid on top and sent me on my way. I had made this trip numerous times and it was no big deal for a young country boy to do this.

I had to walk a couple of miles or so back into the country woods that were behind our little house. When I got to the field, I could see my father plowing the field. He was now driving an old Ford tractor. Mr. Lawson Elder had moved from using mules to break the ground and had invested in tractors for his farm hands to work their field. I am certain, there was a charge associated with the use of his equipment. Mr. Elder was not the kind of man to do something out of the kindness of his heart. His investment had to provide some kind of financial benefit to him.

After I gave my father his lunch, he and I talked for a while and he assigned me a few more things to do when I got back home. He always left something in his bucket for me to eat on my way back to our house. As I was walking up a trail that ran beside a small creek something caught my attention. I looked up in the tree and there was the biggest bird I had ever seen. This bird was huge! It was as tall as I was at the time, if not taller. The bird looked like something I had never seen before. It had a huge curved top beak that turned down over the bottom of its mouth. It had large penetrating eyes, similar to a bald eagle's eyes, but only larger. It had massive big talons on its huge feet. It was looking down at me very intently. It never made a sound. I was not afraid, but something told me to get a weapon, which I did.

I looked around and I saw a fairly large stick and picked it up. I also picked up a large, hard piece of dirt from off the ground and I threw it at this bird and hit him with it. The bird only made a slight flinch, but never took its eyes off me. I decided not to go by the tree where he was perched; instead, I crossed the small creek and went up the small hill that led out into the open field. I stayed close to the fence row that had trees along the side of the field. The bird turned his head and watched me as I walked away. After a while, I saw him flying very high in the sky, going the same direction I was, but only faster. I never saw him again. When I got home I told my mother about the bird, and she later told my father when he returned home from the field. My father got his shotgun and had me take him to where I had seen the bird, but there was nothing there. Since that time, I have never seen any kind of bird that came even close to matching the size of the bird which I had seen.

Based on my research, the largest birds of prey that exist in the world today are either the Eurasian Black Vulture which has a wing span of "8 "to 9.5" feet, or the Andean Condor that can weigh up to 30 lbs. I have seen pictures of both birds and they do not come close to matching the size of the bird that I saw that day.

I am going to guess, because I have no way of knowing, but the bird that I saw was four to five feet tall and very muscular. I would guess that it would weigh easily over a hundred pounds. Its beak was about the size of a large man's hand with the top beak curved down over the bottom. The top beak curved down and was rounded to a point. The feet of this bird was absolutely huge with long black talons that gripped the branch where it was sitting. The feathers were large and were a dark color, brownish grey. This bird was a bird of prey - unusually and abnormally big. It reminds me now of some type of prehistoric bird that an ornithologist (someone that studies birds) would say is extinct. I could not argue with him.

I know that the bird that I saw that day would have had no problem killing me if that had been his intention. I have searched books since that time and have come across only one bird that fits the description of the bird that I saw and it was a prehistoric bird of prey. This is another mystery which is still unresolved.

The Ice Cream Truck, "Manna" from Heaven – Event 4

I remember one very hot summer day, in July or August, 1958. It was in the summer and we were out of school. This particular day I remember it was unusually hot. Keep in mind that back then, a lot of poor people (black or white) did not have refrigerators. To compensate, they would buy blocks of ice to keep their food from spoiling.

That was our situation. We had what was called an old ice chest that our parents would use to keep food items cool. We would draw our water from a well to wash or to cook. Our well had a long metal draw bucket. We would lower the long tube or draw bucket down into the well and the tube would fill itself with the water. We would then raise the tube up by pulling on the rope and release a tube full of water into our container. The tube would hold a gallon or more of water at one time.

On this day, the weather was really hot. It was the kind of heat similar to what the old folks used to say, "You know it's hot when you can look down the cotton fields as you were working, and you see the monkey's jumping." This was an old southern phrase used by poor people to describe a hot day to work. In reality, what they were really seeing were heat waves from the sun hitting the earth and bouncing back up into the environment.

This movement of the sunlight would create the illusion of little monkeys or devils dancing in the heat in the far distance from where you were working. This movement of something dancing out in the distant field is nature's way of letting you know it's going to be a very hot day.

I can assure you this was one of those "monkey jumping" days. We had no air conditioning or window fans in our house. Any relief that we got from the oppressive heat came from the good Lord. He would allow a cool breeze or a quick shower to cool things off. When this happened, it would feel so good to our skin. We used to say, there is nothing better than a "cool breeze" on a hot summer's day.

This Saturday evening at about 4:00 or 5:00 pm, there were lots of kids that lived near us and we were playing together. Girls were playing with girls, and boys were playing with boys. As we were all playing, along came this large ice-cream truck over the hill and it was heading our way. As this truck turned the curved rock road that was directly in front of our little house, the back door of the ice-cream truck flew open, and boxes upon boxes of ice-cream fell out. The truck driver never slowed down but kept driving. I assumed that he never knew that he had just lost over half of his ice- cream delivery.

I will never forget that precious memory of so many hot and thirsty poor kids running to get at what I call the ice-cream "manna" from heaven. There were boxes of popsicles, ice cream sandwiches; chocolate and banana fudge cones, cups of vanilla ice cream, drumsticks, fudge pops and much more. In retrospect, looking back on this little event from my past, it was kind of funny to see and be a part of all those poor, black kids trying to consume all that ice-cream before it melted in the hot Tennessee summer sun. I, along with the rest of the kids, was eating ice-cream as fast as I could and crying because we hated to see the rest of it melt. Boy what a treat! I see this now as nothing but a treat from God. He gives His children a cool treat on an unusually hot day. He works in mysterious ways.

The one thing that I have learned about God is that you will never know what He's up to. You can be the best Bible scholar in the world, but you will never be able to tell what God is going to do. That's why is very important to learn to just trust and obey! He says if I am with you, I am more than the world against you. That is enough for me. My God-is God, and that is all that I need to say on that!

If He can take the time out of His busy schedule to feed a bunch of hot, thirsty, and dusty poor kids all-you-can-eat ice cream, then surely He will take care of all your needs when you learn to trust and obey Him. Hebrews 13:5 says, *"I will never leave you or forsake you."* My, My, My - What a Mighty God we serve!

The Night our House Caught on Fire – Event 5

Our family moved from the Elder's farm onto a farm owned by a man named Mr. Paul Williams. This move was during the early part of 1960. I was ten years old at the time. I did not know why we moved, because our father never told us. It would be years later that I learned the reason that we moved from the Elder's farm was because of a conflict between the landowner and my father.

As a family of sharecroppers, we had worked the cotton fields all that week. My father had promised us that if we did a good job, he would take the family into town on Saturday. I always enjoyed going into town on Saturday. We got to mingle with some of our classmates, and got the chance to see what the grown folks were doing down in the black part of town that was called the hole. The "hole" was where the older, grown black people would go to relax, drink, dance and have a little fun before returning to their hard lives as poor share crop farmers. You could hear the latest R & B or blues songs played on the juke box. Occasionally, a fight or two would break out as a result of someone having too much to drink, and saying the wrong thing to somebody's wife or girlfriend.

Many of the black, farm families only had one day to be free from their work. Usually, this was Saturday. Some Saturdays you would work the fields a half day, go home and change clothes then head to town. People would gravitate down toward the juke-joints. The juke-joint was a kind of tavern which sometimes doubled as a restaurant and grocery store that catered to black people. They catered only to black people because the white people would not patronize black-owned stores. This was a place where some of the men and women would go to party and forget about their troubles.

Some would drink cold beer, dance, and eat Miss Anna May's fried chicken, with a side of green beans, potato salad and some collard greens, and corn bread. The sweet-potato pie or the chess pie would cost a little more. The black folks would eat and enjoy themselves because they knew that come early Monday morning, they would be expected to be back in the cotton fields working from dusk to dawn. The sharecropper lived a hard life. They never had any real freedom to complain, they did as they were told by the farm owners. "Yes Sir" and "Yes Mam", was they addressed the farm owners.

Once when we had worked more than a half day, our father called it a day and we were going to go home and get cleaned up to go in town for the night. Mr. Lawson Elder was driving by in his truck and asked my father why he did not have us in the field working. My father told him what he had promised us. Mr. Elder told my father that he needed to get us back out in the field to work and get his crops in. My father said "those kids are my kids, and nobody can tell me what to do with my kids." Mr. Elder told my father if that was the way he felt, then we needed to find a new place to live.

To show how God can make a way out of no way, He blessed us to find another place to live. Moreover, after we moved from Mr. Lawson Elder's farm, a few years after we moved, his farming business began to go downhill. This is because most, if not all, the black farmers moved off his farm after we left, and he was never quite the same. He took sick a few years later and died. His wife also was not in good health and she died not long after he did. His son got the farm but did not farm it. He worked in a plant like all the rest of us. I never tried to re-establish any kind of relationship with the son, although my mother says he often asks her about the boys that he partially grew up with.

We moved to the Williams' farm. This farm was in an area where only white people lived. I will say that Mr. and Mrs. Williams were very nice to us, as nice as could be expected from white people in the 1960's. They never talked down to us like the Elders did. Mrs. Williams would stop by and she and my mother would talk for what seemed like hours. If she was prejudice, she did a good job of hiding it from us. She was always giving my mother clothes for us to wear and extra food for her to preserve.

I liked the area that we lived in. There was another older, black man and his wife that lived there also. His name was Mr. Tom Jarrett and his wife's name was Mrs. Anna May Jarrett. Both were very nice people. They did not have any children and they adopted us into their family. At times, I felt like I had two sets of parents; we were that close.

Neither of the houses that we lived in was in good shape. Our home was a three bedroom house with a small living room/bedroom and a small kitchen. The back kitchen door opened out to a small back porch, where our well/cistern of water supply was kept. The outhouse was down the hill from our house. The whole house was old and was not air tight. We kept warm by sleeping under heavy quilts and we kept plenty of wood and coal burning in the heaters. One night in the fall of the year, between Thanksgiving and Christmas, our house caught on fire and burned completely down. It was not in the dead of winter, but it was cold enough for us to have had our first snow.

The providence of Almighty God was with us on this night. Our parents were supposed to go to our church for Bible Study, but for some unknown reason, they did not go. When we went to sleep that night, our stove caught the house on fire as we slept. What I am about to share with you is still vividly clear in my mind. I can never forget it and I will carry its memory to my grave.

As we slept in our beds our house was on fire. I remember that a hand touched my forehead just above my eyes while I was asleep. This hand was colder than ice; it was colder than anything that I have ever felt. Yet, the fingers were soft and as each finger made its way down my face, I could feel each one. When the last finger lightly rubbed across my eyes, I was made instantly awake. All I could see was the foot of the bed in which my brothers and I were sleeping and it was on fire and burning. Without thinking, I immediately ran to my parent's bedroom and woke up my father. Daddy, as we all called him, began to get everyone out of the house, which by now, was completely engulfed by the fire.

My father had to forcefully drag our grandfather out because he was trying to get an old trunk from the closet and take it outside with him. We later learned that our grandfather's life savings was in that old trunk. We never knew how much money he had saved over the years. You might ask the question? Why did he have all his life saving in an old, World War I, wooden, army trunk? The answer is simple: my grandfather was born not long after slavery ended in America. He never truly understood why people would want to put their money into a bank system. And he never truly trusted white people to keep his money without stealing it.

In view of what America went through during the first years of the Obama Administration with the banks having to be bailed out because some of them were busy making deals that were detrimental and under-minded the overall economic health of our nation, I guess it is understandable how my grandfather felt. To top it all off, not a single person as far as I know was convicted as a result of the worst banking scandal to ever hit this country since the Great Depression's 1929 stock market crash.

The George Bush years of government caused this nation to suffer serious financial problems and a general loss of world respect as a nation representing the free world. Mr. Bush is the only U.S. President that I know of to have had shoes thrown at him while he was visiting the foreign country of Iran. This act is symbolic of a "complete and utter disrespect" for the recipient of the shoe attack. In this case, it was our beloved President, George W. Bush.

The headlines of December 15, 2008 were:

> "A surprise visit by US President George Bush to Iraq has been overshadowed by an incident in which two shoes were thrown at him during a news conference. An Iraqi journalist was wrestled to the floor by security guards after he called Mr. Bush "a dog" and threw his footwear, just missing the President".

To this very day, we are still not back to where we should be.

Now back to our little family's home burning to the ground. After our father had gotten everyone out of the house, he and my mother counted heads. We were all there, including grandpa. The only clothes the kids had on were their night clothes. I had on white jockey briefs and a thin white tee shirt and no shoes. All the other kids had on similar dress.

What I do remember is that we stood outside on the snowy cold ground watching our house completely burn and implode to the ground. As for myself, I was never cold anywhere on my body. I think the same was true for the rest of the family but I cannot say for sure. Based on how they were standing, I never heard anyone say they were cold.

After our house burned down, our family was scattered among other family members for the first time. The girls stayed with my parents and some of the boys stayed with my uncle Bobby. Bobby was my father's older brother and Aunt Anna Bell was his wife. They did not have any children of their own.

The boys were divided up into two's and some stayed with this uncle, or that aunt, or an old friend of the family. We were apart for about two or three weeks before my father and Mr. Paul Williams found a nice home for us to stay in. Mr. Paul immediately began building a newer house to replace the one that burned down on his farm. The new house was better than the old one only because the wood was newer. Otherwise it was the exact same, small wood frame house built exactly on the same spot of the old house that burned down.

My father was a man of vision. None of us knew that he was working two jobs and farming, all the while saving his money to buy his own home. His plans for home ownership materialized one day in 1966, when he took out a home loan from a bank in a county adjacent to his home county. Thus, the builders began construction on the first Johnson family home.

My father had purchased a plot of ground outside of town on what was called the old Hurricane Hill Road without telling us. During this time, plants and other manufacturing companies began to move into Lauderdale County and my father being the kind of man that he was, applied and was accepted to work in one of those new plants. He was hired to work for the Tupper Ware Company. They manufactured plastic ware and were considered by many to have the best product in their market. My father was now making a living without back-breaking labor, and for the first time in his life, he did not have to smile and grin to get what he had worked for.

I think it was during the Labor Day weekend when most of the black and white people celebrated the holiday that there was some confusion with Mr. Paul and my father over some work that Mr. Paul wanted us to do. My father had already made plans for the family to rest and enjoy the holiday weekend as a result of all the work we had already put in leading up to this day. To make a long story short, when my father refused to make us go back into the field and work until later that evening, Mr. Paul got angry and told him if he could not do as he was told, that maybe it was time for us to be looking for a new place to stay. He did not realize that my father was having a new house built and the house was now complete and ready for us to move into.

They say a picture is worth a thousand words. I wish someone could have captured the look on Mr. Paul Williams' face when my father informed him that he would be moving off his land starting the next day. After he said this, he simply turned and walked away.

I heard later that Mr. Paul did all that he could to talk my father out of moving. When he saw that my father was going to move anyway, he did all he could to find out where my father was moving. When he finally found out that we had moved into our own home, he surprised our family with a visit. Mr. Paul and his wife, Miss Betsy stopped by to see how we were doing and before they left he asked my father how this had happened. I am not sure of exactly how my father answered this question, but knowing him the way that I do, I would venture to say, his answer had something to do with " by the grace of God" this was made possible. I am sure he never told him the details of how or why he did what he did.

Mr. and Mrs. Paul Williams were no different than any other white land owners in the south at this time. They were not bad people per se; they were living out what they had been taught by their parents. They were taught that whites were superior to blacks and that blacks were inferior to them in all things. However, they could not see that things were changing for them. They could not see that the old "sharecropper" black man that had to always respond to any and all white people regardless of age as "yes sir", or "no sir" was on its way out. So we moved and started our new life in a house that was far better than any house that we ever stayed in when we had sharecropped for a living. Thank you, God, for your mercy and your grace.

Death Events that Brought Life

Chapter 7

The four major deaths of my life are short personal stories, the first one starting with the death of my Grandfather. The stories are about the actual death of four people closely related to me and who had a major impact on my life. It is by no means an attempt to minimize and devalue the death of other individuals that have also deeply enriched my life. I am truly grateful and appreciative of the impact that each person had on my early years.

The Death of My Grandfather – Event 6

My grandfather was born on September 16, 1882. His name was Carliss Brooks Johnson. People that really knew him called him Mr. Brooks. I still remember the night my grandfather passed away. He had been sick and was in the hospital. When the telephone rang at 11:30 pm, I knew he was dead. I felt his death all through my body. I suddenly felt sick, and when my mother confirmed what I already knew, my tears were already flowing.

I called him "Grandpa" and he was a special kind of man. I remember him being a gentle man with a genuine patient and humble spirit. He had a very easy smile and was always easy to talk with. He and I spent a lot of time just talking. Some of the most memorable and enjoyable times of my life were spent with him and I sitting outside on our front porch in an old raggedy swing, rocking back and forth and just talking. I would ask him all kinds of questions about life, and then one day he said to me with a slight smile on his face, "Donnell, you may be young in age, but you have an old person's mind." I never quite knew what he meant by that, as I went on to the next question.

Ironically, I find that my youngest granddaughter, Caidyn, has this same habit of asking me questions without end. She never seems to stop, and she enjoys just sitting and talking to me. Sometimes when I tire of all her questions and begin to get irritable with her, I remind myself of how patient my grandfather was with me. So, I try to be patient like he was to me, but I admit I fall short at times. This child has no end to her questions!

As I have said, my Grandfather was born in 1882. He was a devout God-fearing man, and it was evident in how easily he lived his life with contentment and how he carried himself. I spent all of my early life around this man, and I never once heard him say a curse word, or anything negative or bad about anybody-black or white. He loved the Lord and he would always tell me never to grow up doing wrong and telling lies. He always reminded me that God looks after His children. I was not old enough to appreciate what he was telling me then, even though I understood what he was saying.

I did not truly grasp the truth of his words. As an adult with grandchildren of my own, I have truly learned and can testify from my heart to the reality that God will, can, and does take care of His children. I'll share a testimony on this later.

My Grandfather taught me that if you borrow a penny, then you pay a penny back. He would always tell me that the mark of a good man is one who stands behind what he says. He would always tell me to never be known as a liar. "Say what you mean, and mean what you say." He talked to me about always having the correct respect for your elders, women, and white people. He was wise enough to teach me that during this time period between 1950 and 1970, that to disrespect white people could bring unnecessary harm to me personally and to the family. In other words, if you were to say good morning to a white person - let's use our land owner for an example – say, "Good morning Mr. Paul", and this greeting and acknowledgement of him made him feel superior to you. You have not lost anything by giving this person a false sense of security that they are better than you.

What you gained by playing by their rules was a house to live in, help in feeding your family, money to live on, land to grow your cotton or corn, and a place to raise your family. The white landowner had connections with the influential white community members in case there were serious problems that he alone could not handle. Self-pride is one thing, survival is quite another!

During the time of the "Jim Crow" south, black people were only striving to survive and raise their families with little or no help from anyone. This is why so many black families and black people migrated to the north in search of better living and working conditions. My grandfather loved to look up into the heavens as though he was talking to someone. Sometimes he would tell us, "It is going to rain this evening around about four o'clock, so be sure and put the mules in the barn." Now if you did not do this and it rained, it was your fault, because he had already told you what was going to happen. My grandfather was not highly educated, but he had a natural wisdom, that to this day, I still do not understand. For example, he had a way of reading your mind that was uncanny and scary.

My grandfather was a good judge of character. He could look at someone and correctly analyze their nature. When one guy called himself courting my oldest sister, my grandfather walked by him one day and looked at him but never said a word. He later let it be known that this particular young man was not good enough for my sister. He said this person had a mean spirit about him. A few years later we found that my grandfather was correct. This same young man ended up hurting a girl very badly because she broke up with him.

My grandfather loved going to church, and he loved gospel music and good preaching. One of my grandfather's most favorite songs was *"A Charge to Keep I have"*. This is an old gospel hymn that was written by Charles Wesley (1707 – 1788) the brother of John Wesley who was the founder of the Methodist religion.

The words of this song are:

"A charge to keep I have, A God to glorify,
Who gave his Son my soul to save, and fit it for the sky?
To serve the present age, my calling to fulfill
O may it all my powers engage, to do my Masters will.
Arm me with jealous care, as in thy sight to live,
And O thy servant, Lord prepare, a strict account to give.
Help me to watch and pray, and on thyself rely,
By faith assured I will obey, for I shall never die."

I will always remember the teachings of my grandfather. He was more than a grandfather to me. He was also my father, my teacher, and my friend. A sad reality for some kids today is that some of them will grow up and never appreciate the beauty of spending time with an older, loving, and caring grandfather or grandmother.

Sadly, the hustle and bustle of this modern generation teaches kids about texting each other and communicating through Facebook updates. Some of them will never take the time to spend with their older parents. When they die, it will be too late to wish that they could have known them better. Young people, get to you know your family – especially your grandparents. They will surprise you with what they know about life.

The Death of Tommy – 1960 – 1994 – Event 7

The death of my younger brother, Tommy Ray Johnson in August of 1994, came as a complete surprise to our family. Tommy Ray, or "Tommy" as he was called, was a very popular young man. He was an excellent athlete, he wore his hair in a big afro and he was blessed with good looks, very intelligent, and yes, all the girls just loved him. However, one of the most desired attributes about Tommy that I admired was that he was a saved young man.

Tommy got married early in life. He went from the Baptist church directly into a Pentecostal Church of God in Christ at an early age. After his conversion, he was saved and filled with the Holy Spirit. Tommy was a young man who was always involved in the church. He sung in the choir, he and his wife and their three kids were heavily involved in their church activities. That's why his death took everyone by surprise. He was never a smoker or drinker of alcohol, and as far as I know, he never "ever" was involved with illegal drugs.

Tommy became sick one day at work. They sent him to the local hospital. From there he was transferred to a bigger hospital in Memphis, Tennessee. The doctors at this hospital said that Tommy had a heart murmur, and that he was suffering from a type of virus infection in his heart. During an operation on his heart, he died. When I heard the news that my younger brother had passed away, I was beyond words. I immediately made plans to go home and attend his funeral. From where I live in Decatur, Illinois to

Ripley, Tennessee is a drive of about 6 to 7 hours, arriving in Ripley around 4:00 pm.

It was a beautiful, sunny day when I arrived home. As I began to turn left on Highway #19 East toward Brownsville, Tennessee, I met a truck going west in the opposite direction. We were the only two vehicles on the road at the time. When the truck and I passed each other, I just barely got a glimpse of the driver; but he looked like my brother Tommy - same big afro and all. I did a double-take and immediately looked in the rear view mirror to see the old truck that I had just passed. To my surprise, there was no truck there. My car was the only car on the road! I called this event the "visions of Tommy". The reason that I call this a vision is because I know what I saw. I am not delusional. I was not drinking, and it was a clear and beautiful day. I do not know why I was allowed to see Tommy driving this old truck, but I did.

The second event or vision that I was allowed to see as it relates to Tommy happened at his funeral. To this very day it is still a mystery to me. On the day of my brother's funeral after the service was over, Tommy's body was taken to the Springhill Baptist Church cemetery for burial. The graveyard is only a short distance from our church. The pastor was saying the last words and Tommy was being lowered into the ground. The pastor was reading a scripture from John, Chapter 11:25-26. The Scripture reads as follows: "*I am the resurrection, and the life: he that believeth in me, though he were dead, yet shall he live: And whosoever liveth and believeth in me. He shall never die.*"

As people were standing around talking, I noticed my mother talking with one of her friends. She was talking to Myron Driver's mother and his younger sister Debra Driver- Morgan. I walked over to listen to their conversation and to comfort my mother, but I was the one who really needed to be comforted. As the woman talked, I had a strong urge to look over my right shoulder towards Heaven, and boy, what a vision the Lord blessed me to see. I was allowed to see directly up into heaven.

It seemed that as soon as the casket was lowered into the ground, the casket or something that resembled a casket was received in heaven. It appeared as if two figures stood at the foot of the casket, two figures directly beside and behind the casket in the middle, and two figures standing by the head of the casket. Everything was white and somewhat transparent. I could not make out faces, but I could see distinctive shapes of heads, body shapes, and their wings. The wings appeared to be folded and the tips of each hump of the wing were on each side of the head. There appeared to be thousands upon thousands of these small figures. It looked like they were all sitting or standing in a huge coliseum, similar to what you would expect to see at a major football or baseball game.

I could not fully comprehend what I was experiencing because I was completely amazed at what I had just been given the privilege to see. God does not make mistakes! I was allowed to see this vision for a reason.

I was not daydreaming, I was not drunk, and I definitely was not hallucinating. I know what I saw! Why I saw it remains a mystery to this day. Moreover, as I really began to focus on what I was looking at, the clouds of heaven seemed to just "softly and gently" close the view, which might be similar to the closing of the curtains when the first act of a major play is over.

Over the years I have thought about this incident and wondered the meaning of it. A few years later, I told my mother and father what I saw. However, I don't think they really understood or appreciated the meaning of it as I did. Before I leave this chapter in my life as it relates to Tommy's death, there is one more vision that I need to make known.

A few years after Tommy's death, my parents had a family portrait made of all the kids in our family. This was the first official family portrait ever made of the Johnson family. It just so happened that all the kids were home for the Labor Day holiday, and we got together and took a family group picture.

The family's portrait was taken right in the front yard of our parent's home under a beautiful tree. Everybody was there except Tommy. After the portraits were completed, we were all looking at the large picture, when one of the girls noticed something embedded in the picture. The face of Tommy Ray Johnson can be seen in the outline of the tree that we were standing beside. Tommy had a big afro back then and if you look at the tree in this picture very closely, you will truly see the shape and the outline of a man's head with an afro. We still have the original family portrait hanging in my mother's living room. And to this day, you can still see my brother's face in that tree. God is truly awesome!

This picture below is of all my brothers and sisters, with the exception of Tommy. The picture was taken the Labor Day weekend of 2012. We are standing in the front yard of my bother–in–law's home in Henning, Tennessee. You might remember the name of Henning, Tennessee as the boyhood home of Alex Hailey, the author/writer of the book "*Roots*".

The picture above is a snapshot of some of the boys just hanging out in our mother's kitchen.

The picture above is a snapshot of all the sisters in our family. Yes, it's the girl's time to shine.

This picture is of all the boys except Tommy. I suspect he is standing with us but we just can't see him. My mother was really glad to have all her boys and girls together at one time. She cried a lot that whole weekend! She is 85 years young in the pictrure. She loves the Lord and she will tell you that!

This picture is of my youngest brother and my grandmother, Sally Smith, who will be 102 years her next birthday, if God is willing. She does not take any medications, does not wear eyeglasses and can see better than I can. Her favorite quote: **Keep living!**

This is my mother, Mattie Ella Johnson, the woman who bore 18 children with one man, Mr. William Henry Johnson.

Yes, she is still fine!

Death of Mr. William Henry Johnson, My Father – Event 8

When I think of my father, I think of a real life hero. My father was a man who was not very well educated in the secular sense. He only had an eighth grade education, but that never stopped him from learning, growing, and developing himself into a man who was completely responsible, caring, and loyal to his family. There are so many things I could say about by dad. His life's story alone could very easily fill a book.

On one occasion, my father told me that the black man is the best friend that the white man has ever had, but the white man was too arrogant and hateful to know this. He went on to list some pretty interesting historical data to support his position. He went from slavery, all the way to the Civil War, World War I, World War II, and all the wars in between. He told us how the black man had given his life for a country that has never fully regarded his life as worthy.

I will only talk about those characteristics of my father that made him unique to me. I think that it is very profoundly interesting that my father and my grandfather shared the same birthday. My grandfather was born on September 16, 1882 and died on January 10, 1968. My father was also born on September 16, 1923 and died on September 1, 2005.

My father died a few days after Hurricane Katrina struck the Gulf Coast of North America. I will always associate my father's death with the year of Katrina. In case some of you who are reading this book have forgotten, Hurricane Katrina was one of the worst hurricanes to ever hit the city of New Orleans, Louisiana. As a matter of historical records, my research informs me that Katrina was one of the five deadliest hurricanes in the recorded history of the United States. Hurricane Katrina formed on August 23, 2005 and dissipated on August 30, 2005. This hurricane had sustained winds of 175 mph and had confirmed fatalities of 1,833.

This storm was, without a doubt, a major catastrophic event with life-altering implications wherever it struck. Katrina had a major impact on the nations of Cuba, and the United States of America – especially in the greater New Orleans, Louisiana, Mississippi, Alabama, and the Florida Panhandle area. Additionally, most of eastern North America was affected by the storm. In total property damage alone, it was estimated that this hurricane will cost an estimated $81 billion to repair its losses. As of the Labor Day holiday September 2012, there are portions of the city of New Orleans, the Ninth Ward and other areas, that are still uninhabited. Hurricane Isaac of 2012 also hit the city on almost the exact same date as Katrina had devastated it seven years earlier. God works in mysterious ways, His wonders to perform!

What I find to be completely mind-boggling about Katrina is that the people living near the Gulf Coast were advised to leave. Many people living in the greater metropolitan area of New Orleans, Louisiana refused to leave. I remember watching the news about this storm and some of the people were drinking alcohol and planning "Hurricane Katrina" parties. People listen! Planning a party for a level 5 hurricane is like having a death wish. It is not only suicidal, it is just plain dumb. It is like mocking the powers of an Almighty God. Any human who thumbs their nose in God's face, has not truly considered the cost of their action. God will hold them accountable. Hebrews 10:31 warns us that: *"It is a fearful thing to fall into the hands of the living God."* I remember saying, "Lord, My God - what is wrong with us? Are we so blind to sin? Are we so vain in our imagination- that we would plan a party in the face of such a major destruction? O foolish humans do not forget your Creator! He is the Living God.

The weather newscasters listed Katrina as being a level 5 hurricane. My limited interpretation of storms would still cause me to seek the higher ground. Common sense would kick in, it would scream to leave this city. A level 5 hurricane is something we don't see hitting our coast very often. I could not comprehend people making light of a deadly approaching situation. I realize there were people who may have gotten trapped in specific areas and could not escape. Seniors citizens, people with no car transportation, and people in hospitals and nursing homes probably had to ride the storm out. There were also people who chose to stay with their own property because they'd been through similar storms and did not want the hassle of moving. For whatever reason, the cost of staying in the greater New Orleans area and the other outlying areas was very expensive. Some people paid for their decision to stay with their own lives. God works in mysterious ways, His wonders to perform."

Whenever I think of Katrina, a natural catastrophic event of Biblical proportions, I can't help but think of Sodom and Gomorrah. I think of the great flood that Noah and his family survived. I think of the "Passover", the night when God allowed the death Angel to pass through and over the children of Israel. The death Angel consumed the firstborn of all humans and beasts that did not have the Blood of the Lamb over their door post.

I think of God parting the Red Sea and making available the dry ground for His people to cross. Who is like God, I will say it again - who is like our God? When we stop and truly consider all the spectacularly wonderful and fearful things that God has done in history, it causes me to tremble with fear. Who are we humans to ever think or dare to challenge Him? Lord, please forgive us for our "human" pride, arrogance and conceit. Help us to see YOU, who is the real power in this world. My father and mother taught us to always have respect for God, because God is Holy. His holiness means perfection in everything that He does, in righteousness, in judgment, in wisdom, and all things that we can think of. He is perfection personified.

My father's childhood was similar to that of the other poor black families living in the rural south that had to work to make a living. As a result of their poor living conditions, a lot of the black people living in the 1900 – 1960's time frame did not go to college, or even finish high school. They had to work the fields to help feed and support their families. That is why my father, like so many other poor black men, had a sub-standard education. I think maybe that is why he made such a fuss about all of his children getting an education. We all had to at least stay in school and finish high school. This was the rule of law in our home: you would finish high school, and anything beyond that would be up to you.

My father and mother had a total of eighteen kids; three died at birth and fifteen survived. My mother gave birth to eleven boys and seven girls. Starting with the brothers first, I will name all of the kids in the order of their birth - including their nicknames and those who died:

The Boys:

        William Ivory Johnson – *"Peter"*
        James Larry Johnson – *"Tosh/Macintosh"*
        Lafayette Johnson – died at birth
        Curtis Donnell Johnson – *"Pumpkin"*
        Arthur Louis Johnson – *"Chicken"*

Terry Lee Johnson – *"Poonkie" (now called the "Giga Man")*
Thomas Ray Johnson – *"Tommy T"* – died at age 33
William Henry Johnson, Jr. – *"Z Bull"*
Bobby Glen Johnson – *"Baby Boy BB"*
Two twin boys died at birth – no names were assigned to them.

The Girls:

Mattie Lou Johnson – *"Big Sister" or "Big Sis"*
Linda Faye Johnson –
Brenda Joyce Johnson – *"Inquiring Minds Want to Know"*
Anna Francis Johnson – *"Miss Anna"*
Rosie Ann Johnson
Doretha Yvonne Johnson – *"The Professor"*
Deborah Kay Johnson – *"Debbs"*

Do you remember the popular family television show called "Brady Bunch?" Well, let me assure you, the Brady Bunch had nothing on us. Even though we were a large family, we were not clones of each other. Each child had their own distinct personality and style. You could get into trouble very quickly trying to treat us all the same way. That did not work back then and it doesn't work now.

We were a large family and for the most part, we were dirt poor. We, like so many other black and white families of the rural South growing up in the 1940s through 1960s time frame, lived on what was called a sharecropper's income. Living on a sharecropper's income means to actually do the manual labor and to work the farmland and produce such crops as soybeans, corn, cotton, tobacco, etc. After the crops were harvested in the fall of the year, the money would be tabulated and the landholder would take out his cut. Some of the landowners were so unscrupulous, that the poor tenant farmers that lived on the land could never get out of debt, because the landholder usually ended up getting most of the money. The poor sharecropper ended the year in debt, and started the New Year in debt. I cannot begin to tell you how our parents were able to clothe and feed fifteen children, on a sharecropper's income. That, in and of itself, is a miracle. Thinking back over our life in the Johnson household, I cannot remember a time when we went to bed dirty or hungry. Even when we were working out in the fields every day in the hot sun chopping cotton or picking cotton before going to bed at night, our mother made us wash and clean up our bodies.

Looking back over my life in the Johnson family, I can see that the hand of God was the "true glue" that held our family together. Even though we did not have much money, we had love for each other, and our parents had much love for us. Our parents were strong believers in Jesus and the Word of God. Going to church every Sunday in our family was not an option. It was a requirement. The requirement was a condition that if you wanted to continue to live in the Johnson household under the leadership of my father and my mother, you went to church.

My father and mother took their kids to church. And if you wanted to have a bad day, let either of them hear you murmuring about not wanting to go to church. I thank God for my parents, who had the wisdom to teach us about God, at an early age in life. Even though as kids we did not fully understand or appreciate what going to church and good Bible teaching was doing for us, we fully understand its importance now. Our parents taught us many things. The one thing they taught us that continues to stand out from all the rest is: "*Put God first-in all that you do.*" In other words, if you cannot justify to God that what you are doing, or are about to do is right, then don't do it.

If only I had followed their example and life plans. I would have avoided a lot of pain and suffering. However, I can truly testify that I am a living testimony. Had it not been for the mercy and grace of God, I would have been gone a long time ago. Our parents taught us early about the values of work.

You will find biblical references for the value of work in Scripture beginning with Genesis 2:8 and 20:15 that was instituted by God. Before the fall of man, Genesis 2:15 states: *"And the LORD God took the man, and put him into the Garden of Eden to dress it and to keep it. And the LORD God said it is not good that the man should be alone."* In 2 Thessalonians 3:6 we learn that *"if a man did not work, he did not eat."* From Ephesians 2:10 we learn that *"we are God's workmanship, created in Christ Jesus to do good works."* God not only expects us to work, He expects us to produce good work worthy of His acceptance. *To confirm this, the* Apostle Paul said *in* Colossians 3:23, *"Whatever you do, do it with all your heart, as unto the Lord."*

Our mother and father were truly unique people. In addition to instilling into us a good work ethic, they made sure that we knew that lying and stealing and cheating were not of God. I can still hear them saying: "*if you lie, you will steal, if you will steal, you will kill.*" To be called a liar in our family was a big deal. That was one title you did not want to have!

My father's health began to fade in the year of 2005. He had cancer and this infected his lungs in the latter stages. My father was the kind of man who loved the church and loved to sing in the choir. However, because he was on an oxygen machine to help him breath, singing was out of the question; or was it? I was told by several members of our church that before my father died that he asked the Lord to allow him to sing one more time, one more song in the church choir. Moreover, God allowed him to sing three songs in the church choir, and I was told that he sang all three songs with great power.

What's more, on the following Sunday a week later, he was able to sing two more songs. He sang with great power, but on September 1, 2005, he died in his sleep. God truly does work in mysterious ways His wonders to perform. And God does hear and answers prayers that are according to His will. My father died right before the Labor Day holiday. For some reason, it had become a tradition on the part of a lot of black families in Ripley, Tennessee and other counties in Western Tennessee, to celebrate the holiday with a family get together. There are many family reunions planned around this weekend.

I assume that a lot of people in the good old U.S.A. have heard of Memphis, Tennessee. This is the largest city in west Tennessee; however, there are a lot of people [black and white] as well as other races who live and work in smaller communities in western Tennessee, like Brownsville, Dyersburg, Ripley, Henning, Covington and Nutbush. People who now live in various parts of the country and the world, who at one time lived in the smaller communities in western Tennessee, usually try to come home for the Labor Day weekend.

The City of Ripley, Tennessee has a yearly celebration for homecoming activities. Many families schedule their reunions to coincide with the city's homecoming festivities. On Monday, Labor Day and the last day of the holiday weekend, there is a parade. Hundreds, and sometimes thousands of people, line both sides of the streets to watch the parade. There are high school marching bands competing for the best band trophy. There are floats with all kinds of creative designs. The Shriners ride around in their small cars throwing candies to the children and there are people playing music and dancing, and people riding in their fancy cars, trucks, and on motorbikes. The last part of the parade is the horse show.

The horse show is comprised of horse riders and owners who can make their horses perform tricks. Some of the tricks include making the horse dance or prance; some make their horses take a bow after they have finished performing. Some horse riders train their horses to "bend down" or "stoop down" so the rider can get on its back. Then the horse will stand up with the rider on its back. It is all very impressive to see.

The parade finally ends up at Rice Park. Rice Park is for the black citizens of Ripley, Tennessee. At the park, softball games are in full swing, and many food pavilions are open for the adults to eat and mingle with old classmates, family and friends. There are carnival rides for the children to enjoy.

Scheduling the yearly family reunions around the Labor Day weekend is a good way of staying in contact with your family and old friends. It seemed to be the providence of an All-Knowing God, who took my father home a few days before the Labor Day weekend. God knew that my father's health was bad and we had already scheduled a family reunion for the Labor Day holiday. Family members came from California, Virginia, Washington, Illinois, Georgia, as well as other states, to participate and enjoy the long overdue Johnson, Wilsons, Hence, and Boyd families as well as many other family members from across the US and overseas. So what did God do? He turned a family reunion into a" home going" celebration. The family was already home to attend the family reunion. So while we were all home for one function, God added another. God truly works in mysterious ways, His wonders to perform.

I truly felt that God's timing was perfection! God did not allow any of us to go back to our respective homes after the Labor Day celebration and family reunion was over just to turn right around and return for the funeral of my father. This would have been very expensive for those living in states that are far away from Tennessee. God knows what is best. I have learned to trust in Him completely. Even when I do not understand His ways, I will still trust Him. All of His decisions are right, even if we cannot see them at the moment.

On the morning of the funeral, my family and I were staying in a motel. I woke up early that morning. When I looked at the clock in our room it was around 4:30 am. I went outside to get some fresh air so as not to disturb the rest of my family who were still asleep. Once outside, I quickly re-discovered that the Tennessee early morning air is very cool and damp. However, the damp air felt really good on my face, and as I continued to gaze up into the heavens, I began to meditate on my father's death and burial that was scheduled for later that morning.

I felt sad that morning as I reflected on my father. I thought of all the things that he taught us. I noticed the clearest, brightest and the biggest ever Big Dipper Asterism that I had ever seen. Somehow my thoughts connected this heavenly body of seven stars to the death of my father. Each star was very distinctly visible and sparkled like a diamond. I said, "Wow, look at how big the Big Dipper really is!"

I thought about my father as a big dipper of life, and the more I thought about this concept, I wrote the following declaration: *"A Testimony to My Father."* It was a tribute to him that I read at his funeral. I will quote exactly what I feel the Lord laid on my heart to write, in reference to the Big Dipper and my father's status here on earth – in God's eyes.

Please note that I said my father's "status" in God's eyes" not man's eyes. If he were judged by the world's standard, he would be judged as a failure. The world would say, "What is so exceptional about a poor, black, uneducated sharecropper who struggled to feed and clothe his family, a man with less than an eighth grade education, who could barely read and write, a man who fathered 18 children, and whose only claim to fame was a love for God, family and country. Why should the world honor such a man?"

I choose to see my father through the eyes of "faith" in his God – Jesus the Son of the most High God. I see a man who never abandoned his family. He was a man who taught his kids the value of working for a living, and of learning about and trusting in a Holy God. He was a man who never abused his wife or his children. He was a man who sometimes worked three jobs to take care of us. He was a man that always tried to instill in his children, education and the desire to do what is right. He wanted us to always love ourselves, each other and never be ashamed of where we came from.

My dad was a true teacher of life by being an excellent example for us and to all that knew him. What a beautiful example of true manhood to follow. His "motto" about life would be: "Always put God first in all that you do, family responsibilities cannot be allocated or delegated to anyone else, and lastly, honor the rules and regulations of the country that you live in."

"A Testimony to My Father"

When I was a young boy, I used to let my mind wonder sometimes on things that I was too young to fully comprehend. Things like what it would feel like to lose someone that you truly love, admired and respected? As a young child growing up in a poor Tennessee family, I used to envision what life would be like if we lost our father and mother. I remember thinking, "who would want us? Who would want all of these children? Who would want to take care of and feed so many children?" Then, I would begin to worry.

I can remember as a child growing up in a household in which we were all a part of the same litter, yet as children we all had very different and well established personalities. I would speculate on how my mother and father could always find just the right words to settle a dispute or soothe a hurting or broken heart. My mother had her ways, and my father had his. I was constantly amazed at how they always seemed to be on the same page regarding how they would relate to us. We could never pull anything over on them without getting caught. They would sooner or later find out what we did.

They would always ask, "Who did this?", and "woe" to the kid that lied and did not admit his/her involvement. Lying to cover your mistake was not an option to consider in our home. If you lied, and they caught you in a lie, you had to be punished for the lie you told, plus, what you were lying about.

They never punished us without just cause but they did punish us. I do not know about the rest of my family members, but when it came time for getting a spanking, I would rather have it done by my father than my mother. Our father did the majority of the physical discipline. He would talk to you as he was whipping you and then let you go. His spanking was quick, hard and then it was over. My mother, on the other hand, would work overtime on you. She would be very quiet during the spanking process. All that you would see is that strange look in her eyes that let you know she meant business. She would say things like "No, I'm not done with you yet Mr. (whatever you did wrong would fill this space)."

I only remember one of my father's, many spankings. I remember all three of my mother's, but, she would always come back sooner or later and talk to you and make you see that what you did was wrong. She had a way of talking to you that made you wish she would just spank you again and stop talking. That's because the truth, the admitted truth, makes a connection with reality and forever is stored in the mind "under lessons learned." I will never do that again.

As previously stated, at 4:30 am, the day of my father's funeral, I could not sleep, so I got up and went outside to get some fresh air. I was standing outside reflecting on our family reunion, my father's death, and life in general. I looked up into the eastern sky and there was the most brilliant picture of the Big Dipper that I had ever seen.

It seemed to be very close to the earth and it was crystal clear. It dawned on me that our father to us was a "Big Dipper". He was a Big Dipper on having faith in Almighty God and he was a Big Dipper in working hard to support his family. He was a Big Dipper in regard to love, kindness, honesty, and trying to always do what was right. In many respects, he reminds me of Father Abraham, whose faith in God was immeasurable

The Johnson family will surely miss our "Big Dipper" but he was promoted to a better life with God. Scripture tells us that "to be absent from the body is to be present with the Lord." (2 Corinthians 5:8)

Therefore, our biological father is now present with the Lord. However, because he lived his life as a Big Dipper of life, his legacy will live on. If my father were here now, he would charge each of us, his children, with the following responsibility:

1. *Take care of your mother and her mother, Mama Sally, our grandmother.*

2. *Study and learn to understand the wisdom of Scripture. For example, Proverbs 3:5-6 "Trust in the Lord with all thine heart and lean not to thine own understanding, in all thy ways acknowledge Him and he will direct your path."*

3. *As a family, stay connected, in love and fellowship, and continues to cherish each other.*

4. *To any family member, friend or foe, if you do not have a right relationship with God, you need to make it right, while you are yet living.*

5. *To have a right relationship with God, you need to acknowledge that God exists, and confess your sins to Him with a pure heart and a humble and contrite spirit and live right.*

6. *He would advise us to raise our children in the fear of the Lord, to take them to church and teach them about God early in life, because that same God that watched over all of us will continue to watch over our children when we are long gone.*

"Father, I do not know if you can hear me, but if you can, rest assured that as a family we will strive on. We will continue to live up to the examples that you established for us to follow in faith with God. We will hold ourselves accountable to look after our mother, and our grandmother. We will pass on to the next generation the true value of life, which is to fear God, and put Him first in our lives. We will teach our family to learn of Him and to keep His commandments."

In closing, I want to give credit to and recognize other family members of the Johnson, Boyd and the Wilson family members who have gone on before us to live with God.

- *Carliss Brooks Johnson and wife (our grandfather and grandmother)*

- *Uncle Bobby Johnson and Uncle Hewitt Johnson*

- *Uncle Walter and Aunt Jennie V. Wilson*

- *Uncle Sam and Aunt Mary Boyd*

- *Tommy Ray Johnson – our brother*

- *Milton Wilson – my cousin for life*

- *Brian D. Johnson – my only son (and the list goes on)*

A few years ago I lost my son. It took me a long time to come to the realization that he was gone from this earth, and that I would never see him again in this life. I admit that for a long time I blamed myself for his loss. I felt that I was not a good enough father. I failed to see what my son was going through.

Then, that gentle Voice that only comes from above reminded me that God calls all His children home and that only God Almighty knows the fate of all people, and that nothing good or bad happens on this earth without it being a part of His perfect will. I came to the reality that God alone is in control of all our lives. He decides how each of us will leave this earth. If you are a student of Scripture, you will very quickly discover that God is a Sovereign Power. He is God all by Himself. He said, *"Beside Me, there is no other"*. (Isaiah 45:51)

In Jeremiah, Chapter 23:23 God says - *"Am I a God at hand," saith the Lord "and not a God far off? Can any hide in secret places that I shall not see him?" saith the Lord.*

I am so glad that my father and mother taught us the value of serving a true and living God. I will have to admit, I did not always follow the path of righteousness, but I have always believed. It was not until late in my life that God made me aware that I was a part of a blessed family – His family chosen long before I was born, as many of you are here today.

Yes, I said "before" I was born. In Jeremiah, Chapter 1:4, God speaks of His knowledge of us before we were born. He says: *"Before I formed you in the belly, I knew thee."* Although He was talking to Jeremiah in this instance, the same applies to us today.

Of all the things that we learned from our parents, the most precious is that they took us to church and taught us about having a right relationship with our Creator. The scripture says to raise up a child in the way that he/she should go, so if he/she departs from it, he/she will one day return to it. I have found this to be true.

The Death of My Son, Brian D. Johnson – Event 9

It is difficult writing about my son. I thought I could write this short story about him without becoming too emotionally upset with feelings I thought I had under control. After all, he has been gone from us for a while. I was wrong. As I thought about my son Brian, the more I realized what a big, empty hole there is in my heart and my life as a result of his death. I wish my son was still here. I miss his reassuring smile and his easy-going style of life. Nothing seemed to bother him.

If there is anything that can be gleaned from the death of my son, I will say I have learned we never quite fully understand the impact loved ones have on our lives, or the impact we have on another person's life until that person is gone. It is too late to say all the things we wish we could have said or done for that person. Lesson learned! If you truly love someone, tell them so. Do not wait because later may be too late. And if you think they will not appreciate what you have to say, too bad, say it anyway. Just do it! Don't let another hour, day, month or year slip away without confirming how you really feel about the ones you love.

Black men in particular, are bad about holding in their feelings, and not letting their wives, mothers, fathers, brothers, sisters and children know that they love them. Black men should stop being "stingy" with their affection. If you love your wife tell her so. If you love your family, show it. Trust me, they need to hear it more often than you realize. Men, do not make your wife and the rest of your family perform to get your attention. We, as fathers, have been given the God-given assignment to nourish, love and cherish our families. Therefore such a precious a gift from God should not have to guess if you love them or not.

In reference to love - John 3: 16–17 says: *"For God so loved the world that he gave his only begotten Son, that whosoever believeth in him should not perish, but have everlasting life. For God sent not his Son into the world to condemn the world; but that the world through him might be saved."* Now if God Almighty would allow His son to die for a sinner like me, like all of us, who are we to withhold our love from our families, friends and especially all who profess a belief in Jesus Christ. In the book of Ephesians 5:28, God teaches us through the Apostle Paul that *"So ought men to love their wives as their own bodies. He that loveth his wife loveth himself."* So men, the next time when you are given the opportunity to tell your family that you love and cherish them and you fail to do this, you are failing the commandments of God.

Consider how many of our young women have entered into the profession of prostitution because they failed to receive the reassuring love from a father figure in their early life. How many of our young men and women have ventured into a life of drugs, crime and gangs simply because they were never told the word "son or daughter, I love you?" If they do wrong, don't beat around the bush tell them the truth, in a loving and encouraging way. "Yes, you did wrong, but I still love you and will continue to love you through whatever you are going through." That is the way God loves us every day. Pass this love on to others – especially with your own family members starting right now. Learn to be forgiving and show mercy and love whenever you are given the chance.

Now, let me get back to my son. This short story is about him, yet, it is not about him. It would be impossible to summarize the life of my son into a short story. He was gifted. I want to share briefly about my son's life and how the Lord worked to teach me a valuable lesson about caring, and having empathy for others. No one lives in this world in a vacuum. When one person (black or white- any race or national origin) hurts, we all hurt. The death of a mother or father in any family is a tragic event. We need to understand and not see it from the stand point of "Oh well. It's not my mother or father."

My son was a gift from the Lord. To this day, I hurt. I think of him often even though he has been dead since February 13, 2001. There is something unbearable in the heart of a father who has lost his only son. It is like having a dull knife penetrate your consciousness every day. It is like an insatiable longing that can never be satisfied. To lose a son or daughter, especially your only son or daughter, is a life-altering event.

My son and I were very close, yet, we were sometimes confrontational. I was the kind of father that wanted and expected a young man to grow up and act like a man. I strongly encouraged my son to take responsibility for his life, yet in many respects, I failed in this life assignment. My son was born February 12, 1972 and died February 13, 2001. He was a free spirit. Brian was blessed with a keen mind, and he was very artistic. He loved to sing and he was a good singer. My son was very intelligent and he had a very easy laid-back quality I admired. I loved my son, but I did not go around kissing on him and hugging him as some fathers do. I wish that I had that option now.

Brian was saved at an early age. As a matter of fact, he went to church when I was not going. God does work in mysterious ways. When Brian was in high school, he would go to church with one of his friends who happened to live next door to us. I guess the Lord was working through him that he might save the rest of us. My son would go every Sunday. To this day, I regret not doing more with my son in the church. His initiative to go to church also inspired me to get back into the church.

My son finished high school and joined the Navy. Life was beginning to take shape for him. He was happy, seeing some of the world that he had never seen before. He was ambitious and focused. While he was stationed in California, he called me one day and said, "Guess what Pops? I am getting married". I was happy for my son, even though I thought he was getting married a little too young. But he was a man now, so I couldn't tell him what to do. I did not try to talk him out of this, because as I listened to his conversation he was in love with her. Over time the marriage ended in divorce.

■ ■ ■

When my son was honorably discharged from the military service, he came home and started his college career. He moved down to Carbondale, Illinois, to attend Southern Illinois University, commonly known in this part of the state as S.I.U.

My wife and I would drive down to help him adapt to his new life in college. My wife, who is Brian's stepmother, was one of his biggest supporters and fans. As a matter of fact, she was very close to Brian, and he was absolutely crazy about her. There was nothing he would not do for Jane. I was glad to see that my son and my wife had a really positive relationship. My son had lived with us since he was two years old and my wife thought of him as her son. She took the time to let this young boy know that he was not only loved, but was truly welcomed into our home. A lot of stepmothers do not treat their stepchildren with real love. I saw clearly the compassionate heart of my new wife. She went well beyond the call of duty in helping me to raise my son and my daughter Kellie. I respect and appreciate her for helping to raise my kids and for providing a stable environment for my life as well.

Jane was truly a gift from God to me. I always think of her when I read the Proverbs: 31:10-12 *"who can find a virtuous woman? For her price is far above rubies. The heart of her husband doth safely trust in her, so that he shall have no need of spoil. She will do him good and not evil all the days of her life."*

My son "pledged" a fraternity in college and I believe this is where bad things began to happen. It was there that something went wrong for him. It was during these pledge activities that resulted in my son being arrested and taken to jail. This was the first of several arrests. I do not know all the details surrounding the events of my son's arrests. I truly suspect there are others associated with this fraternity that caused my son to go off the deep end of life, because later he was diagnosed as paranoid schizophrenic. My wife and I stood by him, and since he was a veteran, we tried to get him some help. There came a day when my son ended his life on this earth by taking his own life. The coroner shared this information with us.

My son's death completely caught us off guard. We were completely unprepared to deal with his sudden death. I was very depressed, and angry, but not at God. I never blamed God for my son's death. It seemed to me that my whole world just stopped. It was as if everything was moving in slow motion, and my mind was tuning out all the condolences received from other people. My mind and body felt numb.

I resolved to focus on work and get my mind back in gear after Brian's funeral. I decided the best way to start was return to work. At first, I couldn't get my mind to focus on the job that I was being paid to do, but with prayer, and good support of people, and a good employer (who gave me the time to heal while working) things slowly began to improve. I still hurt for my son. I know from firsthand experience what a parent feels when they lose their son or daughter. It is a true saying: *"You never get over the death of a child."*

About a week after my son's death I returned to my job working as a Supplier Quality Analyst for a major company. I was scheduled to go out-of-state to meet with one of our company's machine parts supplier. The company felt this supplier had begun to produce and send inferior parts into our facility that were not to our design specifications.

I arranged the meeting for a Monday morning. When our small team arrived at the campus of this supplier, we were met by their Supplier Quality Manager. We made known our business position and after some small preliminaries, coffee and donuts was served. We headed toward the shop and another colleague and I spent the entire day watching the fabrication and machining process relevant to the part that was causing our company to have major quality issues out in the field. After spending three days observing their fabrication and machining process, we determined the machining process met our engineering specifications based on our plate check of relevant data points. Our plate check results confirmed the parts were machined to meet our specifications. The quality issue at hand had nothing to do with their in-house machining process; the defect was discovered in the fabrication process. They were not welding the parts to correct weld specifications. This allowed the parts to crack or break under designed load conditions. Once the problem was discovered, the supplier did not readily agree with our estimation of the problem, but our engineering department and our metallurgist confirmed that we were right.

Toward the end of our visit the Product Quality Manager began talking about his son. He was very proud of his son. He made references to his son as being a star football player in college, and to all the girls that were chasing after him. He talked about how handsome and how smart he was. He talked quite extensively about his family, especially about his son, his only son. I listened, but each time he mentioned his son, my thoughts returned to the death of my son. I guess the pain of having recently lost my son began to appear on my face.

The Manager asked us to join him back in his office to wrap things up prior to our departure. He stopped to get some files from his secretary, and we had a short conversation. He asked me "are you ok?" I guess he had observed something in my demeanor. He said "you look like something is wrong." (I thought that I was doing a pretty good job of hiding my feelings regarding the recent death of Brian). I was trying to work my job and keep my personal feelings inside, but somehow, he knew something was wrong. Maybe I had a sad expression on my face that I could not see, so I told him about my son. It had only been three weeks since I had buried my son, my only son. And I let him know I was still dealing with it internally, but that I was okay.

It seemed odd that after I had shared this with their Manager, he did not act as if it was a big deal. Based on how he responded, it was like "Oh well". I don't know what I was expecting from this man, but I guess I expected him to respond with some type of human emotion like "I am sorry for your loss, or I am so sorry to hear that." Yet, he went right on with a "business-as- usual" attitude.

Now, I realize that people who didn't know my son Brian would not or could not understand how I truly loved and missed him. I did not expect any major sympathies, because the grieving process is truly personal, and it takes time to heal. But I did expect him to say something other than nothing. Having and showing compassion toward another human who had just lost a loved one is the correct human response. He didn't do any of that.

Early the next week, a few days after we returned to our facility, I received a phone call from the secretary of this Product Quality Manager. What she shared really shocked me. She told me that when we were in their plant, she overheard me telling her boss about the death of my son. She also recalled that he did not show me any consideration by offering to say anything or to offer any personal condolences for my loss. I thought to myself, apparently I was not the only one to think this quality manager's behavior was odd when I told him I had just recently experienced the death of a close loved one in my family.

The secretary went on to tell me that the weekend after we left their facility, the son of this manager was killed in a car accident. Apparently the man's son and some of his college friends had been out partying and drinking and had a head-on collision with another vehicle. It was a very bad accident in which several people were killed. This manager's son was the driver of the car that caused the accident. I was completely saddened by this. All I could say at the time was "wow". I thanked her for telling me and I sent a card and an email to the Manager, offering him my condolences at the loss of his son. The thoughts flashed across my mind that when I had shared with this man about the death of my son, he showed no emotion. Now that he had lost his son, his only son, could he now better understand what I was going through that day in his office? I wonder if he knows now what it feels like to lose a son. God does work in mysterious ways, His wonders to perform. God knows the heart of all. It could have been that this man's heart had zero compassion for others. Only God knows for sure. Maybe God allowed him to feel what I was feeling. Like I said, God works in mysterious ways. Only God know for certain what the future holds for each us.

The Vision While Driving Home from Work – Event 10

On a beautiful day in 2005 I saw this vision. I got off work and made it to my car and began to make my way home. When I left the plant, I turned right at the light and proceeded to go west on Pershing Road. At the intersection of Pershing Road and 22nd St, I turned left at the stop light. While driving past the old Firestone Tire & Rubber Plant which is now closed, something got my attention. Looking out the right side of my car window I saw something spectacular. As I looked up in the sky, I saw the most beautiful vision that I have ever seen in my life. It was so breathtakingly beautiful, I can barely describe it. My attempts to describe what I saw will not be acceptable; it was that beautiful. As I continued to look at this vision in the sky to my right, it seemed that "time" somehow stood still. I was staring at the majestic beauty of something that was completely incomprehensible.

I saw what seemed to be a "sea of glass" that had no beginning or end. This sea of glass was so gorgeous; it sparkled like the brightest stars on a moon-less dark night. The sea sparkled just like polished diamonds. The sea of glass diamonds reminded me of the world's choicest and finest crystals; the kind of fine hand-crafted crystal you would expect to find in a very expensive, upscale jewelry store. However, this sea of glass far exceeded anything man could ever dream of making. The sparkling vision of a large "sea of glass" is reminiscent of stars that twinkle and shine so brightly on warm dark summer nights. The vision to me was similar to the reaction of a child when seeing the Grand Canyon or the Atlantic or Pacific Ocean for the first time. They are just speechless. The vision that the Lord allowed me to see was a mouth-dropping experience. There are no human words I can use that would adequately convey, or make clear to you what I saw that day. Words like "magnificent", "picturesque", "majestic", "dazzling with splendor", "gorgeous", and "stunningly beautiful", are not good enough.

As I continued to drive home trying to watch the traffic and drive all at the same time, I found it impossible to take my eyes off this vision. At the very end and far in the distance of the "sea of glass," there appeared to be something that resembled a stairway leading up to heaven. This stairway had rows of what looked like small fluffy clouds on both sides of narrow steps. The stairway was inclined in a 45 to 65 degree angle, which reminded me of the moving steps seen on an escalator at the shopping malls. The steps went all the way up into heaven. At the very top of the steps, I could see something, but I could not determine what it was. What I saw appeared to be seats. As I continued to look, the clouds closed and the vision was completely hidden from my view.

I tried to make it home so that I could get my camera to take some pictures, but I was not successful. By the time I made it home, the vision was long gone. I shared this with my father before he died, but I could not explain it very well. My father sat quietly and listened and felt it was meant only for me to see. The vision made me think of the scripture in 1 Corinthians 2: 9, *"But as it is written, Eye hath not seen, nor ear heard, neither have entered into the heart of man, the things which God hath prepared for them that love him."*

"Lord, I thank you for allowing me to see just a small glimpse of your glory that day. I may not know why you allowed me to see it. It is my hope that by sharing what you allowed me to see, that some lost soul will begin to seek you. I hope and pray that unbelievers reading this book will give their life to you. Amen"

Expect the Unexpected and Watch God Move!

Chapter 8

Abortion is Not the Work of God – Event 11

On June 22, 2002, the Lord blessed our youngest daughter with a beautiful daughter, who was our second grandchild. She was a healthy girl of 7lbs. At this time in my life I was not living for the Lord. I was running the streets, getting into things that married men should not be indulging in. I was gambling, not only with my money, I also was gambling with my life and with my marriage. I was living a sinful selfish lifestyle, yet, on the surface I was doing fine, but, I was not happy. Something in my life was missing and I did not know that Jesus was the missing piece of the puzzle. My life had a hole in it, a hole that only Jesus could fill. I did not have a real relationship with the Lord, and I refused to consider Jesus as the answer to all my sinful problems and declining lifestyle.

My insecurities, my negative outlook on life, combined with the poor way I was treating my family, were all the result of a sinful worldly lifestyle. And all the money in the world could not solve that problem. If anything, having money seemed to make a sinful lifestyle worse, not better.

I had just lost my only son in 2001. I am not trying to make excuses for my behavior, but the truth is, I never really got over his death, and to this very day, I still grieve for him. I sometimes feel I was not there for him when he really needed me. I failed to see what I should have been looking for in his life. Not long after his death, I developed a "I don't give a shit attitude." My personal choices reflected this negative attitude about life.

It was about this time that my youngest daughter, who was a senior in college, became pregnant. One night, she and the father of the baby came to discuss the matter with me and my wife. I thank God for my wife. She always stood by me no matter what. She always was and still is an independent thinker and is not afraid to voice her own opinion.

Note: For the duration of this chapter and throughout the remainder of this book, any reference to the baby's daddy will be designated by the initials "BD".

The boy who got my daughter pregnant did not want the child. He told our daughter that the baby was not his. He did not want to admit that he had fathered a child and he did not want to accept responsibility for his actions. This made me very angry, because we knew that our daughter really loved this boy. We also knew that our daughter was never a wild child; we had never allowed her to run the streets. My daughter was not perfect. However, she was not allowed to act any way she wanted while she lived with us. Our daughter was always a quiet girl, who took after her mother. Thank God for that!

The boy knew that the baby was his; he was just trying to avoid or get out of his responsibilities. At the time he got my daughter pregnant, he was a big man on his college campus. He was one of the university's main superstar basketball players. When he mentioned an abortion, he made me think. He left our home, and after discussing this at length, I realized my wife, daughter and I were not on the same page. What really hurt me more than her being pregnant was the hurt look on her face when this boy that she loved and the boy that she thought loved her rejected her and his child?

I am pretty sure my daughter and my wife wanted her to go through with the pregnancy. I, on the other hand, was pretty much considering the abortion option. My thoughts were: 1) My daughter is a senior in college, her last year of school, 2) the father of this child doesn't want to be the father, and 3) the father is not claiming any responsibility, so why should my daughter get stuck raising a child by herself? I was also considering how expensive it was to bring a child into this world. Yes, the abortion option was looking better and better. As I went to bed that night, this was my position and my thoughts.

I am sorry to admit it now, but it is the truth. I was considering abortion for my daughter's pregnancy. However, when I was asleep that night, a voice came to me in a dream and asked me this question: "So you say it is okay for your daughter to have an abortion, am I hearing you right?" I answered back and tried to explain why I was of the opinion, and this voice just talked right over my voice and became louder, deeper and clearer. The voice repeated, "Are you saying that it's okay for your daughter to have an abortion? Am I hearing you right?" The voice went up to a higher octave. I woke up and I knew that the decision that I was contemplating was completely wrong.

I am so grateful to God for letting me know how evil and selfish my decision was to ever consider abortion as a viable option to His precious gift of life. My granddaughter is truly a special and beautiful gift from God. When I look at her now, I cannot help taking her in my arms and holding her tight and kissing her. Yes, she doesn't like me to baby her, but I do not care; I want her to know that she is loved. I think this child has a special calling on her life. I do not know what it is, but time will tell. I just pray that I am around to see it. I am doing all that I can now to help raise this child in the fear of the Lord. I made many mistakes when I was young raising my own children; I don't plan to make the same mistakes with my granddaughter. We talk about God all the time, and she listens.

In Proverbs 6: 22, the Bible teaches us that *"Train up a child in the way he should go: and when he is old, he will not depart from it."* I completely receive and accept this wisdom from the Lord through Solomon. I, too, was brought up in the church. I spent 18 years in the Springhill Missionary Baptist Church, and yes, I did stray away. But the Lord God brought me back. Thank you, Jesus!

My daughter had her baby, and with our help through God, she was able to finish college. The "BD" went back to his carefree life as a senior in college, playing basketball for one of the major universities in the State of Illinois. He had plans of becoming a professional basketball player in the NBA, and was pretty much a shoo-in. At the time of all this, I was told that he was number two in the nation in scoring. He had teams like the Los Angeles Lakers, the Atlanta Hawks, the New York Knicks, and the Boston Celtics interviewing him.

My daughter was in the process of getting her life in order after she finished college and moved back to our community. She was able to find a job, and we helped her to move back to Decatur, and to find her own apartment. This is where things really begin to turn ugly. One Saturday evening the father of our grandchild came to my home for discussion. He still didn't want to have anything to do with my daughter and was still denying that the child was his. After he had finished speaking, something came over me because I began to speak in the spirit. I prophesied to him that as long as he did not honor his child, nothing good was going to happen to him. Here is what happened. He went from being number "two" in the nation in college basketball. He was injured during the last game of his college career breaking his arm in the last game of the season, which resulted in him missing the pro-draft.

A few weeks later, this young man had two cars and each one caught on fire. He was in the second car that caught on fire, and it could have been serious. He was slightly burned on his arm. After this, he started to give some support to his daughter and things began to turn around in his life. Our God is an awesome God. He is the ultimate Judge!

Even the Moon and Stars Obey Him – Event 12

After our granddaughter was born, I planned a trip to take her and my daughter south to visit with my family. My father was very sick with cancer, and I wanted him to see another great granddaughter, and the newest addition to our family. My father loved to see babies born. He would just smile and hold their little hands.

During the week I had worked a lot of overtime working 12 hours days. I thought that I could handle the 6-7 hours' drive from my home to my father's home in Ripley, Tennessee. I had made this trip so many times; I felt I could handle the extra hours of work and the drive home. I left my home that night at about 10:30 pm and drove to Glen Carbon, Illinois which is close to St. Louis, Missouri. This is about a 2 hours' drive from my home. I drove this part of the trip without any problems.

I picked up my daughter and the baby and packed their things in the car and off we went. My daughter had classes that day, so she and the baby went right to sleep. Two or three hours later as I continued to drive, my eyes started to get really heavy. I was doing all sorts of things to stay awake, but none of them were working. I stopped and got some coffee, but it did not help. I did not want to pull off the side of the road and sleep, because people have been known to get carjacked when they were parked in out-of-the-way places sleeping.

I continued to drive and the longer I drove the sleepier I became. I found myself starting to nod off behind the wheel. I would, immediately jerk myself back to consciousness. Out of desperation, I said, "Lord, please help me to stay awake. I know I am tired, but it's not safe to stop." I did not want to wake up my daughter who was now snoring and sleeping soundly. As I prayed to the Lord, I begin to notice the drowsiness leaving my body. It suddenly dawned on me that the moon looked to be very close to my car. As a matter of fact, from St. Louis, Missouri to Cape Girardeau, Missouri is a straight shot south on Interstate 55. The truckers call this interstate the "double nickel". I have driven this road many times, and I have never before seen the moon directly in front of the interstate. Normally, the moon at night is to the east of this interstate and high up in the heavens. On this night, this big, pretty, and bright moon was dead center of Interstate 55 and it looked like I was driving into it. This moon was so big that I could see details of its surface.

The moon up close and personal is a beautiful thing to see. One thing I know was that as I was driving, it was now impossible to sleep because my eyes stayed focused on how beautiful and mysterious the moon was. It reminded me of a big huge liquid amber ball as it appeared to move away from me to match the speed that I was driving.

The moon stayed in this position until I got close to Dyersburg, Tennessee. Then, I noticed it had moved. The moon returned back up high in the shy and east of my location. I was now only 18 miles from my father's home and very awake. God is just awesome!

When you stop and consider how majestic and "above description" He really is, you will come to the conclusion that He is worthy to be praised! Let's take into account just one divine attribute of God into contemplation. For example, I once heard it said that there are over 6 billion people living in the world today. Yet, God can hear the voice of one of His children who has put his/her trust in Him. He not only hears them, He sees them and depending on the situation, if it suits His good pleasure and His will. He makes a way out of no way. That is why I want to serve and please Him. Think about it, over 6 billion people in this world and He knows all there is to know about each one. He even knows the exact number of hairs on each head. People, we serve a Mighty God! A God that does hear and answers prayer, and a God that works in mysterious ways His wonders to perform!

There is Wonder-Working Power in Prayer

Chapter 9

In 1992, I purchased a brand new Yamaha – Venture Royale, 1300 cc's, motorcycle. This was my first big motorcycle and it was very powerful. I loved this bike. On weekends, I would sometimes spend hours washing, polishing and shining all that chrome. I would take my bike on trips to Tennessee, a distance of about 350 miles one way.

At this time in my life, I was not living a saved life. Yes, I believed in God, but believing in the Almighty alone is no substitute for living a consecrated life, a life that is set apart and totally committed to Him. This biblical truth is revealed in many examples in scripture. It is especially clear in James 2:19–21 which states: [19] *"Thou believe that there is one God; thou doest well: the devils also believe, and tremble.* [20] *"But wilt thou know, O vain man, that faith without works is dead?* [21] Was *not Abraham our father justified by works, when he had offered Isaac his son upon the altar?"* The Apostle James is letting us know that even the demons, our enemies, believe in God, and tremble at the sound of His Name. How then should unbelievers, as well as all professing believers, stand in "awe" of an all-powerful, all-knowing, and everywhere-present God.

James says that "faith without works is dead". Works activate and allows you to stand on your faith. I had to learn this the hard way. Most people who say they are saved have works that testify to the contrary. This also works the other way around when people have done good works and they occasionally brag on their personal contributions, yet they lack genuine faith in God. For some people, they put their faith in their power and money. Some are quick to tell you "Look at all the wonderful things I have done to help others". I say it's a good thing to help someone, but your help is in vain and of no spiritual value if you did it in the name of "self" and you still do not believe in God. You have already earned your reward which is the praise of men. My God knows the conditions of the heart. He does not see as men see. Man looks on the outer appearance of a man but God looks on the heart.

I have always believed in God. When I look back over my life when I was riding that motorcycle at speeds of over 100 miles per hour, sometimes, having consumed alcohol and other substances, I wonder why God still allowed His arm of protection to cover and shield me from accidents or death. "Oh Lord, I thank YOU. Where would I be without your mercy and your grace?" I can honestly see how foolish it was for anybody to ride on two wheels without a real relationship with their Creator. A lot of things can happen to you when you are riding a large motorcycle on the open road. One of the main things that black motorcyclists must be aware of is racism. There are still pockets of racism that will cause some Caucasians to try and hurt and/or kill a black motorcyclist. Some will pretend they did not see you, and cut right in front of you. I have had some semi-drivers run me off the road, under the false statement "oh, I am sorry, I did not see you".

Sarcastically I think, "It is okay good buddy", even though it's a beautiful day, broad day light, the sun shining brightly and it's just you and me on the interstate. As I was attempting to pass, you swerved over into my lane and then back into your own lane". Dead is dead. If it had not been for the grace of God, death would have claimed my life many times while riding my bike. But you need to know this. The same God that protected me that day also knows what you tried to do. You will have to answer to Him for what was in your heart.

The Memorial holiday of 1992 was just a few days away and I had planned a trip to my parents and was really looking forward to the ride south. The weather was nice, with no predictions of bad weather or thunderstorms. On the day of my departure, I kissed my wife and kids good bye, loaded up my Yamaha and headed south. The weather was good and I was cruising at highway speeds of 75 to 80 miles per hour. Big bikes can cruise at this speed without any hesitation. I stopped to rest my legs, and to top off the gas tank, just enjoying the thrill of my motorcycle out on the open road.

I took the bypass around the St. Louis metropolitan area, and it was clear sailing on Interstate I-55 south to Tennessee. Each time other motorcyclists in the north bound lane passed, they would either wave or flash their head light. This is something bikers do to recognize each other and communicate to other bikers that are also traveling along the interstate. After a couple of hours I began to notice that the majority of motorcyclists that were going north on Interstate 55 – were, as they say down south, hauling ass. The bikers had on their protective rain gear, however; where I was, it was still a beautiful day. As I topped the hill, I saw why the bikers and the cars were going so fast. I was heading right into what looked like the development of a powerful thunderstorm. As my eyes scanned the horizon, as far as the eye could see from east to west was jet black. This blackness did not look like the kind of blackness you see when you go outside at night. This blackness looked like a deep dark blue "wet" blackness that appeared to be full of rain and fury.

The temperature dropped, and the wind immediately began to shift from normal to strong wind gusts. I was afraid. I have always been afraid of lightning since I was a kid riding on our neighborhood country school bus. It was storming and I just happened to be looking out the bus window, and during this hard rain there was also loud thunder and lightning. I focused on a small group of cows that were standing in some farmer's field. I saw a bolt of lightning strike a cow. The lightning bolt looked like the finger of God Himself coming down from heaven and struck the cow directly on its head. I saw the cow tremble and shake as though it was full of Tennessee corn whiskey and fall to the ground. I also saw smoke coming off the cow's head and horns. Since that day, I have been deathly afraid of lightning. My father was also afraid of lightning. As a kid growing up in our home, our father would tell us to turn the radio and television off and get somewhere and sit down, be quiet and be still. He would say that when God is passing by and doing His work, you are to be quiet. He meant every word. Woe to the child that forgot to get somewhere and was not quiet. Usually, that child was disciplined immediately.

I remember one occasion from my child hood when I was probably 8 or 9 years old. We had just sat down to dinner, and a storm came up suddenly. There was furious rain and hail, combined with loud thundering and lightning. One of the loud thunderous outbursts was really loud and came very close to our little home. The power went off and everything went black. When the power came back on after a few seconds, I noticed that our father was not sitting at the head of the table. At the sound of that last thunderous outburst, he had quickly jumped under the kitchen table. I thought this was funny and started to laugh at what my father had done. In retrospect, I now realized that was not too smart of me. For one thing, you never laugh at your father. My father proceeded to pick me up by the seat of my pants, and when he was finished with me, I never again laughed at him. I had to learn the hard way.

I was riding the motorcycle and seeing the sheer size of the storm and looking at how "wet" with blackness the whole east, west and south, I began to look for a place to pull off and to put on my rain suit. I saw a very small overpass, a country highway overpass over Interstate 55, and pulled off the road and decided to wait out the storm under the overpass. This was the only protection available here on the open road. I prayed, "Lord God, You know how afraid of lightning I am. Please watch over me and protect me from this storm." That was all I said. In the distance, I could see this storm was quickly approaching me. I could see big lightning bolts striking the ground as the storm continued to advance toward my position. However, after I prayed that prayer to God, I noticed a quietness, like something was about to happen. It seemed to me, that it got eerily quiet. I also noticed the black clouds were still there, but the lightning had stopped; at least, I could not see any more lightning strikes. I saw the rays of the sun trying to penetrate the wall of blackness that was coming my way. As I continued to look, it was the sun, and the sun appeared to be consuming and eating through the black clouds. In about 15 minutes, the entire terrible- looking storm was gone.

It did not dawn on me what had just happened. I did not fully comprehend that I prayed a prayer from my heart to God, asking Him to protect me from this storm. Not only did He hear my prayer, He made the storm to disappear. Who is like our God? As powerful as He is, He can still hear the voice of one sinner like me whose heart was crying out to Him for help. He (God) truly works in mysterious ways, His wonders to perform.

Who is like our God? I beg you non-believer, rethink your position on God. He is just what He says He is. If after careful consideration, you still do not believe in Him, I pray that you never come face-to-face with a "mega" storm. Who would you call on for help? If you called me, all I could do is pray, and since you do not believe in prayer, I would have no other way to assist you.

Again, I thank God for teaching me that day that He is God all by Himself! God sits high and looks low. He hears the cry of His people; even when we are not doing what we should. His mercy and grace defy human understanding. His love and patience with people like me can never be fully appreciated by our human minds. His love is love perfected. This was proven when His only Son was sent to die for us. Yet, we as a people do all that we can sometimes to take that love for granted. Lord, help me to never lose focus of what YOU have done for me and my family. It is my prayer that YOU would bless me to do something to reach people that are lost, and those who do not know Jesus in the pardoning of their sins.

God made a believer out of me with this passage of scripture in Isaiah 54:14-17. When I say that God made a believer out of me, I am not saying that I was not a believer before. I am saying that God took me through a valley, a low point in my life, and it was here that He caused me to really trust Him and to see that He is a God who answers prayer. I hope this makes sense to you. These scriptures - Isaiah 54:14-17 - will be with me until the day God calls me home. It is with this specific section of scripture, that God truly got my attention. Again, I am not trying to say that God did not already have my attention. My point is that sometimes in life, God will take you through something in order for you to really appreciate and give genuine reverence to Him. I call this the "Jonah experience".

There is power in prayer and as I share the continuation of the drama with the "baby daddy drama", you will understand what I mean. After our daughter finished college and moved back home, she met a new boy and they began to date. The old boyfriend, BD, had decided that he did not want anything to do with my daughter or baby. We advised our daughter to move on with her life and we would continue to stand by her and help her raise the child.

It had been two years since DB abandoned my daughter and his child. My granddaughter was two years old. Now, DB wanted back into the picture. He had been trying to get our daughter to take him back, but when she refused he became hostile. He started calling her negative and disrespectful names and threatened her and the new boyfriend. He was doing all that he could do to make her life unbearable. He called her cell phone and left insulting and nasty messages, some of which I took to the police. When my daughter said that she was going to report him to the police, his response was (expletive) the police, they could not do anything to protect her nor her father. All of this was recorded and turned over to the Chief of Police.

When my daughter and her new boyfriend would go out on a date, we would keep the baby for her. BD would sometimes show up and stalk them as he was trying to scare off the boyfriend, and keep my daughter in a constant state of harassment. He was operating off the assumption that if he could not have her then no one else could. This was a situation that caused my daughter and our family to lose respect for BD.

One Friday night around 10:30 pm, our daughter was home alone, when she called us crying. BD was trying to force his way into her apartment. My wife and I drove over to our daughter's apartment. When BD saw us coming, he left. This happened three times. We'd to go over and stay for a while, then leave. And as soon as we left, he would come back and cause more trouble. He was playing games. This night, it went on until 1:00 am. Around 12:45 am, (the fourth time we had been called to assist our daughter), we got there and I was already not in a good mood because of his childish behavior and the way he was acting. I had enough of BD's drama and it was time to confront the situation. We were calling the police for assistance, but this was a busy weekend and they were slow in responding to a domestic-related call.

When my wife and I arrived at my daughter's apartment, we could see BD standing outside the security door of the apartment complex. We got out of the car and my wife went inside the apartment. I began to try and talk with BD and after about ten minutes of him cursing, I realized that talking to this man was foolish and a waste of my time. It was evident to me that BD wanted to fight me and demonstrate to my daughter what a tough man he was. When he and I began to squabble about my daughter, I advised him to leave her alone. BD started off yelling that he was not allowed to see his daughter. Yes, that's correct, his daughter. The same man that refused to admit that the child was his daughter, the same one that refused a pay a penny on any of the hospital bills, the same man that wanted my daughter to have an abortion, the same man that was not providing any financial support to his daughter, now wanted to claim that she was his daughter. I guess he thought the child was expected to survive on his love.

I told him that his concerns could and would be settled in the court system, but for now, he needed to leave. The argument really intensified and he told me that he was not going. For the next ten minutes, he and I had a serious get-acquainted session. We both used words that were wrong and improper. At some point during this argument, I realized I was talking with a fool. I turned around and left him in the middle of the street still cursing me and calling me names. Before I unlocked the outside security door to go inside the apartment complex, I told BD that I was through talking to him. I told him that if he kicked in my daughter's door, it would be the last the last thing that he did on this earth! And I truly meant every word. He continued to curse and threatened to call his father as I closed the door in his face.

When I stopped to think about it, I had to wonder about the mentality of some of our young men today. This young man alleged to love my daughter, yet he cared nothing about cursing out the father and the mother of the child he claimed to love. The mentality of some of the young men today is that they do not respect what the father and mother says, and think that they can come into your family and take over. Excuse me, young men, but that is not how it's done.

BD continued to use foul language against me, but I decided to go inside the apartment. We called the police again. My wife and daughter had been calling the police repeatedly, but as I said earlier, they were slow to respond. By now BD had also called his father, who, as I later found out, was a major drug dealer in our community. When BD and I were having our argument, he had repeatedly said he was going to call his father and said "You won't talk to my father the way you talk to me." I recall thinking to myself, "your father is not the problem - you are the problem." It was obvious that he was trying to enlist and recruit the assistance of his father into resolving his problem with my daughter and me.

The only problem that I could see was this man wanted to dominate and control my daughters' life. When that did not work, he tried to use force. And you can never force anything or anyone to love you; not a pet, and certainly not a human.

When I went inside my daughter's apartment, I was very upset. I really wanted to hurt or do some serious harm to BD! While my wife was continuing to call the police again and again, I poured out my soul to the Lord. I prayed, "Lord God, please help me. Help us. I do not want to kill this young man and I do not want to be killed by him either. Please God, please help me."

Immediately, after I said the words "please help me," I started to get very sleepy and became so tired that I could not hold my eyes open. What's more, I felt like something was gently pushing my head to lie down on the sofa. I tried to fight against this urge to sleep and not to lie down, but it was like fighting against the Pacific Ocean, trying not to move when a strong wave moves against you. I finally lay down on the sofa and realized some peace in the midst of the storm. I had about twenty minutes of rest and that was all I needed. All the anger that I had in me was now gone from my mind. I can't explain how a person can go from one extreme to a relaxed frame of mind, but that is what I did. When the police finally arrived, BD's father had also arrived. I went outside to talk with the police and give them my side of the story. They resolved the situation by asking BD and his father to leave the premises. They also told them both not to return; and if they did return to the apartment complex, they would be arrested. BD's father thanked me for calling the police on his son and for not fighting with him. I recall thinking that his father had more sense than the son.

The police left and my wife stayed the night with my daughter. I went back home. It was now well after one o'clock in the morning, and I had to be at work by seven. I did make it to work, but I was still upset from the night before. I was trying to hide my feelings and emotions, but my coworkers knew that something was wrong. Each time a coworker would ask me if I was okay, I would lie and say I was okay, however; I was far from okay. I made it halfway through my shift by the grace of God. The whistle sounded at the start of our lunchtime. Since the Saturday's work schedule is sometimes worked at a slower pace, I had some time to think and to reflect. I used this time wisely by reading the Scriptures and trying to meditate on the Word of God.

I was reading and studying in the book of Isaiah, but my mind could not focus on the reading material. I tried to concentrate on the scriptures but my emotions were still out of control. It seemed I could not focus on the words. But when I got to Isaiah the 54th chapter, verses 14 through 17, something mysterious and unexplainable happened. As I was about to close the book and have some lunch, something came over me, and I could not close the book. I had this insatiable desire to read the passage again. This happened three times and I could not close the Bible. I would re-read this verse of scriptures. After reading it the third time, I still had no inkling as to how those four verses were about to change my life forever.

I still did not have a clue or an understanding of what God was doing. I was still focused on BD and my desire to bring him harm. However, whenever I was about to close the Bible and break for lunch, the words on the page literally jumped in Isaiah 54:14-17. I rubbed my eyes to make sure that I was seeing correctly what I had just witnessed, and read the scriptures again. I tried to close the Bible again, however, this time the words stood up on the page and laid back down. Actually, they sat back down. The words actually stood up, and then they sat back down on the page. I am not making this up. I actually saw the letters and the words on the page move with my own eyes. As I looked at the words on the page, I thought to myself, I am seeing things that are not real. But it did happen! What I had just seen did not make any sense to me because words cannot move like that. The only thing I could do was to read the verses again. As I tried to close the Bible for the sixth time to break for lunch, the same words stood up, got big black and gold and laid back down the page. I was now fully aware of what I was looking at. I finally realized that God was telling me something, although I was not sure at the time what it was. I had no idea how this would affect my life.

A couple of weeks later BD's father was found dead. He was killed by one of his own drug dealers. It finally dawned on me what God was telling me that day when the words of the Bible moved, stood up, and sat back down. The Scripture that spoke to me was Isaiah 54:14-17: *"In righteousness salt though be established: thou shalt be far from oppression; for thou shall not fear: and from terror; for it shall not come near thee. ¹⁵Behold, they shall surely gather together, but not by me: whosoever shall gather together against thee shall fall for thy sake. ¹⁶Behold, I have created the smith that bloweth the coals in the fire, and that bringeth forth an instrument for his work; and I have created the waster to destroy. ¹⁷No weapon that is formed against thee shall prosper; and every tongue that shall rise against thee in judgment thou shalt condemn. This is the heritage of the servants of the Lord, and their righteousness is of me, saith the Lord."*

My rationale was that if BD and his father were in a conspiracy against me, that what he really wanted his father to do was to take care of this situation by taking care of me. God over ruled that plan if that was his intent. Be careful what you say before a Holy God. For out of your own mouth He will judge you. I do not ever want to try and speak for God. He tells us in Psalm 7:15 *"He made a pit, and digged it, and is fallen into the ditch which he made."* It is not wise to plot to do someone harm. Our God knows the hearts of men. He is a God of love and mercy and He is also a God of Judgment.

When you study the book of Esther, the wicked Haman wanted to destroy all the Jews, just because one man, Mordecai, refused to bow and pay homage to him. Haman built a seventy-five foot high gallows in which to hang Mordecai. But the providence of God had already resolved the problem before the wicked Haman could execute his diabolical plan.

Let me share my thoughts with you:

- I truly receive and accept the wisdom of God's words into my life. I am not saying that I am so perfect that God is automatically on my side. Not at all! I too have sinned and fallen short of God's glory. On the other hand, I do not look down or condemn anybody for how they live their life. If you are a prostitute, my prayer for you is that you stop. I love you in the Name of Jesus, but I hate the sin that has you bound. My prayer is for you to get to know Jesus Christ and through Him, overcome the sin that has you bound.

- If you are a drug dealer or drug user, I do not hate you. I hate the sin that has you bound. Sin is sin. My prayer for you is that you stop dealing drugs or using them and get to know Jesus Christ. He died for your sins and mine.

• Whatever your sin is, my prayer is for you to get to know Jesus Christ. He tells us in 1 John 1:8-9 *"If we say that we have no sin, we deceive ourselves, and the truth is not in us. If we confess our sins, He is faithful and just to forgive us our sins, and to cleanse us from all unrighteousness."*

• I personally do not have a heaven or a hell to send anyone. I just want to confess what God has done for me and my family. I just want to shout it to the world that I thank God for saving me, and I want the same for you.

I have learned to stop trying to second-guess what God is doing. I, like anybody else, might offer my opinion, but that is all it is - just my opinion. God is God. Therefore, whatever He resolves to do is alright with me. I have learned to trust and obey Him. When you trust Him to lead and guide you, you start to see things differently. A good example is what He teaches us in Romans 8:28 - *"And we know that all things work together for the good to them that love God, to them who are the called according to his purpose."*

I am going to trust Him even when I don't understand what or why God is taking me down a path. I am going to trust Him when I am up; I am going to trust Him when I am down. I know He is righteous, and whatever He decides to do or not to do in my life is okay with me. I am still His child. Again, "*all things work together for the good to them that love God, to them who are the called according to his purpose.*" God has taught me that just because you are saved, do not mean that you will not have tribulations, trials, and bad days. Just look up, and fall to your knees when the trials of life get too heavy. He has already promised in His Word that He will never leave us or forsake us.

He tells us in Psalms 50:15 *"And call upon me in the day of trouble: I will deliver thee, and thou shalt glorify me."* I am a living testimony to the fact that when I called on Him when I was deep in trouble He did just what He said He would do. He delivered me out of my deadly life-altering situation. He calmed the storm that was raging out of control in my life. God is a good God! When you strive to get to know Him, I promise you, you will not regret it.

Can you share this prayer with me?

Most Holy God, I feel very blessed today, I am happy to have a relationship with You. I pray that you would bless me to be a seed-planter for the kingdom of God. Lord, teach me how to serve and please Thee. Lord, teach me how to give my all and live a life that is pleasing to Thee. Lord, I pray Thee, teach me how to be wise and win souls for the kingdom of God.

Lord, my prayer is that you never take your hand from me, but draw me ever closer. Oh precious Lord, if you will be my leader, teach me how to hear and know when the Holy Spirit is leading and guiding me. Teach me Lord to be sensitive to the needs of others and to be humble at all times, and to always know right from wrong. Lord helps me to not commit any wrong, and to walk before Thee in righteousness and truth.

Lord, I pray Thou would please guide me in goodness and mercy and in righteousness for the rest of my life. I pray that my whole life will be lived to please Thee. My Lord and Savior, I pray that when my time on this earth is over, that my spirit will rejoice in the bosom of my Master and Savior Jesus Christ forever. Amen.

What's So Special about the Number Two?

Chapter 10

The more that I think about the subject of this book - The _Two Doors of Life_ -the more I think about the number two. I begin to turn over in my mind the spiritual significance of the number two.

The following is just a few of the possibilities that I came up with.

1. For starters, sin and death (I call them the two evil twin spirits), entered the world as a result of Adam and Eve's failure to obey God. Consequently, they chose to disobey the Word of God and to believe the lie of Satan and eat of the forbidden fruit as mentioned in the book of Genesis 2, verses 16 and 17.

In these two short verses, God gave man and woman a choice about how they were to live their life. That God-given choice was represented by two trees - the Tree of Life and the Tree of Knowledge of Good and Evil. In the Garden of Eden, God gave unmistakable instructions. He told Adam and Eve they could freely eat of every tree in the garden; however, they were warned not to eat from the Tree of Knowledge of Good and Evil. The book of Genesis records the punishment for the sin of disobedience that Adam and Eve fell victim to. The consequences and the punishment for that sin can be found in Genesis 3:13 -19. God will punish sin. He told Eve that as a result of her sin, He would greatly multiply her sorrows and her conception during childbirth. Additionally, He told her that her desire would be to her husband, and that the husband would rule over her.

God told the serpent – used by (Satan), *"Thou art cursed above all cattle, and above every beast of the field; upon thy belly shalt thou go and dust shalt thou eat all the days of thy life"*. He also told the serpent that He would put enmity between his seed and the seed of the woman. He also told the serpent, *"it shall bruise thy head, and thou shalt bruise his heel."* The providence of God was correcting what the devil thought was a fatal blow to God's creation. Jesus fulfilled this prophecy at Calvary when He died on the cross for the sins of all mankind.

Finally, He told Adam that because he listened to the voice of his wife and failed to obey God's commandment not to eat of the Tree of Knowledge of Good and Evil, that *"cursed" is the ground for thy sake. In sorrow shalt he and his family eat of it for all the days of their life?"* He said the earth would bring forth thorns and thistles and they would eat the herbs (plants) of the field.

In addition, God told Adam that by the sweat of his face shall he eat bread until he died. God was telling Adam and Eve that if they wanted to eat food, they would have to now work and produce and grow their food to survive.

2. The Prophet Amos 3:3 raised a specific question in his book. The question that he asked is, *"Can two walk together, except they be agreed?"* The answer is "no". Therefore, the twin spirits of sin and death were, and are still united in their fight against God's creation - man. If anyone allows himself or herself to be overtaken and controlled by sin, it is only a matter of time before the evil twins (sin& death) show up to claim their victim. If a man is involved in the game of death (i.e., murder for hire, or drug dealing, idol worship, just to name a few), the sole reason for being involved with this type of activity is a direct link to sin.

Let's take a look further:

- The power of life and death.

- Heaven and Hell

- It requires two people to get married.

- It takes a male and a female to produce a child.

- When God created the heavens and the earth, He created a greater light called the Sun, and a lesser light He called the Moon.

- Humans have two feet, two legs, two arms, two hands, two ears, two eyes, two nostrils, two kidneys, two lungs, etc.

- When Noah built the Ark, God told him to put two of every animal, male and female, on the boat.

- There are really only two kinds of people in the world - those who believe and those who do not.

- Deuteronomy 17:5-7 says, *"At the mouth of two witnesses, or three witnesses, shall he that is worthy of death be put to death; but at the mouth of one witness he shall not be put to death."* (In the Old Testament, God used the number two or more to establish truth.)

- Numbers 35:30 says, *"Whoso killeth any person, the murderer shall be put to death by the mouth of witnesses; but one witness shall not testify against any person to cause him to die."*

- Matthew 18:16: *"But if he will not hear thee, then take with thee one or two more, that in the mouth of two or three witnesses every word may be established."*

- John 8:17: *"It is also written in your law, that the testimony of two men is true."*

- *"After these things the Lord appointed other seventy also, and sent them two and two before his face into every city and place, wither He himself would come."* Luke 10:1

- Mark 6:7: *"And He called unto him the twelve, and began to send them forth by two and two, and gave them power over unclean spirits."*

- Hebrews 6:17-18: *"Wherein God, willingly more abundantly to show unto the heirs of promise the immutability of his counsel, confirmed it by and oath; that by two immutable things, in which it was impossible for God to lie, we might have a strong consolation, who have fled for refuge to lay hold upon the hope set before us."*

These are just a few examples of the significance of the number two.

It is my strong belief that the two doors of life - though invisible - are absolutely real. A question that we need to be absolutely sure about is this, on the day of our death, when we enter into eternity, which door will our past life allow us to open? Will we open the door that leads to heaven? Or will we open the door that leads to eternal damnation and separation from God?

This question calls for major consideration and we must be sure, very sure, of our final position before we leave this earth. I do not know about you, but as for me and my house. I choose to believe, serve, and obey the Word of God that is plainly spoken in the Book of Wisdom, the Bible.

Joshua said it best when he told the people of his day in Joshua 24:13-15 *"Now therefore fear the LORD, and serve him in sincerity and in truth: and put away the gods which your fathers served on the other side of the flood, and in Egypt; and serve ye the LORD. [13] And if it seem evil unto you to serve the Lord, choose you this day whom ye will serve; whether the gods which your fathers served that were on the other side of the flood, or the gods of the Amorites, in whose land ye dwell: [15] but as for me and my house, we will serve the Lord."*

The Judgment of all Mankind – A Certainty of Life

Chapter 11

As we go through this life, there is one thing that I know for certain: just as certain as we were born, one day we are all going to die. I do not know of anyone who can lay claim to immortality in the flesh. Death does not discriminate. Money and power will not stop us from dying. Our good looks, our association, our job, or our profession will not keep us living forever. It doesn't matter if you are a male, female, young, old, popular, unpopular, believer, nonbeliever or even a member of the most prestigious country club in America – it is all vanity. When death comes to collect, there is no negotiating.

Let's look at the death of some internationally well-known people. Whenever death occurs to the rich and famous the world acts like this is not supposed to happen. "Oh this is just terrible", I have heard them say, or they act like the death of the rich and famous has somehow robbed the world of their presence and unique contribution.

The death of two megastars, Michael Jackson and Whitney Houston, are two examples. There are many others, but for a short discussion, let's just focus on the impact of these two and consider what the message from God is to the rest of the world. God tells us in Luke 12: 40 and in Matthew 24:44 to be ready. God did not say, nor has He ever indicated, that money, fame, good looks or being a non-believer will keep you from death. In Luke, He said *"Be ye therefore ready also: for the Son of man cometh at an hour when ye think not."* And in Matthew, He says, *"Therefore be ye also ready: for in such an hour as ye think not the Son of man cometh."*

And for clarity of argument, I am not implying or suggesting that Michael Jackson and Whitney Houston were not believers in God. It is not my place to judge them. My sole purpose for discussing their death is that I hope to lead someone to Jesus Christ through the sad and tragic loss of their lives. I was a fan of both of them. Their voices were a gift from God. They had talent that seemed to defy normal ability. However, I am reminded of the scripture which says, *"What would it profit a man if he could gain the whole world and loose his soul."* All the money, fame and prestige mean nothing if you give all your energies to the world and nothing to the Lord. *"For in him we live, and move, and have our being; as* certain *also of your own prophets have said, for we are also his offspring."* (Acts 17:28)

When the death of a rich and famous star occurs as in the case of Michael Jackson or Whitney Houston, the world puts on a big show implying that it truly loved them and will miss them. The world glorifies the big name star for a while, but over time, the world will eventually start to dig into the celebrity's back ground and reveal how this person actually lived and died. This is because after the world system has used someone up, it will spit them out and move on to the next victim it may devour. Sound familiar? The point I want people to understand is the world system of man does not love anybody. It was this same world system of man that crucified the only righteous and sinless man to have ever walked this planet, and that is Jesus Christ.

That same world system that crucified Jesus is actively present today. When you work in this system and you represent the world with your God-given talent, you are in a position to lead others into serving the world as you have chosen to live and do. The world will honor you for a while; however, that honor is never permanent. Do not think that your fame will be eternally preserved in this world. The world system of man does not, and cannot, eternally honor and glorify anyone. The best the world system can do is to list the attributes and the contributions of the rich and famous in the annals of man's recorded history. What people remember fades away eventually. There is no eternal value for man's achievement if they are not to the glory of God. It is only what we do for Jesus Christ that will last eternally.

Whitney Houston's funeral was televised to the nation and the world on February 18, 2012. I think this was the right thing to do for a person who had achieved world-wide recognition as a world-class professional singer and recording artist. However, there were some people in the state of New Jersey who did not share the Governor's sense of doing the right thing. The Governor of New Jersey, Chris Christie, had the flag flown at half-staff to honor Whitney Houston, who was from New Jersey.

As I watched some of the televised events surrounding the death and funeral of Whitney Houston, I could only pray that she was saved and had committed her life to Jesus Christ. I am not writing to judge her or any other person. The point I want to make is this: she was blessed with a voice that was a gift from God. She used that gift to achieve great wealth, status and fame in her short life. However, if she failed to know Jesus, by walking away from her early church schooling, and died in her sins, God will be her Judge. I loved to hear Whitney sing. I have failed many times in my life, but I have come to realize the eternal significance of walking before God in righteousness and truth to the best of my abilities. This is not to say that I am perfect, because the truth of the matter is, I am far from perfect. But I have come to the conclusion as so eloquently spoken by our very wise brother Solomon in the last two verses of Ecclesiastes 12: 13–14 with reference to the question of life. He said: *"Let us hear the conclusion of the whole matter: Fear God, and keep his commandments: for this is the whole duty of man. For God shall bring every work into judgment, with every secret thing, whether it be good, or whether it be evil."*

I wish the same for Whitney and for anyone who leaves this world. I pray that anyone who dies has a right relationship with God through His Son, Jesus. Anything less will not do. All the crying, the great and powerful words of love and adoration, the huge funeral with celebrities giving their testimonies of how great the deceased person was, the money , the fame, the battle with sin, is soon over. Nothing man can do or say can go beyond the grave. God's Word says that after death comes the judgment. That is what I want to drive home to the living. There is nothing I can do for Whitney Houston or Michael Jackson, but, if I can say something that might result in one soul being saved, that is my prayer before God.

Prayer for the Lost:

"Lord, I pray that if there be anyone who does not know you in the pardoning of their sins, they would get to know you. I pray they would seek you with a pure and contrite spirit and a real desire to repent of their sins, and turn from their wicked and unrighteousness ways. Lord, I pray that people will commit to serving Christ through studying the Word, through prayer and meditation on the Word, and becoming a doer of the Word.

God, let each person learn that the world's offer of fame, money, power and prestige are a poor substitute for the eternal blessings of God which you bestow on all who have chosen to live for you. Lord, your mercy and grace are too wonderful for us to really fathom. I thank You Lord, for being longsuffering toward us, and not wishing any of us to die in our sins and enter into eternal separation from You. Amen"

There is hope if you are part of God's family. The Lord tells us through His Apostle Paul in 2 Corinthians 5:8, *"We are confident, I say, and willing rather to be absent from the body, and to be present with the Lord."* This verse is saying that once we pass from this life, our spirit will be present with Almighty God in Heaven, and then comes the judgment. What judgment you might ask the question? The answer is the judgment of life in reference to how you lived your life. How do we know that there is a judgment after death? If you study and believe the Word of God as presented to us in the Holy Scriptures, Hebrews chapter 9:27 says *"And as it is appointed unto men once to die, but after this the judgment."* Additionally, we learn from Acts 17:31 – *"Because he hath appointed a day, in which he will judge the world in righteousness by that man whom he hath ordained; whereof he hath given assurance unto all men, in that he hath raised him from the dead."*

Yes, there is coming a day of judgment. In 1 Corinthians 11:31 we learn, *"For if we would judge ourselves, we should not be judged."* At this judgment seat we all will stand in front of a Righteous Judge who makes no mistakes. You will not be able to buy your way out; you will not be able to call your powerful friends to get you out of trouble. You won't be able to cash in your nonbeliever status symbol as a mistake. You will not be given a second chance to live your life over and make things right. If you are a racist, you will be going to judgment as being a racist. The same holds true for all activities associated with sin. If you were a drug dealer all of your life, and you died in your sins, you will go into judgment with those sins. The same would be true for any horrible sin that you refuse to stop in your life whatever it may be - adultery, murder, rape, racism, pedophilia, covetousness, nonbeliever, and the list continues. Keep this in mind. There is coming a time in the life of all people, believers and nonbelievers, that we will be judged. Depending on which door of life that you opened and depending on how you chose to live your life, will have major significance on how you are judged in the afterlife. As an example, if you entered into the big, black, door of life, and your time here on earth was spent having a good time partying, drinking, self-pleasures of lust, power, position, money, and covetousness, you will be judged accordingly. You could have been a corporate CEO who controlled the destiny and lives of thousands upon thousands of people who worked hard for your company for years, it doesn't matter. Everyone will be judged.

You could be a very powerful politician thinking that the world belongs to you, I have one book for you to read, and it's called the Book of Esther. This book focuses on the misguided efforts of Haman's wickedness. You might be a poor man or poor woman that refuses to learn of God and His righteousness. If you are that person who never took the time to find out and know that salvation is by grace through faith in Christ Jesus, now is the time, while you can still make a change. If you are the one who for years has had all the best things the world has to offer, i.e. money, power, status and admiration of men and women, it will not sway the judgment of God. Do you not know that the saints, will judge the world? I Corinthians 6:2 tells us, *"Shall judge the world? And if the world shall be judged by you, are ye unworthy to judge the smallest matters?"* The scripture states the saints will judge the world, not your friends, your connections, your money, nor your race.

When you are face-to-face with the Righteous Judge, Jesus will judge us based on how we lived our life. You're going to hear the summation of your life's trial in front of the mercy seat of the throne of Jesus. Jesus will read from The Book of Life, and He will declare to those who worshipped and served Him faithfully, *"Well done my good and faithful servant."* But to those who rejected Him, and chose to live their life their way, He is going to say, *"Depart from me, you are a worker of iniquity, I know you not."* We are told this in Matthew 7: 22-23 that *"Many will say to me in that day, Lord, Lord, have we not prophesied in thy name? And in thy name have cast out devils? And in thy name done many wonderful works? And then will I profess unto them, I never knew you: depart from me, ye that work iniquity."*

In Matthew 7:15, we learn that *"Beware of false prophets, which come to you in sheep's clothing, but inwardly they are ravening wolves."* A wolf in sheep's clothing is still a wolf. His goal is to destroy you. What is God telling us with this verse? I believe He is telling us that a false prophet or teacher is a very dangerous person to have in your midst. He or she seeks to weaken the doctrine of Jesus Christ and to lead people astray and away from the truth. Some church doctrines now openly allow homosexuals to be a part of the clergy. I have seen and read about gay bishops, pastors, teachers, and others. I just want to stand on the Word of God and say to all who claim to be saved and yet are actively engaging in a homosexual lifestyle, you are going against the Word of God. If you are teaching that it is okay for two men or two women to marry, you are teaching a lie. God is very clear on His views of marriage.

In the Old Testament Book of Leviticus 18:22, God said *"Thou shalt not lie* with *mankind, as with womankind; it is abomination."* Yet, when we turn on the television or read the newspapers, we continually see people engaging in this alternative lifestyle without any shame. We see them parading on every channel. Our Congress has now passed new laws that make it completely acceptable to marry your same sex partner. America needs to wake up and get back to what made this country great. God judged Sodom and Gomorra because of it wickedness. God is very capable of doing the same to America or any other nation that "snubs" its nose at the words of God. Question: was Katrina an act of nature or an act of God's judgment?

The year 2011 will go down in history books as one of the worst years on record for weather. There have been more tornados, storms, fires, droughts, floods, and hurricanes than any year that I can remember. Yet, we go on, as if God is powerless to control what man does. We all would do well to read and understand the warning given to us from Galatians 6:7-8 *"Be not deceived; God is not mocked: for whatsoever a man soweth, that shall he also reap. For he that soweth to his flesh shall of the flesh reap corruption; but he that soweth to the Spirit shall of the Spirit reap life everlasting."* I think that man is playing a very dangerous game, and going against the Word of God which has been the foundation of morality in this country for centuries.

I am going to read to you a very disturbing article that I found in the Decatur, Illinois Herald and Review.com. This particular article was found on page 84, and the date of the article was Friday, December 9, 2011, Decatur, Illinois. I want to quote the article exactly as I read in the paper. The title of article was in bold black letters: "Bill Would End Military Sodomy Ban."

"Recently passed Senate legislation would make sodomy and sex with animals legal under military law, ending long-standing prohibitions and triggering cries of perversion from conservative groups.

The bill, which the Senate passed 93-7 last week, would repeal article 125 of the uniform code of military Justice that states any person who engage in unnatural carnal copulation with another person of the same or opposite sex or with an animal is guilty of sodomy. Guilty of sodomy would be subject to court-martial.

Senate Armed Services Committee Chairman Carl D Levin, D-Michigan, said Thursday that they repeal was simply a legal change because it's no longer constitutional. A 2003 Supreme Court decision struck down a Texas ban on sodomy. The committee said that changes in the law were recommended by the Joint Services Committee on Military Justice and the Secretary of Defense.

Senate negotiators are working to reconcile the version of the bill with the house-passed measure and produce final legislation that sets policy for the Pentagon. House Republicans opposed the repeal. Conservative groups angered by the end this year of the ban on gays serving openly in the military were outraged by the proposed repeal.

"Now, in its rush to accommodate the left, Congress may have inadvertently opened the door to even more perversion," Tony Perkins of the Family Research Council said.

Wake up America! We are at war, and the enemy is sin! The leader of this army of sin is the devil himself. Therefore, allow me to borrow a phrase from one of America's most powerful military geniuses, Gen. Douglas MacArthur, who once said: *"there is no substitute for victory in war"*. When it comes to the things of God, to holiness, to righteousness, and being a part of the kingdom of heaven, there is no substitute for victory over the enemy the devil. There is absolutely no negotiating with unrighteousness, sin, un-holiness, or giving in to the kingdom of darkness, which is the home of Satan. There is no cease-fire or working relationship with the flesh, sin, or with the devil. We are to overcome and conquer them, or they will overcome and conquer us. There is no truce with the enemy of our soul. As a good soldier, we are to live or die standing on the Word of God.

Here is a warning call to all who will listen. The Lord has placed all these words on my heart to tell the world - The day of the Lord is coming! Allow me to directly quote from five mighty men of God that at one time walked this earth, and left us their prophecy of what is to surely come. Joel 2:1-2, says, *"Blow ye the trumpet in Zion, and sound an alarm in my holy mountain: let all the inhabitants of the land tremble: for the day of the LORD cometh, for it is nigh at hand; A day of darkness and of gloominess, a day of clouds and of thick darkness, as the morning spread upon the mountains: a great people and a strong; there hath not been ever the like, neither shall be any more after it, even to the years of many generations."*

True believers know that the day of the Lord is coming. This day, when it arrives, will not be a day of business as usual. The world cannot, and will not, be able to blow it off just as a freak accident of nature. Man will know immediately that the Son of the Living God is making His Second Coming known to the entire world. Jeremiah said in chapter 30:7 of his book, "Alas! For that day is great, so that none is like it: it is even the time of Jacob's trouble; but he shall be saved out of it." Man will not be able to pretend that all is well on this special day of the Lord. On that great day, who will be able to stand? None but the righteous will stand.

In Daniel 12:1-4 regarding the day of the Lord, we learn: *"And at that time shall Michael stand up, the great prince which standeth for the children of thy people: and there shall be a time of trouble, such as never was since there was a nation even to that same time: and at that time thy people shall be delivered, every one that shall be found written in the book. 2 And many of them that sleep in the dust of the earth shall awake, some to everlasting life, and some to shame and everlasting contempt. 3And they that be wise shall shine as the brightness of the firmament; and they that turn many to righteousness as the stars forever and ever. 4But thou, O Daniel, shut up the words, and seal the book, even to the time of the end: many shall run to and fro, and knowledge shall be increased."*

From the teachings of Daniel we learn that the day of the Lord will be a time of trouble, a kind of trouble that no man or nation has ever seen before. It will be a day that the dead will rise to be judged. Some will go into everlasting life, others into everlasting separation from God. What a day that will be! It is my prayer that all who read this book will be saved through Jesus Christ. Only He can cleanse and wash away sin. The goal of this book is to point all non-believers, toward our Savior Jesus Christ.

The Apostle Peter said in 2 Peter 8-10, *"But, beloved, be not ignorant of this one thing, that one day is with the Lord as a thousand years, and a thousand years as one day. 9The Lord is not slack concerning his promise, as some men count slackness; but is longsuffering to us-ward, not willing that any should perish, but that all should come to repentance. 10 But the day of the Lord will come as a thief in the night; in which the heavens shall pass away with a great noise, and the elements shall melt with fervent heat, the earth also and the works that are therein shall be burned up."* He exhorts them to holiness of life.

Peter is telling us that our loving God is longsuffering towards us. He does not want to see any of us go into judgment with unrepentant sins. Do not confuse His loving kindness with weakness or slack concerning His promises. God is going to judge us all one day. It is though His loving kindness that He is merciful to us sinners but note what Peter says in verse10, *"the day of the Lord will come. And when it comes it will come as a thief in the night."* This means He will come when you least expect Him. People, don't let God catch you with your work undone. If you are not saved, get saved and start a new life in Jesus Christ. It is referenced in the book of Acts 4:12 *"Neither is there salvation in any other: for there is none other name under heaven given among men, whereby we must be saved."* His Name is Jesus. If you do not know Him, you need to get to know Him; and you need to get in a hurry to know Him. We do not know the date, the time, nor the hour of His return.

In Matthew, our Lord and Savior made a reference to the day of the Lord. His words talk about a great tribulation that will occur after the rapture of the saints. He said in Matthew 24:21, *"For then shall be great tribulation, such as was not since the beginning of the world to this time, no, nor ever shall be."*

We have heard the words of five great men of the Bible, including words from the Son of God himself informing us of what is going to come upon the world. Knowing this, what excuse do you have for not believing in God? What makes you as sure as a non–believer that you are correct in your belief that God is not real? This reminds me of a saying I had on my desk when I was working. It was something that was shared by the well-known and respected Bishop T. D. Jakes, He said *"I would rather live my life as if there is a God and die to find out there isn't, than live my life as if there isn't a God and die to find out there is."* I do not know if Mr. Jakes actually wrote this, and it does not matter, it is the wisdom of the message that's gives it substance. I wish that all of our men, both black and white, Latino or whatever, that are in street gangs or thinking about joining a street gang would memorize this saying.

Allow me to quote a passage of scripture directly from the King James Version of the Bible. I am speaking directly to any and all non–believers and specifically to all the gang-bangers, drug dealers, prostitutes, pimps and "wannabe" players in this gift of life we have received from God. To all racists, murderers, robbers, child molesters, and finally, to anyone who needs to come to know Jesus in the pardoning of their sins, now is the time to listen attentively to what the Lord is saying.

If you don't have a Bible, please get one, and if you have a Bible, turn to the book of Acts, Chapter 10: 36-48.

36 "The word which God sent unto the children of Israel, preaching peace by Jesus Christ: (he is Lord of all :) 37That word, I say, ye know, which was published throughout all Judaea, and began from Galilee, after the baptism which John preached; 38How God anointed Jesus of Nazareth with the Holy Ghost and with power: who went about doing good, and healing all that were oppressed of the devil; for God was with him. 39 And we are witnesses of all things which he did both in the land of the Jews, and in Jerusalem; whom they slew and hanged on a tree: 40Him God raised up the third day and shewed him openly; [41]*Not to all the people, but unto witnesses chosen before of God, even to us, who did eat and drink with him after he rose from the dead.* [42]*And he commanded us to preach unto the people, and to testify that it is he which was ordained of God to be the Judge of quick and dead.* [43]*To him give all the prophets' witness, that through his name whosoever believeth in him shall receive remission of sins.* [44]*While Peter yet spake these words, the Holy Ghost fell on all them which heard the word.* [45]*And they of the circumcision which believed were astonished, as many as came with Peter, because that on the Gentiles also was poured out the gift of the Holy Ghost.* [46]*For they heard them speak with tongues, and magnify God. Then answered Peter,* [47]*Can any man forbid water, that these should not be baptized, which have received the Holy Ghost as well as we?* [48]*And he commanded them to be baptized in the name of the Lord. Then prayed they him to tarry certain days."*

After reading these twelve verses of scripture, we have the Word of God to confirm that Jesus Christ was sent from God, and Jesus Christ is Lord of all. Study each verse very carefully and take this diligently to heart what the God of Creation is saying regarding His Son, Jesus. You will find that you have two choices, (there's that number two again); you can either: 1) Reject the Word of God as presented in Acts, or 2) have complete acceptance. If you truly accept the Word of God as presented, it will manifest itself in a changed lifestyle. You will also repent of all your sins and ask God to forgive you and come into your life. You will commit your life to Him and your life will be forever changed. Find a good God–fearing church to join as you begin to study and grow by reading and learning the Word of God.

The End Result of Sin
Chapter 12

To the gang-banger and all who chase after money (by any means necessary), love, power, and lust of the flesh, I have one scripture for you. Please memorize it. It comes from the study of Job 1:21 *"And said, Naked came I out of my mother's womb and naked shall I return thither: the Lord gave; blessed be the name of the Lord.* In case you failed to grasp the meaning of this short verse, allow me to enlighten you. Job is saying if it were possible for you to gain all the money, all the love, affections, power, and all the lustful cravings of the flesh that the world has to offer, what good would it do you if you ended up going to hell as a result of the poor choices you made in this life? The writer of Job is also telling us it does not matter how much money, power and fame that you achieve in this life, you will die one day. And all that you worked so hard to accumulate materially will not follow you into judgment. I once heard a pastor say, "You will never see a U-hall moving truck following behind a hearse in a funeral procession." That is not going to happen.

I'm reminded of a story that I once heard and I thought it was very funny. There once was a man who was very wealthy. Yet, he was a miser with his money. He always bought things at second-hand stores, rummage sales, and items that were used or on sale. He was a very stingy man and when his wife complained he would always remind her that he was the moneymaker of the family–not her. The money belonged to him. It was his money and his rules. She would remain silent because she knew he was the one making the money and she did not have a job. It had been his decision for her not to work. So over the years this man's money continued to grow, yet he lived like he was in poverty. One day, the man was walking home from work because he refused to buy a car. He was attacked by some street thugs and severely injured. He was injured because he refused to hand over to them the five dollars that he had in his pocket.

While in the hospital, the doctors told his wife that his injuries were very critical and that things may not go well for him during the surgery. The doctor advised her and the rest of the family to get their house in order. In the hospital room prior to the surgery, the man told his wife that because he had worked very hard to amass the huge savings they had in their bank account, he wanted her to promise him in writing that if he should die, she was instructed to withdraw all the money out of his bank account. He wanted all his money to be buried along with him. The amount of money he had arranged to leave her was less than five percent of the total amount accumulated. She finally agreed and signed the release. As fate would have it, the man died. As the wife was telling the lawyer and the banker what she wanted to do, the lawyer said, "Excuse me madam, please tell me that you are not going to go through with your husband's request of drawing all that money out of the bank and to putting it in the casket with him. Please tell me that you are not going through with that ridiculous demand."

The wife was so browbeaten from years of abuse at the hands on this very mean and stingy husband that she raised her head ever so slightly and said in a small low sweet voice, "Yes sir, I am going to honor my husband's request. He wanted all the money to be buried with him and that is what I agreed to do. So please write me a check for the full amount, and if he can cash it, I will have done my part." The moral of this story is the wife was not as dumb as the husband thought she was.

Gangbanger, I see you walking down the streets, talking on your cell phone, with your pants sagging as you flirt with every female you meet. I see you checking on your money and running your part of the block. You are a different kind of black man; you are what people call a master of the streets. Nothing or nobody had better dare mess with your paper. To you, making ends meet and getting paper is what life is all about. "Pay attention", you tell all the young kindergarten "wannabe" future gangsters. You show them how to be a big man in the streets, by kicking in another brother's teeth, breaking a few of his ribs; all because he lost some of your paper. It never occurred to you that the reason he failed to pay on time, was that he used part of the money to keep his mother who is sick with cancer from being evicted in below-zero weather. He was not, as you had said, trying to disrespect you. He is just another misguided young black kid who was led away by sin, by the bait of making fast money, slinging dope. However, his heart simply is not as black as yours. He still feels emotions and love for a few people like his mother. You, on the other hand, never knew your mother or father. You were raised in the poorest of orphanages, in the heart of the ghetto in one of the largest cities in the USA. Poverty, corruption, and crime are constant reminders of a youth spent just trying to survive. Love for self and hate for others is embedded in your DNA.

Your "modus-operandi", Mr. Gangbanger boss, is doing whatever it takes to make your paper grow. Killing someone who happens to get in your way, is just a part of the game you are in. You have killed people so many times, you have lost count. You are the kind of person that is mentioned in 1st Timothy 4:2 which says *"Speaking lies in hypocrisy; having their conscience seared with a hot iron."* Your conscience left you a long time ago, now it's all about you and you see your narcissistic personality disorder (NPD) as an asset. You are not only living your life behind the black door, you are a solid citizen. A person of power and authority actually knows and recognizes you when they see you. All the girls love you because you have large sums of money all the time and sell only the best drugs. Your crew is well organized, and if you decide to cancel someone's contract, they are as good as dead. In your mind, you operate by your own rules. You view anybody who holds down a typical 9-5 job as a sucker. You decided a long time ago that you were never going to work for anybody Work is for suckers, at least that is what you tell all your little kindergarten admirers who all want to grow up and be like you. You are like the "reprobate" that Paul described to us in Romans 1:28-32. He *said: 28"And even as they did not like to retain God in their knowledge, God gave them over to a reprobate mind, to do those things which are not convenient; 29Being filled with all unrighteousness, fornication, wickedness, covetousness, maliciousness; full of envy, murder, debate, deceit, malignity; whisperers, 30Backbiters, haters of God, despiteful, proud, boasters, inventors of evil things, disobedient to parents, 31Without understanding, covenant breakers, without natural affection, implacable, unmerciful: 32Who knowing the judgment of God, that they which commit such things are worthy of death, not only do the same, but have pleasure in them that do them."* Paul has just described you correctly. Do you care? No, is your reply. You are making major paper, and on your way to becoming one of the main players of life behind the black door. As a matter of fact, things are going so well for you that you are going to have to branch out. You make thousands of dollars a week from your drug, prostitution, extortion, and gaming operations. You have a high profile attorney at the ready to come when and if he's needed. But he is never needed because you are in the real, what the smooth jazz R&B singer Sade sings about - you are a smooth operator. One week you fly to Bangkok, Thailand, the next week, Paris. You have to be in New York for a major conference with members of the underworld, and after you relax for a while in the Big Apple, you send one of your guys to Brazil to make connections on new shipping routes for your product.

Yes, things are going well for you. So well that you and your crew had a meeting. You now decide that at the rate you are moving, you will need to move all your assets overseas and start a new fictitious account under an assumed name. You use a name that cannot be traced or linked directly to you. Therefore, if you are ever caught, they will never find the money. You tell your crew that after three more years in the business, there would be enough money for everyone to sit back and enjoy life and take it easy

There is one stumbling block that you did not see coming and had been watching you all the time. He is God Almighty. Yes, that God that you cursed when that old lady called on Him as you took her life when you were 13 years old. She only had six dollars in her purse. Yes, that same God who saw you when you raped that mother of two and then pistol whipped her husband because he owed you two hundred dollars for crack cocaine. You were 21 years old when this happened. Yes, that God that allowed you to be sent to prison so that you might redeem your life and rehabilitate yourself, however; after you served your three years for armed robbery and drug possession, you came out of prison more determined than ever to make it big in the drug business. And make it big you did.

Yes, the same God that silently watched as you mercilessly killed and robbed all your competition in the drug business. You were completely ruthless. Even the people in the drug underworld were afraid of you and your crew. Over the years, your fame as a serious drug dealer and gangbanger grew. You now have a small empire that was on the verge of major expansion. Yes, the same God who silently watched all the horrors of your life, and gave you chance after chance to repent and change your life, now called you the rich fool. You lived your life similar to the rich man we learn about in Luke 8:16-21. The scripture is listed here. [16] "And he spake a parable unto them, saying, *the ground of a certain rich man brought forth plentifully: [17]And he thought within himself, saying, what I shall do, because I have no room where to bestow my fruits? [18]And he said, 'this will I do: I will pull down my barns, and build greater; and there will I bestow all my fruits and my goods. [19]And I will say to my soul, Soul, thou hast much goods laid up for many years; take thine ease, eat, drink, and be merry. [20]But God said unto him, Thou fool, this night thy soul shall be required of thee: then whose shall those things be, which thou hast provided? [21]So is he that layeth up treasure for himself, and is not rich toward God."*

One thing that we need to make absolutely clear, if God calls you a fool, you are most definitely a fool. And to the gang member, and to all the gang members, there is going to come a time when we all will come face-to-face with an all-powerful, all-knowing God! All of your years of unbelief will evaporate. The Lord tells us in Romans Chapter 14:11-12, *"For it is written, As I live, saith the Lord, every knee shall bow to me, and every tongue shall confess to God. So then, every one of us shall give account of himself to God."* Therefore, if you have been a member of a powerful street gang all of your life and your motto has been "no fear". You will now learn fear that has no limits. Your buddies will be as weak and powerless as you are when they come face-to-face with an all-powerful and Almighty God.

Sin is like cancer. If undetected, it will continue to grow and spread to all parts of the body. If the wages of sin is death, then the end result of cancer is also death. There is no negotiating with either sin or cancer. They must be completely removed from the body, if the body is going to continue to function in the capacity it was originally intended by its Creator – God!

Before I leave the gang-bangers, the prostitutes, the drug dealers, drug users, and the alcoholics, I have a sad confession to make. These people are lost in their sins and if they do not repent and turn from their wicked ways, they are going to die in their sins and go straight to hell. The depressing thing that I hate to admit is, the drug dealers and users, and unbelievers in general, while they lived, they seemed to be more loyal and true to their gods. Who are their gods? The god of drugs, lust and sexual perversion, and the god of money are their gods. In many ways they are more committed to their particular god than many of our Christian brothers and sisters who attend church and claim to be disciples of the Most High God.

I call these Christians "fair-weather" Christians. You know them – we have them in all of our churches. A fair-weather Christian is only responsible for going to church during good or fair weather. Do not expect to see them if the weatherman says rain, or if inclement weather pays a visit or it turns cold. Do not expect to see them if it's too hot, because they will say it's too hot in the church. Do expect to see them during the Easter and Christmas programs. They will be in church to show off their new outfits and their hair styles. They will want their kids to be on the program so they can sit up front and take pictures and be seen in their new clothes. It doesn't faze them in the least that a lot of the older mothers in church are sometimes forgetful and say to them, "who are these people, and do they go to our church?" The pastor is also asking the same question. A fair-weather Christian is going to leave right after the church service is over, and they will not be back to church again unless it's a major program like a revival or a big event.

You can forget asking a fair-weather Christian to come back to Bible Study, or any program out of the normally scheduled church service. Additionally, they are not going to come in early to attend Sunday school. However, they might send their kids to Sunday school if the church bus comes and picks them up. They will expect the church to feed their kids a snack, and bring them back home after the service is over.

It is my personal belief that fair-weather Christians are one of the main reasons sinners and unbelievers fail to come to the church. Why? It is because the fair-weather Christian's lifestyle in many ways is no different than the sinner's lifestyle. In other words, the fair-weather Christian does not carry him or herself like a committed saint, one who has the discipline to worship and praise God twenty-four hours a day, seven days a week. A real disciple of Christ does more than just praise God on Sunday for a few hours then the rest of the week you hear the same kind of loud and gutter-filled music coming from their home as from the committed sinner and unbeliever's home. How can a fair-weather Christian tell a sinner about Jesus and the ministry of reconciliation, if they are not truly committed themselves? The first thing the fair-weather Christian needs to do is strive to get him or herself ready. Jesus tells us through the Apostle Paul in 2 Corinthians 6:17 *"Wherefore come out from among them, and be ye separate, saith the Lord, and touch not the unclean thing; and I will receive you."*

A Christian, who is striving to be true to God's Word, must stay true to His teachings. Jesus says to make a difference between clean and unclean. Now I am not saying that as Christians we are to walk around with our chest stuck out and our noses in the air. Nor, should we act as though we have a God-given air of superiority that looks down on our fellow man. Our behavior should be just like Jesus' behavior which was never based on pride or arrogance. Jesus' behavior was the exact opposite of pride because it was based on love. We are to humble ourselves out of love for Jesus. We are to use our God-given gift of salvation through faith in Jesus to help a soul that is lost in sin and bound by the devil. As a Christian do we not know that as disciples of the most High God, we are not of this world? However, until God calls us home, we are to live in this world as God's representatives. We are the salt of this dying world!

I want to say this again, the true sinner seems to be more committed to their unique brand of sin than the fair-weather Christian is to his calling or his faith. Allow me to share a real life personal story to illustrate this point. I know a man who is now in his mid-sixties. This person is a committed heavy smoker; he is a substance abuser of marijuana and is addicted to crack cocaine and alcohol. He is also bound by the lust of the flesh and has a strong sexual addictive spirit that drives him to seek sexual gratification when he is high. This man once told me that I should thank my God that I do not have a crack addiction problem because it never goes away. I asked him to explain to me what and how it felt to have an addiction that never goes away. He said, "do you remember the kind of winter we had a few years ago when the weather temperature was below zero and freezing for several days?" He said that on this particular Saturday night it was 25 to 35 degrees below zero and the wind chill factor made it even colder. He said that he and his crack girlfriend were partying and at about 2:15 in the morning they wanted to buy some more crack cocaine and other drugs. They called their dealer who lives miles from their house. The dealer told them he was done making deliveries for the night because the weather was too bad. He also said that if the man wanted the drugs he would have to come and get it. The drug dealer said that he was getting ready to go to bed and he would not be accepting any more calls this night, so if he wanted the drugs he had better be on his way. My friend said that he told the drug dealer that he would be there in about twenty minutes. Crack addicts always think they can get somewhere in a few minutes. The truth of the matter is it might take him an hour or more to walk where he had to go because at this time, he had lost his car.

I have seen how addictive crack cocaine can be. It does not discriminate. This drug is an equal opportunity destroyer. This drug (CC) will make slaves out of all races of people. It does not care how old or young you are. If you get hooked on crack, it will enslave a child just as it will an adult; age is irrelevant. I have seen college- educated and professional people flocking into dirty and abandoned neighborhoods to make contact with their drug dealer in order to get their medicine. Some of these same professionals wouldn't have anything in common or have any contact with a low-living, low standard, low-pants-wearing, uneducated street crack cocaine dealer, yet, their addiction will make them bow to him and risk their very lives by going in a crime-infested neighborhood. People have been robbed and killed leaving an area after they have purchased their drugs. I call this insane behavior.

Why would a person who has spent thousands of dollars going to college to get a degree in some high tech field turn right around and allow this drug to make him or her a slave to an uneducated, non –believer in God, and polluter of all that is righteous? The answer is not because the drug dealer is so gifted that people willingly give all their accomplishments in life just to serve him. It is because of the product that he is selling. If you are hooked on crack cocaine, heroin, methamphetamine, powdered cocaine, marijuana, or any illicit drug, this drug has become your pimp. It controls you.

I understand why the police and law enforcement agencies call hard core drugs controlled substances. It is because this drug has the potential of controlling its victims. That is why they are called mind-altering drugs. They call drugs "dope", because it dopes people into slavery and then society calls them dope-heads because their minds have been fried through heavy and prolonged drug use. As an addict, you come when the need for the drug calls, and you do what it demands. If you have to sell your body as many prostitutes do every day to get this drug, you will. If you have to use robbery to get this drug, you will. Even if you have to kill someone to satisfy your habit, it is not a problem for you at the time of your urgent need for the drug. If you have to hurt your mother, father, sisters, or brothers, it will happen all in the name of love for your crack dealer's product. It is no wonder that when the police do catch up with you, they have to use their Taser gun which sends 50,000 volts through your body just so they can safely handcuff you. You still fight like a wild man trying to get away.

The moral of this story is, that whoever controls the most addictive drugs also control the lives of the people who are addicted to those drugs. This is why I have a huge and perfect hatred for drug dealers. They, and the product they sell, destroy families. They get rich at the expense of young lives (stolen innocence). They eat well and can buy whatever food they have a taste for, however; many of their victims and their children barely get by. Addicts sometimes sell their monthly Link card (a food allowance) to buy drugs. The drug dealers create such a strong dependence on the addict's life some are so strung out that they act and look like zombies. When they are craving this drug, they flock to their drug dealer's locations early in the morning. All throughout the day, all times of night, and into the early morning. In many ways they are reminiscent of Pavlov's classical conditioning experiment of the early 1900's.

In one particular crack house in our neighborhood, the crack dealer will hang a bright red curtain or some type of crepe paper to indicate to his victims (crack addicts) that he is open for business. As long as the addicts see the bright red design they flock to his location. When he is out of products, he takes down the bright red crepe paper design and the crack addicts just hang around this area like starving dogs until the man reopens his crack business in the same manner.

I do believe that there will be a special place in hell for the drug dealers, for pimps, and for any illegal business owner who makes money by illegal gains and by making slaves out of God's creation. God loves all of His creation. This is why He sent His only Son to die for us. John 3:16-18 are verses that should remind us all of the tremendous sacrifice Jesus made for us: *16"For God so loved the world, that he gave his only begotten Son, that whosoever believeth in him should not perish, but have everlasting* life. *17For God sent not his Son into the world to condemn the world; but that the world through him might be saved. 18He that believeth on him is not condemned: but he that believeth not is condemned already, because he hath not believed in the name of the only begotten Son of God."* God sent His Son to die for a sinner like me, like all of us. One question - what more can He do? God is the Source of all life for the good of His creation. The drug dealers and pimps prey on life for their own good. They want God's creation to serve them. This is the exact same desire that Satan has. The devil wants God's creation to worship and serve him. It was the pride of life of the devil that got him kicked out of heaven. He has been waging a war on God and His creation ever since. But fear not the devil; our Jesus has prevailed against the demon. If we are standing on the promises of God, and walking in His commandments, we need not fear the devil. The devil is truly our enemy, but he is a defeated foe. His time is coming to an end and he knows it. You should take note that I did not say to ignore the devil, but as children of the cross, our God is God!

Only a foolish and unwise servant would tell you that the devil is harmless. The devil is not harmless; he is a power to be respected in this sin-sick and dying world. As children of the kingdom, we are to watch as well as pray, and keep our focus on Jesus Christ. Remember, as long as we are in the flesh, and are committed to serving and obeying God's will, the devil will view us as his enemy. Never forget that. Allow me to borrow a phrase from a mighty military warrior for God by the name of Joshua. Joshua once told all the Israelites who were doubtful and wavering in the faith. He said in verse 15, *"And if it seem evil unto you to serve the LORD, choose you this day whom ye will serve; whether the gods which your fathers served that were on the other side of the flood, or the gods of the Amorites, in whose land ye dwell: but as for me and my house, we will serve the LORD."*

I want to finish the story I was relating about a friend of mine who is a crack addict. This man told me that he put on all the clothes that he had, and with no gloves, walked across town in below-zero weather to buy crack cocaine and then walked back home. How many believers do you know that would get out of their nice warm beds and comfortable homes that God has blessed them with to attend a 2:00 am prayer meeting during a blizzard of cold and snowy weather? Yes, there would be some, but my point is the sinner man seems to be more committed to his sin and unrighteousness than the Christian man is committed to being saved and living a righteous life. That needs to change and change in a mighty hurry. We need more Christians with the faith and determination of Daniel and the three Hebrews boys, Shadrach, Meshach, and Abednego.

When I was working, I would sometimes have to go in early. On my route to work, there is a liquor store that opens at 6:00 am. The majority of time that I passed by this liquor store, I saw a lot of people, males and females, standing outside the establishment smoking cigarettes and waiting for the liquor store to open. On the street where I live there is a crack house apartment that sells drugs. I know this because some of the people that I see standing outside of this apartment building are known heavy drug users. Since I am retired now, I have the opportunity to observe and pass by this house sometimes several times a day. It is unbelievable the amount of people who just hang around this apartment building. Some of the women I feel so sorry for and I pray for them. They look lost and addicted to the "devil's candy".

The drug dealers are so brazen they sometimes stand outside of their apartment building and actually try to stare down each car that pass by their operation. They try to intimidate the people who live directly in their immediate area. Their unspoken threat message seems to be "if you call the police, we will take care of you and your family". Judging by how they act, it seems to me that they are saying "Yes, I am a drug dealer and what are you going to do about it?" I sometimes think, "If I can discern what they are doing, why can't the police? I want to believe that their day is coming, because the police often make their busts when they have all the evidence they need, at least is what I think they are doing because the police are not dumb. Their job is to protect and serve, and they cannot protect and serve if they are not aware of what's going on in their community.

I see all drug dealers as parasites. They get rich at the expense of addicting some poor-minded soul to using and becoming hooked on their product. They are killers of their own people. They do not care about the many families they have destroyed. They do not care that after a young girl or a young mother gets hooked, many will sell their precious body to buy more of the drug that has them enslaved. I see the drug dealers standing on street corners, or riding around town in their shinny "pimped" out cars with big

24 inch tires and mag wheels. The rims of their cars have rotating spinners on each tire. They sell a product that destroys a person's life and self-esteem and makes prostitutes out of our children. They represent everything in life that I hate. They are shiftless, lazy, brute beasts, but they are very cunning and sometime merciless killers who think evil of anything righteous. Just think of all the many murders and crimes that have been committed in the name of some drug dealer not getting his or her paper (money) as promised. The friend that I mentioned earlier, told me that a man he owed $40 on a past due crack cocaine bill told him that if he did not pay him his money in the next hour, that he was going to kill him and his girlfriend. The dealer said this as he pulled out his gun and cocked it to fire. My friend had to make an emergency phone call to a family member and beg him to bring him the $40 ASAP! When the family member arrived with the money, the drug dealer was standing out in front of the man's house with his gun in his hand. Since it was almost dark it was easy for the drug dealer to hide the weapon, but it was obvious he had a gun in his hand.

As I said before, I think that there will be a special place in Hell for the true unrepentant drug dealers. They will get the chance to see all the many lives they have destroyed and caused to be addicted to their insidious product. Crack cocaine, heroin, methamphetamine, cocaine, marijuana, alcohol, are just a few of the deadly drugs used to enslave God's children. The list is endless. The sellers of these deadly chemicals have no mercy, therefore; in the day of their judgment, they will receive no mercy. I am sure one day I will wake up to read in the newspaper about a huge drug bust in our immediate area. God will judge sin. My faith is in Him. Man has a habit of saying one thing and doing another. God will do what He said that He will do and you can depend on it!

There have been many examples of people, some famous and some not famous, that during the course of their everyday life, opened the wrong door of life never to return. Some call these particular incidents as fate, some say it's just the luck of the draw. The truth of the matter is, we do not have a clue as to why some people doing that exact same thing, opens the wrong door and lives to tell about it. One example of a fateful opening of a wrong door had a life-ending result for a famous rock and roll singer - Sam Cooke.

I know that a lot of younger people may not remember Sam Cooke, but he had one of the most beautiful voices to ever hit the recording industry. In my opinion, no one comes close to singing with the pure clarity and tone of voice as Sam Cooke. His records sound just as good today as they did years ago.

Sam Cooke was born in Clarksdale, Mississippi on January 22, 1931. But in 1933, his family moved to Chicago, Illinois. It was in Chicago that Sam Cooke began to polish his beautiful singing voice. However, fate or the luck of the draw had a different encounter with this very popular and fast-rising soul singer. Sam Cooke was tragically killed in the city of Los Angeles, California on December 11, 1964. He was 33 years old at the time of his death. Before his rise to fame in the R&B world, Sam Cooke was a gospel singer. He started out singing in the church as a child, and later he became the lead singer for gospel groups, two of which were The Highway Q.C's, and The Soul Stirrers. After he crossed over and started singing R&B songs, his popularity took off. He would sing with other up and coming recording stars of 1960's period, stars like: J. W. Alexander, Lou Rawls, Bobby Womack, just to name a few. Sam Cooke wrote a lot of thought-provoking songs, but one song that he wrote shortly before his death had a subtle warning in the song. The name of the song was: *"A Change is Gonna Come"*. This song became very popular after his death. Some of the lyrics of the song are as follows:

> *"I was born by the river in a little tent, oh, and just like the river I've been running ever since. It's been a long, a long time coming, but I know a change is going to come."*

> *It's been too hard living, but I am afraid to die, because I don't know what's up there beyond the sky. It's been a long, a long time, time coming, but I know a change is going to come."*

I don't think Sam Cooke ever knew the real meaning of the words of this song, because the change that came to him shortly after he wrote this song was his death. There are some people who associate this song with the violent "race riots" of the 1960's and they could be right. My personal view is that fate or death itself made its intention known for Mr. Cooke's life in the words of that song. Before you say that's crazy, think of how our songs and music come to us. We don't buy them in a store; they come through the channels of our mind. We create them after we receive thoughts from various sources, and we record them. We do not know exactly where our thought processes comes from. Some of our greatest musicians are referred to as musical geniuses or masters of composition. People like Ludwig van Beethoven who, at seven and one-half years of age, gave his first public performance. Johann Sebastian Bach, Wolfgang Amades Mozart, Pyotr llyich Tchaikovsky, and Johannes Brahms are just a few of the musical architects of our time. They were ahead of their time musically and people around the world still marvel at the complexity of their compositions.

Sadly enough, it seems that many of our truly gifted musical artists live short lives. This seems to be the one unexplainable paradox associated with greatness. This short life is seen across a wide range of musical, artistic, entrepreneurial political greatness, and the list does not stop with these fields. Musically speaking, think of all the short lives associated with musical greatness, i.e., Jimi Hendrix, Janis Joplin, Buddy Holly, Charlie Parker, John Coltrane, and Michael Jackson. The list is endless.

So where am I going with this analysis? My proposition is as this. When God gives man a talent for greatness, and man turns around and uses that talent or skill not to glorify God, but to glorify the world and self with worldly pleasures and rewards like money, power, prestige, and lust of the flesh, the end result is a tragic loss of life and monetary gain which is left behind for someone else to enjoy. In 1 Timothy 6:9-11, we learn: *9 "but they that will be rich fall into temptation and a snare, and into many foolish and hurtful lusts, which drown men in destruction and perdition. 10 For the love of money is the root of all evil: which while some coveted after, they have erred from the faith, and pierced themselves through with many sorrows. 11 But thou, O man of God, flee these things; and follow after righteousness, godliness, faith, love, patience, meekness."*

God works in mysterious ways and we need to realize something; it is not fate that decides man's destiny, but the Creator of life itself - God Almighty! God makes all decisions as to what, when, why, where and how we will leave His earth. It has nothing to do with family, money, race, or cultured or uncultured upbringing. It has everything to do with your acknowledgement and understanding of the Person of God Almighty! Man can get so wrapped up in his great success and achievements, that over the course of time, he forgets who gave him this great ability. It is during this period of life, the rejection and non-recognition of God Almighty, that He allows tragic things to enter our lives. He sometimes gives us a warning to change course, and when we fail to see or heed His warnings, suddenly out of nowhere tragedy strikes. Then we wonder what happened. What happened is that we failed to see the invisible hand of God working in our lives, and we refused to heed His warning signs. A brief research and analysis of the wrong door that Mr. Cooke opened and the resulting consequences for opening that door is briefly summarized below. Here is what I learned about Mr. Sam Cooke.

Sam married his high school sweetheart, Barbara Campbell, in 1959 and they had three children. Tragically, Vincent, their youngest, drowned in their swimming pool at age four in June 1963. In 1963, Cooke's 18 months old son, Vincent, wandered away from his mother's supervision and drowned in their front yard pool while Sam was away from the home. With their marriage already in trouble largely due to extramarital affairs by both Sam and his wife, Barbara, the distance between them deepened as Sam blamed Barbara for their son's death. Cooke retreated into a deep depression, and asked that no one wear black to the child's funeral. He found his escape in out-of-town performances, which he agreed to at every opportunity.

On the night of December 11, 1964, Cooke was set up to be robbed of Christmas money he'd withdrawn earlier in the day for gifts. After the robbery, he was murdered by Motel Manager, Bertha Franklin, who'd shot and killed a man six months earlier at the same motel. That night, Sam picked up Elisa Boyer, a call-girl. They went to a seedy motel in Watts and registered as Mr. and Mrs. Sam Cooke. After going into the room, Cooke was clubbed in the head and knocked out. Boyer grabbed his clothes and ran to the motel office and split the money with Bertha Franklin.

When Cooke came to, he was pant-less and without his wallet. He stumbled to the motel office and saw Boyer and Franklin counting his money which was around $2,500. In 1960, that was a lot of money. He demanded his pants, money and wallet back. When they didn't open the door, Cooke knocked on it as hard as he could and it came off the hinges. After the robbery, he was murdered by motel manager, Bertha Franklin. She then instructed Boyer to run down the street and call police from a phone booth. Boyer told them a phony story about a rape and left the scene and subsequently disappeared. Sam was dead when the police arrived. The coroner's inquest was a slam dunk; not one pertinent question was asked by an investigator, or background check of Bertha Franklin's shooting past. They simply took her made up story for what actually happened. Sam's murder was just chalked up to just another unidentified "rapist" killed in Watts. A reporter the next morning found out that Mr. Cooke was registered at the motel.

Lesson learned here is Sam Cooke is not the first man to get hustled by a woman. Many men, who are way from home on a business trip, make the sinful decision to hook up with a prostitute. Many women give into their desire of the flesh to have a one-night stand, only to end up opening the wrong door never to return. **It happens!** The one question that we cannot answer is why death takes some and spares others who make the same mistakes. I am just as guilty when it comes to making poor decisions in life.

One thing that I do know is to truly acknowledge God for watching over me and keeping me from hurt, harm or danger when I was living a foolish life. And for all those who love to look down on others and judge and condemn, let me remind you of what God has already told His children who believe in Him. He says when it comes to sin *"For all have sinned, and come short of the glory of God."* (Romans 3:23) People, when God says all, He means "All" have sinned, and that means you too, Mr. Reader. You have sin in your closet and sin that you want to keep secret. Well, here's a news flash for you, God already knows your little secret. What you need to do is to confess your sins to Him and repent. That is the only way to be forgiven for sins; you can say all the "Hail Mary's" you want, but only God can forgive man's sin.

Wrong NEVER Conquers over Right

Chapter 13

For the first time in its history, the United States of America elected a black American to become its President. Barack Hussein Obama is the 44th and current President of the United States. He is the first African American to hold the office. Obama previously served as a United States Senator from Illinois, from January 2005 until he resigned following his victory in the 2008 presidential election. Born in Honolulu, Hawaii, Obama is a graduate of Columbia University and Harvard Law School, where he was the president of the *Harvard Law Review*. He was a community organizer in Chicago before earning his law degree. He worked as a civil rights attorney in Chicago and taught constitutional law at the University of Chicago Law School from 1992 to 2004. He served three terms representing the 13th District in the Illinois Senate from 1997 to 2004. The actual election of a black man to fill one of the highest positions on earth was something black people and people of color around the world thought would never happen. I guess we all forgot that God was in control; not man. It is God who rules in the affairs of men.

In Genesis 3:15, God's plan for man's salvation and redemption was mysteriously concealed, yet foretold. All throughout the Old Testament, His mighty hand is at work building a nation of peculiar people, His chosen inheritance, and His nation of priests who are to honor Him and be a blessing to the world. We see Him guide His chosen people out of bondage in Egypt and into the Promise Land. We see Him dealing directly with rebellion, and judging His people in their forty-year walk in the desert. God was at work with His people after they entered the Promise Land known as Canaan and drove out the inhabitants of the land. The providence of God was revealed through Moses as He gave His people the godly standard of living that is required for all people who will live in His kingdom – the Ten Commandments. He also established the law for His people to live by and follow. God's mighty hand is everywhere in the Bible, silently leading His chosen generation.

Later in the Old Testament we come to the part where the people of God wanted their prophet Samuel to appoint a man or king over them. This bothered the prophet Samuel a great deal because he knew that Israel had a King. His Name was God Almighty! God told Samuel to go ahead and honor the people's request. As a matter of clarity, God told Samuel the people were not rejecting him, they were rejecting God and to explain to them what this human king would do to them. The people did not listen to Samuel's counsel, and the providence of God allowed Samuel to elect Saul, a Benjamite was as the first human king of God's chosen people. As you read the story of Saul, you will come to the conclusion that God is always right. If He tells you something, wisdom should cry out STOP, LOOK, LISTEN, and OBEY!

The Election Experience

When we consider kings and leaders of great nations of the world, it is good especially for people who believe in God, to remember the name of King Nebuchadnezzar, the leader of the then Babylonian nation [602–562 B.C.] This great king, like Saul, the first appointed king of Israel, had to learn a universal reality, that the divine right of the Creator will always take precedence over the desire of man. In Daniel 4:17 regarding the providence and the divine will of Almighty God we learn that: *"This matter is by the decree of the watchers, and the demand by the word of the holy ones: to the intent that the living may know that the most High ruleth in the kingdom of men, and giveth it to whomsoever he will, and setteth up over it the basest of men."*

What this scripture is clearly saying is that it was not man's decision to elect Barack Obama, it was God's. As I was studying Deuteronomy, the Lord made a passage of scripture crystal clear to me of the events that were taking place in the presidential election of 2012, which actually started in 2011. He showed me this verse as it related to Barack Obama. Deuteronomy 28:7 states, *"The LORD shall cause thine enemies that rise up against thee to be smitten before thy face: they shall come out against thee one way, and flee before thee seven ways"*.

I believe the one constant that all the seven Republican candidates have in common is their seemingly complete dislike and rejection of President Barack Obama. They all seem to spew venomous and poisonous statements regarding his policies. The one thing that I find interesting about the 2012 Republican Caucus is that they do not want to talk about the failings of George W. Bush and the entire global mistake he, or should I say the Cheney administration, made during their eight non-productive years in the Oval Office. The truth speaks for itself.

Very few presidents start their term of office in the manner that President-elect Barack Obama did following on the heels of George W. Bush. Some of the issues left over from the Bush/Cheney Administration were: fighting two wars, major Wall Street corruption, banks closing, stock failures, and people losing homes and jobs, and the ever-increasing resentment of Americans on the rise throughout the world both foreign and domestic.

At the time I was reading this scripture, the Republican Party had seven nominees that were having televised national debates about who should face President Barack Obama in the 2012 elections. The Republican Party members were James Richard "Rick" Perry, Herman Cain, Michelle Marie Bachmann, Richard John "Rick" Santorum, Newton Leroy McPherson, Ronald Ernest "Ron" Paul, and Willard Mitt Romney. Three of the seven, Cain, Perry and Bachmann had fallen by the wayside. The central fact was they failed to convince the majority of Americans to continue to support them. In the end, they were found to be just "paper tigers" without substance. All of them were just talking heads who loved to spew venom against the only president in my life time that seemed to care for all people, blacks as well as whites, the rich as well as the poor.

During the election primaries, it is okay to voice your opinion against the incumbent, and it is quite alright to run against your competition. This is democracy! But when we in the public see and hear what appears and sounds like racist comments, we can discern what is really at issue. Self-serving comments like those below are divisive and do not promote unity in our nation:

- We are going to take back our country.

- Our top priority is to make President Obama a one-term President

- President Obama is a welfare president.

- President Obama is not a United States citizen.

- President Obama is a communist.

- President Obama is against religion-especially the Catholic faith.

- President Obama is a liar.

- President Obama is a Muslim.

- President Obama is out of control.

- President Obama is anti-American.

- Referring to the President as Obama rather than President Obama

They do not want to see that regardless of this man's God-given race, he is still our President and we are one nation under God. It is together that we are able to stand. If we do not stand as a nation, we will fall as a divided and conquered nation. If that happens, your Tea Party affiliation will mean nothing. The Republican Party and the Tea party remind me of two deer hunters. They have the best equipment, have read all the sporting magazines, and they have access to the best hunting land which is open only to members of their own rich party members. None others need apply. They spend huge amounts of money on clothing and equipment; they hire the best guides and they give the appearance that they are a true professionals. They brag to the wife and their friends back home of the rugged and harsh conditions they had to endure to get that trophy big game elk or buck. In reality, they sleep in an air-conditioned motor home, and travel by ATV to get to the hunting location. Once there, they use a block of salt to entice the big game animal to come close enough to shoot. The professional hunter is there to complete the kill just in case the big game hunter missed his shot and only wounds the animal. After the animal is killed, pictures are taken of the successful hunt and sent back home to family and friends. The truth of the hunt is the animal was tricked into his death by the irresistible taste of salt that all animals love. The hunter did not outwit the animal, he cheated to win. That is the way I see this election process. When you don't measure up to the competition, what do you do? You cheat by changing the rules of the game. You do this by changing the dynamics of the voting process, and by trying to make the voting process harder for some people, while trying to discourage others. You spend large sums of money perpetuating a fraud on the party that you are trying to defeat. And this is done with a smile on your face as you claim to be a Christian.

God sees and knows everything. Nothing, absolutely nothing, escapes His attention. The Lord said I Chronicles 16:22 *"touch not my anointed ones, and do my prophets no harm"*. When they wage war against their incumbent President, God will hold them accountable for their words, their actions, and their treatment of His chosen elected official.

I believe Hurricane Sandy was God's way of letting the power brokers of American politics, and the 2% of truly rich and influential Americans, know that God Almighty rules in the affairs of men. Hurricane Sandy occurred on October 30, 2012 just a little more than a week before the November 6, 2012 election. On the one side you had a black man by the name of Barack H. Obama who was running for re-election for a second four-year term. His challenger was a Mormon Bishop by the name of Mitt Romney.

The campaign was nasty from the very beginning. During the first televised debate between the two, Mr. Romney was disrespectful of Mr. Obama. As a matter of fact, the white power structure unleashed diabolical attack ads against President Obama. They attacked his race, his family, his character, his birth, and on and on. The rich and famous quickly mobilized their power and attacked on all sides. Collectively, they spent well over a billion dollars to make sure that Mr. Obama would not win a second term. Additionally, they tried to rearrange the entire voting process in key states to make sure that the Republican Party would carry the states. They tried to stack the deck by changing the requirements of the voting process in key state districts. You name it, they tried it. Their arrogance was so matter of fact they failed to see the invisible hand that was protecting the President. They failed to see the God over all creation. In Romans 13:1-3 Paul tells us, *"Let every soul be subject unto the higher powers. For there is no power but of God: the powers that be are ordained of God. Whosoever therefore resisteth the power resisteth the ordinance of God: and they that resist shall receive to themselves damnation."* All things work according to His good will.

The opposing party joined forces and tried to demonize the name of President Obama. It got so bad, that well-known actors and TV personalities went on record to show how ignorant they really were regarding their lack of support. It was in your face racism that many in this country thought was behind us. We were wrong. That old spirit of racial pride and the self-entitlement privileges that many people think is their American birthright stood up. It stood up and proudly proclaimed to the world that the white man was taking back their country. They were so bold in their attempts to destroy President Obama, that Mr. Romney said that he did not need a concession speech. Well, again they failed to see the divine hand of providence covering the life and actions of Mr. Obama.

The Hurricane Sandy Experience

Again, I believe Hurricane Sandy was God's way of letting the power brokers of American politics know that God Almighty rules in the affairs of men.,

There was so much hatred going on when Hurricane Sandy hit. The storm was so big that it was estimated as being from 1000 to 1500 miles wide. The storm did major damage to the East Coast. It completely shut down parts of New York, and many other areas in the state of New Jersey, Pennsylvania, Virginia, and the state of Delaware.

In terms of the estimated financial dollar damage, three months after this storm, a majority of people living on the East Coast were still living without power during the winter months of 2012 and into the new year of 2013. One report said the storm damaged or destroyed 305,000 housing units and disrupted more than 265,000 businesses in New York State. About 14,000 housing units have been repaired so far through New York's Rapid Repairs program. In New Jersey, 346,000 housing units were destroyed or damaged, and 190,000businesses affected. Nearly 18,000 households have received aid for repairs from FEMA.

It was the FEMA program which stands for the Federal Emergency Management Agency, that Mr. Romney said that he would dissolve if he were president. I guess if Mitt Romney had his way, the entire East Coast would have been left to fend for itself without any assistance from the Federal Government. I call this major arrogance and zero sympathy for thousands of Americans needing help during a time of a major catastrophe. The people who were directly affected by Hurricane Sandy needed help, not a cold and uncaring president.

The keynote speaker during the Republican Party National Convention was the Governor of the state of New Jersey, Christopher J. Christie. Mr. Christie launched a very elegant and bold attack against President Obama. In many ways his disrespect for the president set the stage for many others to follow suit and disrespect the President with negative and racist comments, attack ads, and demonization of the man's name and family. They failed to see the divine hand of the Almighty on the life of President Obama and all the people who believe and trust in him. Mr. Christie should have read Psalms 105:15-16, *"Touch not mine anointed, and do my prophets no harm? Moreover he called for a famine upon the land: he break the whole staff of bread."* These two scriptures show what God did in the Old Testament to nations that sought to harm His chosen people. Man seems to always forget, that money and power do not impress God.

As a result of Hurricane Sandy, Governor Chris Christie had to eat a large slice of humble pie. I will give him credit, he was man enough to say on national television that the President was doing, to use his words, "a good job in responding to the catastrophic conditions that the state of New Jersey was experiencing as a result of Hurricane Sandy". This man had to admit that he needed the help of the man that he demonized during the Republican Convention. God has a way of making even your enemies your friends when He wants to show who is really in charge. To God truly be the glory!

Mr. Romney was so deflated as a result of losing his election to a black man. He will go down in history as the presidential candidate who said that he did not care about the poor people in this country; he said there are programs for them. However, he failed to mention that the few programs that existed to help the poor, he would work to reduce or eliminate. He also was recorded as saying that forty-seven percent of the people in this country were under-achievers and wanted the government to take care of them. He once worked for a company whose major claim to fame and fortune was corporate raiders of companies who stripped them and sold them to the highest bidder. They were also heavily involved in outsourcing many American jobs overseas for cheap labor. I thank God for helping this country elect a leader who truly is for all the people, not just the rich and privileged.

President Obama won both the electoral and the popular vote. In our system of government, a candidate for the office of President must have 270 electoral votes to win the election, Mr. Obama had a total of 332 electoral votes and Mr. Romney had 206. This was a clear and decisive victory for President Obama which gave him a second term in office. What made this victory "exceptional" was the fact that over 1 billion dollars had been spent by the Republicans to fund political action committees (PACS) to initiate attack ads and strategies to divide and diminish the vote for President Obama. God Almighty rules in the affairs of men. It is God who builds up nations and it is God who brings down nations. I think we sometimes forget, or in some cases, refuse to recognize that God is still on the throne. He is a God that loves righteousness and is faithful and just to those who put their trust in Him. That, in my humble opinion, was the downfall of the opposition party to unseat the President.

Actions that Affect Others

It is one thing to be against something or someone, but when you label your attacks under a veil of racism and hatred, it is a totally different agenda. As a result of outright bigotry and hatred for the first black president of the United States of America, one hundred and forty-four elected members of the G.O.P. (Grand Old Party) on October 1 through October 16, 2013, were willing to allow the government of the United States of America to default and become non-operational. This conspiracy was set in motion by a Tea Party newcomer from Texas by the name of Ted Cruz. The Republican House Speaker, John Boehner and the Republican Senate leader, Mitch McConnell, failed to do the right thing for their country. They were cowards and tucked in their tails to a conservative Political Action Committee. They failed to have the backbone to face down young tea party radicals who are striving for personal fame at the expense of the country they were elected to represent.

Ted Cruz and the majority of his fellow Republican members forced 800,000 federal workers to lose their jobs due to closed federal parks, buildings. They collectively chose to withhold social security benefits to millions of our older Americans. These and other negative tactics were used under the disguise of defunding the Affordable Health Care Bill. It still boggles the mind, that a group of elected officials could be so easily lead by a small group of extremists who would do harm to their own country, and its people, just to try and make the first black President in United States history look bad. They were calling themselves the victims by saying that President Obama would not negotiate with them. In many ways, these one hundred forty-four G.O.P. Tea Party-controlled Republicans were acting more like domestic terrorists than leaders of a democracy. They refused to compromise with the Executive Branch for the good of the country. They refuse to work with the President or consider any points of view that were different from their own. They refused to govern and control their own party members. Their agenda was and is control. They want to run the country their way. The Tea Party motto is: "we are going to take back our country".

People fail to comprehend one very important point. It is God Almighty that controls the affairs of man. *"Then he answered and spake unto me, saying, this is the word of the LORD unto Zerubbabel, saying, not by might, nor by power, but by my spirit, saith the LORD of hosts."* (Zechariah 4:6) It is not man alone who controls the destiny of this great nation. By God alone, we stand or fall. The Tea Party is a small group of people, some with deep pockets whose objective is to divide and conquer a nation. Their strategy is simple. They make up words that enflame the hearts and minds of the unlearned into actions that divide a nation. This small group of people call themselves real American conservatives. They see themselves as losing their vision of America to undesirables, like the poor people of the land. It seems as if the G.O.P. has sold their positions of authority and power to the highest bidder. In this case, rich industrialists who bank roll anti-Obama activities. These so called politicians masquerade around our nations' Capitol doing nothing but trying to do in the President.

I cannot find one positive thing they (the G.O.P) have done since their candidate Mitt Romney lost his bid for the Presidency in 2012. Their main focus has been to position their party to take back the White House in the 2016 elections. They are behind the re-districting of states that are changing the laws to make voter registration and voter participation much more difficult. In short, when a person figures that they cannot win an election fairly, they seek ways to change the rules to benefit them. That is what criminals do every day. Some elected politicians don't seem to have any integrity. They are for sale to the highest bidder, just like a prostitute is for sale to the highest bidder. God help us when our leaders fail to govern for the people and by the people.

It is God who has the last say in political matters. It is really God that they are upset with. Maybe one day God will open their eyes. Until that happens, they will go on like wild animals spewing hatred to all who will listen.

In spite of all the sin, corruption, and wrong in our world, God is still on the throne. He still desires to save and heal. He is a miracle-working God and I want to share with you miracles He has performed in my life.

Miracles of a Magnificent God

Chapter 14

My wife and I got married on January 1, 1976. She was born on January 4. I still think that the reason she wanted to get married on January 1, 1976, was she wanted to celebrate her anniversary, a wedding, and her birthday, all within the same week. Oh, she is a crafty little devil. I do believe that my wife wanted to have a yearly major celebration equipped with husband at home with plenty of presents, and she was able to make this happen with good old fashioned planning. We had been married for 25 years when the dreaded disease we humans have come to loathe as cancer, decided to stop by our home and pay my wife a visit. The year was 2001 when this disease raised its ugly head. I was not living a saved life, and I was definitely living a life behind the big black door.

I had just recently lost my only son on February 10, 2001. I was working, but I was not happy with myself. I knew that my life was missing something, but I was never quite sure what that was. I was missing something. Over the years, I have come to the realization that Jesus was the missing piece of the puzzle in my life. Only Jesus could fill the void in my life that I was facing after the death of my son.

One Monday morning, I was working at my desk at 6:30 am when the telephone rang. It was my wife. She had just regained consciousness after having passed out at home. She was not steady in her conversation with me and barely coherent. When she talked to me on the phone, she asked me to come home immediately and take her to the hospital. I immediately jumped out of my seat and made a mad dash to my car to get home as quickly as possible. When I got home, Jane was still having problems. I helped her to finish getting dressed and took her to Decatur Memorial Hospital. The doctors ran many tests, one of which was called a CT-Scan. After the results of the tests were completed, the doctors wanted to do what they called exploratory surgery to remove what appeared to be two tumors which the tests indicated were on her ovaries.

Surgery was scheduled immediately. The surgery lasted six hours with three hours of recovery time. I was really afraid for my wife and my family. I asked our local church to pray for her, and they did. I was now a member of a local holiness church. To this day, I think God allowed me to join this church to grow my faith in Him and increase my desire to study and learn of Him. I prayed during the long surgery and recovery. One of my wife's best friends and my daughter was with me. I remember that the night before the surgery, I was dreaming and crying and praying for her in my sleep. At this point, I had never in my life talked in "tongues". Talking in tongues is something that saints do on a regular basis when the Holy Spirit comes upon them. This is sometimes especially noticeable in the older, more seasoned saints. I, on the other hand, had never actually experienced this form of worship from my mouth. Speaking in an unknown tongue is something that you do not want to pretend you can do. I am not hypocrite. There are some things in life that you do not want to fake. Being saved is one of those things. Saying that you are saved and pretending to speak in tongues just to impress the pastor or your neighbor in church is very hypocritical of you if it's not genuine. I will not fake talking in tongues when I know it is not of the Spirit. I actually heard my own voice utter sounds, groans, and other words that were foreign to my mind. I was saying words that I never voiced before in my life. They were words that were not of a known human language. Even though I can't speak French, German or Russian, when I hear them spoken, I may not know what the person is saying, but I will know the sounds of the words. I had never before heard the words that I was speaking that morning spoken any place in my life. They were strange sounding words to me in what I assumed to be a dream. However, as I began to slowly wake up, I wrote down one of the words that I heard being repeated over and over again by my mouth in my dream. To the best of my knowledge, the words that I was speaking over and over again were "Elliasha'A –kaeillaha'de" I do not know their meaning or if I spelled them correctly. I tried to spell them like they sounded. It almost sounded like I was saying the prophet's name of Elisa, although I cannot confirm that.

When I took Jane to the hospital early the morning of her surgery, I was walking directly behind her and talking to her trying to keep her spirits up. As we got closer to the entrance of the hospital admittance main door, I saw this white lady walking in our direction. She seemed to just float around my wife. If Jane recognized or even noticed this woman, she did not act or respond like she did. This lady looked directly into my eyes and held my gaze as we passed each other. When she was directly beside me, she reached over and grabbed hold of my hand. She whispered to me, very assuredly, "Everything is going to be all right."

A few seconds later, it dawned on me what she had just said. I recall thinking to myself how did this stranger know what I was thinking, or what my wife and I were about to go through? How was she able to pin-point my exact thoughts? I turned around to see the lady that had just passed by me, and she was not there. There was no way this lady could have disappeared that fast. When we passed each other, I only took two or three steps before I looked back at her. Where had she gone so fast? I recall the intense look that she had in her eyes. Her eyes were very penetrating and focused on me as she very briefly said what she said, "Everything is going to be all right." Even though this thought did occur to me at the time, later on when I had time to reflect on the lady that passed me and gave me some encouragement, I was reminded of what I had read in Hebrews 13:2, where it says *"Be not forgetful to entertain strangers: for thereby some have entertained angels unaware"*. To this day, I think this lady was an angel of God sent as a messenger to let us know that my wife would be okay during her surgery.

After the surgery I talked with the team of doctors that were caring for my wife. The surgery had been long and some of them looked to be tired as well. After the three-hour recovery was complete, I was allowed to visit my wife in the recovery area. Later she was moved into her own room. She was very weak from the surgery, otherwise, she was okay. She was in the hospital for over a week, but with the help of my Lord and Savior, she recovered.

What I am about to share with you now continues to bring tears to my eyes. Our God is a good God, and will and can do marvelous things to those who believe. My wife had a lot of tubes connected to her, and the most watched machine was the monitor that was used to stabilize her breathing.

The nurses and the doctors kept a close watch on this machine. I am told that a normal person will breathe anywhere from eighteen to twenty breaths per minute. My wife was only breathing at a rate of about two or three breaths per minute. They had her on a breathing machine that monitored her lungs for correct breathing. This machine made a sound each time Jane failed to breathe correctly and this made her try harder to breathe correctly.

From the start of her surgery of six hours with three hours of recovery, it was now well past 6:00 pm. I was allowed to go to the recovery room to see her as they moved her to a special care room, and the time slowly began to fade back into reality for us. Around 9:30 pm, I could see that my wife was not doing very well. Her breathing had not improved, and the nurse's constant watch gave me cause to worry. I noticed her complexion was turning a pale white color, as if she had no blood or life in her body. I tried talking to her, but she was too tired and too weak to respond. This went on for about two more hours to around midnight. At that point, I decided to go into the visitor and family lounge to get a little sleep. When I woke up shortly after 2 am, I returned to my wife's room and found that she had not improved. She appeared to be getting worse. The color in her skin on her face was all gone, her cheekbones or facial cheekbones were sunken in on both sides of her face. She was still very weak and barely breathing. She had her head tilted back on her pillow with her eyes fixed on the ceiling. I was scared that I was losing my wife.

The thought came into my mind and said, "why don't you pray" and that is what I did. I took her hand and knelt down by the side of her bed, and I began to pray to God. I prayed a prayer of surrender to the Lord. I do not recall the words that I said, but I do know, that at the moment I finished praying to God, and before I could get up off of my knees, I saw my wife's upper body and her breast cavity move. Her whole body began to move, similar to a car tire that is low and air is applied from an air hose supply line. This was how fast my wife's upper body cavity began to rise as if it was being filled with air. I saw her upper body, her stomach and lungs, greatly inhale air and expel air as if she was being given a large dose of something. She raised her head off her pillow, looked directly at me, and smiled and then fell off into a deep and much needed sleep. However, before I got up from my knees, I looked up and said in a loud and strong voice, "I may not be able to see you, but I know God is in this room". As Jane continued to sleep, her breathing immediately began to improve. The color came back into her face from the sickly-looking pale white to normal, healthy-looking skin. For then and now, I say "thank you, Lord. Thank you for your blessing, and being with us through this ordeal. Lord, I am truly thankful." I thank God for His mercy and His grace, for allowing my wife to successfully make it through the surgery and the recovery phase after the surgery. After the surgery my wife had six treatments of chemotherapy, one treatment every three weeks. There are some unpleasant side effects when a person is undergoing chemotherapy. However, my wife never complained. She had a difficult time trying to adjust her body temperature, for example, she was cold and the next five minutes she would be hot. There were days when she would be very nauseous. But overall, the Lord was with her and she made it through all her treatments. Thank you Jesus!

The Return of Cancer – 2006

The cancer returned in 2006. This time, my wife was having a constant and consistent pain in her right side. She went back to her oncologist and after they took additional x-rays, the doctor discovered that her cancer had returned. More tests were completed which included a biopsy of the suspect tissue cells which were found to be malignant. She was scheduled for another surgery. The cancer this time was discovered on her large intestine. The doctors did a colon resection, a complete hysterectomy, and an appendectomy. This surgery lasted three hours with two hours of recovery. Thanks to God, she made it through the surgery, and after a short stay in the hospital, she went home to begin additional treatments of chemotherapy. She was scheduled for six treatments, one every three weeks. I was learning from all the surgeries my wife was going through to trust more in God. I cannot say it enough that God is truly worthy to be praised!

After my wife completed her chemotherapy treatments she was able to return to work. During her recovery she worked from home each day. This woman truly has the heart of the lion.

The Cancer Returns – November 2010

In November of 2010, the cancer returned. Jane had a scheduled exam and the x-ray revealed a spot in the stomach wall area. Jane's oncologist wanted her to have it removed, so more surgery was scheduled. We prayed about this. My prayer to God was that the surgeon would find nothing cancerous in my wife. I prayed that prayer over and over. On the day of the surgery, all went well and the doctors performed a short exploratory surgery to remove a cancerous growth from the wall of Jane's stomach. They could not find any growth. The doctors went to the exact location during the surgery that the x-ray technician indicated there was a cancerous growth. But the surgeons could find nothing, and stopped the surgery. He told me that he had good news and bad news. I told him to give me the bad news first. The bad news was he had to do surgery on my wife to investigate the oncologist's report of a growth on the inner wall of her abdomen. The good news was they couldn't find anything. After I thanked him for his report the thought hit me! Our prayer the night before the surgery was answered! Our prayer was that the doctors would find nothing, and they found nothing! God heard us. We prayed this prayer, and I know that my God does hear and answer prayer if it's according to His will. Lord, thank You.

The oncologist was still saying that there was a growth on the inner wall of Jane's abdomen. Another surgery was scheduled, which this time would be more intrusive. The doctor performing the surgery wanted to use a new technology that involved using a guide wire that would better pin-point the exact location of the cancerous growth. After all the preliminaries were completed, the surgery was scheduled for early the next morning. Again, I was very concerned for my wife. She had by now gone through so many major surgeries and was about to go through yet another. We held hands and prayed together again and ask God to be with us, and we put all our fears in His hands. On the day of the surgery, all did not go well or according to plan. When the doctor had finished his operation and was removing one of the metal guide wires, it broke or to use his words, the guide wire exploded. The doctor had to do more surgery to remove the metal guide wire fragments and this added another one to two hours to a three hour surgery. However, the doctor was able to find and remove all the metal guide wire fragments and complete the operation.

Liver Cancer - 2011

During the summer of 2011, my wife found out that she was going to need liver surgery as a result of cancer. Yes, cancer had been discovered on her liver. We were completely taken off guard by this depressing new development. I was hoping that she was done with all the cancer.

This was going to be a major operation with a 50/50 success rate. This was definitely not the news that we wanted to hear. I have to tell you, my wife really inspired me. She showed no fear at all. In her "as usual and positive" way, she smiled and asked the doctor to schedule the surgery. The doctor in our community could not perform this type of surgery as it was beyond his technical know-how. They arranged to have the surgery done by an expert in the field of liver surgery. The surgery was at Barnes Jewish Hospital which is in St. Louis, Missouri. A day was scheduled for our initial consultation with the specialist at Barnes Jewish Hospital. He told us about his success and failure rate for this type of surgery and felt the procedure he was going to try would be successful. The surgery was scheduled for a week later. On the day prior to her surgery we spent the night at the hotel that was adjacent to and connected with Barnes Jewish Hospital. This made it easier to get straight into the hospital without the hassle of trying to drive through traffic at rush hour for the early morning surgery.

We prayed together before going to bed and asked God to watch over us during this rather complicated surgery. During the night, I began to hear a voice in my dream that said, "I Am, I Am." It would become a little bit stronger "I Am," "I Am," "I Am," "I Am," "I Am." I am not sure how many times I said the words in my dream. I just know that it was like a continuous sound. I Am, I Am, I Am who I Am. As I began to wake up from my dream, I recall thinking it was a strange dream to me. Why was I dreaming about the words - "I Am"? As I further began to focus and wake up completely, I realized what had just happened. The words" I Am", is a reference to the Name of God. I realized that God was telling me that He was with us and everything was going to be all right. I got up and began to write the thoughts that had gone through my head in what I perceived to be a dream. And those words are as follows

The "I Am" Dream

God told Moses in Exodus 3:14, "I Am, who I Am". He told Abraham also that His Name was "I Am". That is a very unusual name. Have you ever wondered what it means? Well, the Lord showed me time and time again what it means. It means, "I Am _____ (you fill in the blank). I Am means anything you need when you need it, "For I Am the Lord Your God, is there anything too hard for me?" So if my God is named "I Am", my name is "let me be _____ (fill in the blank). For me it means anything you want me to be to serve You, Lord. I thought to myself, The Lord was telling me that He is with us. He was going to be with my wife, Jane, during her moment of need. I could go back to sleep because through faith, I knew "I Am" would be with us and guide us through the surgery. "I Am" was all that we needed to get through this procedure.

We arrived at the hospital at 7:30 am. Jane was taken directly into the pre-opt area and by 8:30 am she was on her way into the operating room. By 11:00 am she was back from surgery, and this was followed by a two-hour recovery. I was allowed to go see her around 1:30 pm after her recovery was complete. The doctor found me after the surgery and told me that the surgery was a success. I said to myself, "thank You, Jesus". She was weak, but was doing well. I thought of the words I heard in my dream - "I Am, I Am, I Am". God moves in a mysterious way, His wonders to perform.

My Turn to Face Cancer - 2011

The year of 2011 was not turning out to be a good year for me and my wife. I found out on February of 2011 that I had prostate cancer. My PSA cancer screening exam numbers were 742. According to my doctor, that number was too high. After a battery of tests, the diagnosis was confirmed. The cancer had not spread throughout my body. I was told that it was contained within the prostate, gland itself. I thank the Lord!

To say the least, I was scared to death. Why? Let me tell you something. It is one thing to be supportive, and to provide a shoulder for someone else to cry on as you offer your love and comfort to someone when it's not you going through a difficult and potentially life-altering situation.

However, when that same shoe is on your foot, you begin to know exactly what the other person is feeling. When that same traumatic experience has embedded itself within your life, it is a completely different reality.

During the initial stages of the prostate cancer consultation with the oncologist, my doctor and the staff at the cancer treatment center in our community, I was provided with information as to the steps in the treatment options. My spirits were down and I could not think straight. The doctor gave me a booklet with the different types of treatment options, and frankly, none of them made sense to me. For the first time in my life I was hearing such medical terminology as: Radical Prostatectomy (the complete removal of the entire prostate gland plus some of the surrounding tissue cells), Radiation Therapy (there were two kinds to choose – external and internal therapy), Hormone Therapy (Androgen Deprivation Therapy), Orchiectomy – (the removal of the male testicles), and Luteinizing hormone, a releasing hormone process.

My doctor did a good job of explaining the advantages and disadvantages of each treatment option, but my mind was still in a fog as to which option to choose. The doctor gave me material to read and wanted me to get back with him within two weeks with my choice of treatment. I came home from the doctor's office in a depressed state. All I could think about was that life for me was over and coming to an end. I had never dreamed that I would end up with prostate cancer. For the next two or three days I moped around the house feeling sorry for me.

Please pay close attention to what I am about to share with you regarding the Providence of God Almighty in my life. As I said, I truly believe God works in mysterious ways, His wonders to perform. I remember I was in my bathroom being depressed about how my life had suddenly evolved. I could not shake that negative feeling about this being the end for me. When I was thinking those negative thoughts, something spoke directly to my heart and mind. It was similar to having a radio program on and all of a sudden, someone turned the radio program off or down low and spoke directly into your mind. After this voice had finished speaking, the radio program returned to its normal volume. I was thinking negative thoughts, and somehow, something removed all the negative thoughts away from me as it said to me "it's not over until I say it's over"! Immediately, I knew that the voice of Jesus had spoken directly to my mind. I felt relief from what I was going through and from that day to this, I have never felt depressed about the diagnosis of prostate cancer. This I know, for God I am going to live, and for God I am going to die; blessed be the Name of the Lord! I am going to glorify Him with whatever time He allows me to continue living on this earth.

My phone rang later that day. It was a pastor friend of mine who was also our insurance agent. This man is a very good person. He invited me to go with him to a four-day religious retreat at a church in Decatur. This religious retreat was to help God's people better understand the working of the Holy Spirit. I was excited about going. It could not have come at a better time in my life. The retreat started on Thursday and ended on Sunday. People from all across the U.S. were at this conference. It was at this retreat that I met a doctor from Atlanta, Georgia. He was a very nice man. I feel now after looking back at the whole prostate cancer situation that God placed this doctor within our religious work group for my benefit.

The time allowed me to interact with a professional doctor one-on-one about what I was going through. I felt it was the divine providence of God at work in my life that led this doctor to me whom I had never seen in my life. The man took the time to answer my personal questions about which prostrate option to consider. The doctor had just recently gone through the cancer screening process, and he was now a prostate cancer survivor himself. He chose radiation therapy, external beam therapy in lieu of the other options. The doctor explained to me why this was his choice. The Lord Jesus sent this man to me because as a doctor and a fellow servant of the Lord, he knew which option was best. I decided to go with the same choice that the doctor had chosen - the radiation therapy, external beam procedure. I went through the radiation treatment and at the end of my treatments, my PSA was normal.

The prostate cancer that God allowed me to go through has provided me with a deeper understanding of who God is, and what He is to me. I now have a more mature understanding of what the Apostle Paul meant when he told the Philippians in 1:21 *"For to me to live is Christ, and to die is gain."* I know now, that it is not death itself that I am afraid of, it's living without Christ being the head of my life that makes life itself not worth living. I have found that God will take His people through different crises in life, because when we go through a crisis point in our lives, it will truly draw us closer to Him. After seeing what my wife was going through with cancer the past eleven years, and going through prostate cancer myself, I can truly say that I completely trust God, and that is all I need to know about this life to keep me motivated.

Cancer Update and God's Vision

As an update to my prostate cancer, as of February 1, 2013, I have had three post-prostate cancer checkups to determine if the cancer has returned. Thanks to the blessing of my God, the cancer is still in remission. The last PSA numbers were 0.62 and holding. In addition, my family doctor wanted me to have a colonoscopy examination. He felt that men and women should have this procedure as part of the aging process to check for colon cancer. My doctor made the appointment for me to see a specialist in this field, and after our initial consultation, the date was set to have the examination. The doctor wrote me out a prescription for a prep kit. This was the worst part of the whole process. I was given a mild sedative and all I remember is waking up thirty to forty minutes later back in my room. The doctor told my wife that all was well and everything looked good, except they found a polyp the size of a pencil eraser. They removed the polyp and sent it off to check for cancer. My test results were negative, and I thank the Lord God for the results.

The Cancer Returns

The hand of the enemy, Satan, is always against us. If he and his coworker death can't steal, kill or destroy you in one way they will try another. It was during the quarterly exam that my wife's oncologist discovered that her cancer had returned again. There was a mass of tissue that seemed to be growing and spreading in her liver. The doctors made all the necessary tests and arrangements for Jane to return to Barnes Jewish Hospital in St. Louis the see a specialist. She saw a surgeon who specializes in gastrointestinal cancer and pancreatic cancer. He is the same doctor who did the surgery on her two years ago when the Lord came to me in a dream with the words "I Am". We made the two-hour drive from Decatur, Illinois to meet the doctor and discuss treatment options. In this case, based on all the completed test results, surgery was the best option for removal and eradication of this cancerous disease that was spreading in Jane's body. The doctor was very matter-of-fact about what Jane was facing. He told her that he would do the best that he could, but the surgery would be serious. He said that he did not anticipate any major problems but that all could change depending on what he found during the actual surgery process. We had to sign papers which gave the doctor authority to do more invasive surgery to remove other cancer cells if they were discovered.

We drove down the night before the surgery, because we had made hotel reservations for eight days to stay at the Parkway Hotel. This hotel is linked to Barnes Jewish Hospital (BJH) through crosswalks. This makes it easier to park your car in the parking garage and walk to the hospital.

On the night preceding the surgery, we met some friends that lived in the St. Louis area and went to dinner with them. They are very nice people and they were very concerned about this surgery as should be expected. We had a long diner and conversation about the realities of life. We talked about what this family had been going through with family members, and health issues that had impacted their lives. We talked about God and all that He had done for us. We ended the dinner and returned to our hotel room.

My wife did all the preparatory work she was asked to do prior to having major surgery. We discussed our life, and I made her laugh about the many times I seemed to get things wrong and it was Jane who seemed to always make things right. She is that kind of a person. I must admit that after 37 years of marriage, I love her more today than I did when we were younger. She knows how to make me smile and I know just what she needs to keep a smile on her face. We discussed all the ramifications of this surgery, but I would not allow her to end our conversation on a negative note. I told her that nothing is over until God says it is over. We were going to put our trust in Him through faith in the Word and promises of God. We ended the night with prayer of faith in God to see us through her surgery that was scheduled at 7:30 am. We had to be at the hospital at 5:30 am for all the preparatory work before the actual surgery started.

On August 20, 2013, the morning of the surgery, we took a cab over to BJ-South because it was too far for Jane to walk. After the various doctors came and explained what was going to happen, they prepped her and got her ready for surgery which started at 8:20 am. Family members who have loved ones in surgery at BJ-South are housed in a huge, very comfortable, waiting room. BJH has this part of the procedure down to a fine science. You are given a hand-held monitor that is assigned a number. If either the monitor lights goes off or the number is called, they will give you up-to-the-minute information on the person who is having surgery. They do this every two hours. Additionally, they have a board with your loved one's name by a number that only the family knows and this tells you the progress of the surgery. I thought this is a first class operation.

My wife's surgery was five and one-half hours long. She had a two hour recovery. After her surgery was complete, the doctor came to talk to me and my daughter. The doctor explained to us the procedure and drew a picture of the area of Jane's body where he removed the cancerous cells from her liver. He also went on to say that he removed a cancer cell that was adjacent to her liver. The doctor looked tired and I told him that I was praying for Him as well as for Jane. He seemed surprised to hear that someone was praying for him, but he thanked me, smiled, and told us that as soon as they had a room in the ICU (intensive Care Unit – of BJ-south) they would be calling me to come up and visit. We received that call at about 3:00 pm.

My daughter and I found Jane heavily sedated as was to be expected. The main thing was that God had blessed her to still be here. She was very groggy and tried to smile after she called out my name and my daughter's name. She immediately went back to sleep as a host of nurses constantly monitored her vitals. My daughter left to drive back to Decatur. I did not want her driving back at night by herself. Yes, I know she is grown, but some father's instincts and protection never goes away. Jane spent the first night after her surgery sleeping, or at least trying to sleep, because it seemed as soon as she would fall asleep some nurse wanted to check this, or give her a pill, or take a blood or urine sample. This, combined with all the monitors constantly going off, made me wonder how any sick person could sleep or rest in a hospital. This activity never stopped.

The second and third days after her surgery were the worst days. She was in a lot of pain and very nauseous. She was very restless and her color did not look good to me, but she was maintaining the best she could. It was during this time when all the nurses were out of the room, I was reading my bible in the book of Hebrew, when I looked up and there appeared to be what looked like a transparent form of a body standing to the left side of the recliner chair where Jane was sitting. There was definitely something there and it allowed me to see its shape just for a moment or two. The back of Jane's recliner faced the window that was adjacent to the helicopter landing pad on top of one of the buildings. The form of a man's body standing to the left of Jane's recliner allowed me to see right through his body through the window and see the helicopter landing pad.

I stared at this for a few seconds and then it disappeared from my sight. This did not scare me and for some strange reason I was not afraid. But I know what I saw. I rubbed my eyes to make sure that I was seeing what I was seeing and it did not go away. About thirty to forty-five minutes later, I saw this same vision on the other side on Jane's recliner, this time on the right side. It was just standing there and I could not see a face, nor could I tell what it was doing. It made no sound. The vision never allowed me to look up and see its face. I only saw from the shoulders down and it was like looking into a mist or fog that was   light to dark gray in color. I cannot adequately describe what I saw. About an hour or so later when the nurses were out of the room, and as I was reading my Bible and I looked up in the corner of the room across by the door and there stood the image of a man's body with both his hands coupled in front of his body. Again, there was no sound made, and the vision allowed me to see it just for a second or two before it disappeared from view. God is truly awesome.

I had shared with Jane toward the end of her stay in BJH what I had seen, and as we were talking, the vision walked right by my left shoulder as I was sitting facing Jane as she sat in her recliner. The vision or image just appeared without any sound and I noticed it just seemed to float right by me and stand by the recliner. It allowed me to see it just for two or three seconds and disappeared from my sight, I told Jane that she had a visitor, but she could not see it. This was the last time that I saw the vision. Jane was released early from BJH on Sunday August 25, 2013. As a result of such a serious surgery, she was expected to stay in the hospital from eight to nine days, but with the help of the good Lord she was able to come home three days early. My, what a Mighty God we serve!

What a valuable lesson I learned! Serving the Lord will pay off. Don't let the world convince you that God does not exist, because to the world He does not exist. God rewards those who seek Him. I, for one, will go to my grave telling all that will hear me, my God is real. The visions that I have just described are real. The five and one-half hours of life or death surgery that my wife went through at BJH is real. The sad thing about people who claim that they do not believe in God is they act as if their nonbelief is going to somehow make God go away in their minds. They fail or refuse to realize that their nonbelief can't and will never diminish the fact that God is still God whether they believe it or not.

On September 9, 2013, my wife had post-surgery follow up in St. Louis. We made the two hour drive back to St. Louis so the specialist could discuss with us all the pathology tests Jane had undergone. We learned that not only did the specialist remove all cancerous cells from the impacted area; the surgeon also took samples from other areas that had the potential of developing into cancerous tumors. After all that my wife and I have been through, we were not looking forward to hearing more bad news. Yet we had to endure and follow through with this appointment. We prayed and asked God to be with us again and to help us get a good report.

This is the beauty and intimacy of having a right relationship with God. Unlike humans, He is never too busy for His children to come to Him in prayer. As a matter of spiritual fact, we are told in Philippians 4:6 that, *"Be careful for nothing; but in everything by prayer and supplication with thanksgiving let your requests be made known unto God."* I have learned to trust in God. I am not ashamed to tell the world how wonderful and precious He is to all of us. He is truly worthy to be praised!

The doctor and his team came into our little waiting room and examined Jane's surgical wounds. He was pleased that they were healing well. He told us that all the pathology lab results were back and that they all were negative for any cancerous cells. That was indeed good news to hear and I thank God for this. He also told Jane and me that based on his observation during the surgery and with the pathology reports, that as far as he was concerned she was cancer free. Hallelujah and Glory to His Name! Don't misunderstand my gratefulness; I am truly appreciative of all the hard work and specialized service that the doctor provided. But I know that God is the real Source of this positive outcome. A skilled physician is only a tool to be used in the Master's hand. And when the doctor says he has done all that he can do, that is when faith and the real Physician Jesus steps in. Because, it is never truly over until He says it's over. I thank Jesus for what I have learned over these past few years. God is my Shield. He is a Light in a dark place; he is the Perfect Captain during a major storm in life. He is the Master Physician in the operating room! He can make a way out of no way!

- He is my Jehovah-Jireh, - God will provide.

- He is my Jehovah-Nissi, God is my Banner,

- He is my El-Shaddai- I will walk before Him as blameless as I know how, for He is worthy.

- He is the very Ancient of Days – the Great I Am. Bless His holy Name.

As we left the doctor's office, I was amazed at what God had done for me and my family. He answers prayers. All wisdom comes from God.

Only One Way
Chapter 15

The God of Abraham, Isaac, and Jacob-Israel, is real. Remember the old saying, "what's in a name?" Look at how God's name is embedded all around Israel, (God/Israel- is real). Israel is still God's chosen people, regardless of what they do or don't do. I am not saying that we are not highly favored. But the Jews were and still are His unique inheritance. Man needs to understand that when you seek to destroy the Jews, you are seeking to destroy God's anointed people.

God is real. That is the first thing we humans need to get completely straight. God is who He says He is, and your belief or unbelief is not going to change that. In Isaiah 42:5-8, God's promise is revealed. *5"Thus saith God the LORD, he that created the heavens, and stretched them out; he that spread forth the earth, and that which cometh out of it; he that giveth breath unto the people upon it, and spirit to them that walk therein: 6I the LORD have called thee in righteousness, and will hold thine hand, and will keep thee, and give thee for a covenant of the people, for a light of the Gentiles; 7To open the blind eyes, to bring out the prisoners from the prison, and them that sit in darkness out of the prison house. 8 I am the LORD: that is my name: and my glory will I not give to another, neither my praise to graven images."*

The above verses tell us and show us who the Lord God really is. I know there are people who will still reject the Bible for a variety of reasons. To those people who say they reject the Bible, please understand, in reality you are rejecting the Word of God. Whoever rejects the Word of God also rejects God Almighty. Let me ask you this question, "What do you base your unbelief on?" Whatever you are basing your unbelief on, it better be something that you are willing to live eternally in hell for, because, that is where your stubborn belief is taking you. Jesus says to us in Matthew Chapter 10:32-33, *"Whosoever therefore shall confess me before men, him will I confess also before my Father which is in heaven. But whosoever shall deny me before men, him will I also deny before my Father which is in heaven."*

The message to all unbelievers is this, if you deny Him, He will also deny you before His Father. Be very sure of your convictions, because they have eternal ramifications. I also understand that if you do not believe the Bible, you will not accept the words of the Bible. Therefore many people will continue to live their life behind the big, black, door of life, living their life as it pleases them. Life behind this door is a carefree life. A life lived without a care for your fellow man, and a life that continues to reject God. A life that laughs, mocks, and makes fun of God's people who are followers of Jesus Christ. Many of the unbelievers have rejected Jesus Christ and they refuse to have anything to do with God. Some are so confused in their belief that they go as far as to join larger and more powerful atheist groups. With bigger financial resources they are able to collectively use their money and resources to challenge any law that seeks to function in a godly manner as unconstitutional.

Many God-hating groups are the reason why prayer was taken out of our schools. Yet we fail to see the increase of kids with no godly foundation doing creatively crazy things like killing their teachers, parents, and fellow students. Remember this, when we take God out of the classroom, guess who walks in unannounced? The devil!

Murders

Allow me to give a few examples of what happens when we take God out of the home, out of the classroom, and out of the hearts and minds of our senators and congressmen who pass laws that govern our country. One example is Godless behavior.

1. On April 20, 1999, two students, Eric Harris and Dylan Klebold, who attended Columbine High School which is located in Columbine, Colorado, went on a killing spree that resulted in the death of 12 students and one teacher. They also injured a total of twenty-one other students. They both committed suicide. Their atrocity was the fourth deadliest school massacre in the history of the United States of America.

One major question that will probably never be answered is – "why"? I will not try to guess why this terrible, cruel, and hateful situation developed. I don't know if the parents of the two young boys raised them in the fear of the Lord. I just don't know. They may have, and I'm not trying to pass judgment, but that much rage and that much anger could not possibly come from a heart that's in tune with the heart that loves Christ Jesus. We are taught in Proverbs 4:23 *"Keep thy heart with all diligence; for out of it are the issues of life."* This means we are not to store up hatred, jealousies, and racism in our hearts. If the heart of a man is bitter, the man himself will also be bitter. We see examples of this every day. We turn on the television and we watch all the terrible crimes people are committing. And we wonder why. The answer is sin. When we as a nation, as a people reject the righteousness of God as taught to us in His Word, and we fail to teach them to our children, immorality will continue to raise its ugly head.

How can we call ourselves a God–fearing nation when the laws that are passed are not of God? Laws that sanction same sex marriages as being okay are not found in the Holy Scriptures. Yet, we now have passed laws that say it is alright for two men or two women to get married and live together as man in wife. The judges or politicians who favor and made this human desire into a law are thumbing their noses at the Word of God. This is clearly spoken against in the Old Testament and the New Testament. Old Testament: Leviticus 20:13, *"If a man also lie with mankind as he lieth with a woman, both of them have committed an abomination; they shall surely be put to death; their blood shall be upon them.* "New Testament: Romans 1:22–28, *22 Professing themselves to be wise, they became fools,23 And changed the glory of the incorruptible God into an image made like to corruptible man, and to birds, and four-footed beasts, and creeping things. 24 Wherefore God also gave them up to uncleanness through the lusts of their own hearts, to dishonor their own bodies between themselves: 25 Who changed the truth of God into a lie, and worshipped and served the creature more than the Creator, who is blessed forever. Amen.26 For this cause God gave them up unto vile affections: for even their women did change the natural use into that which is against nature:27 And likewise also the men, leaving the natural use of the woman, burned in their lust one toward another; men with men working that which is unseemly, and receiving in themselves that recompense of their error which was meet.28 And even as they did not like to retain God in their knowledge, God gave them over to a reprobate mind, to do those things which are not convenient."*

So my question is this, do we have reprobate politicians and judges making laws superior to God's law? Heaven forbid! If this is the case, and I suspect it is, God is not mocked. In Galatians 6:7, we read "Be not deceived; God is not mocked: for whatsoever a man soweth, that shall he also reap." There will be a day of reckoning for the unjust laws passed that are against a Holy God's moral statutes. Rest assured on this!

2. The Bath School disaster happened on May 18, 1927 in Bath Township, Michigan, and is the worst and deadliest mass murder in a school in United States history. Thirty-eight elementary school children, two teachers, four other adults, and the bomber himself were killed. Most of the children were in second to sixth grade (ages 7-14 years of age).

    The bomber's name was Andrew Kehoe, age fifty-five. He was also a school board member. After he committed these atrocities, he killed himself. I am not going to try and guess the why of Mr. Kehoe's actions that day. I will say that what he did was not of God. I know this because God is love and for life lived more abundantly. It is the work of the devil to kill, steal and destroy. You decide.

3. On April 16, 2007, a single or lone killer by the name of Seung-Hui Cho killed thirty-two people and wounded twenty-five others. This is now remembered as the Virginia Tech Massacre. The shooter took his own life after he had committed mass murder.

Again, the question that begs for an answer is why? What caused this person to do this? What in his life changed that would allow him not to regard human life as sacred? Yes, he could have had a mental condition, yes, he could have just snapped. But to execute or mass murder people requires preparation and planning. This is indicative of a person with a diabolical nature. I would say that this young man did not fear the Lord, because the fear of the Lord is the beginning of wisdom. I would argue where is the wisdom in the mass murder of helpless college students just trying to get an education and become productive members of society? No, this young man was not of God, certainly not of God on the day he chose to carry out his plan of mass murder.

4. On August 1, 1966, Charles Joseph Whitman, while a student at the University of Texas at Austin, shot and killed sixteen people and wounded thirty-two others. Before he went on his killing spree, he had already murdered his wife and mother at their homes. He was shot and killed by an Austin Police Officer.

I am certain that if I searched long enough, I would find a psychological report or some type of police written narrative that explains the why of this terrible situation. I would be really shocked if anything mentioned "failed to fear God". I have become convinced that human nature without God is dangerous. In other words, a life that is completely devoid of God is a life to stay away from. A person that can kill his own mother and wife is a very dangerous individual. To arrive at this mindset did not happen in just one day. This person did not go to bed one night and the next morning decide he would commit mass murder. No, there must have been signs along the way. There must have been signs that should have indicated that this person was heading in the wrong direction. Maybe he was a racist who talked of killing all blacks or Jews. Maybe he hated women and only pretended to love them to his benefit. Maybe he had a short fuse and a hair-trigger temper, or it could be he just developed a desire to kill people.

He may have thought that he loved his mother and wife at one time or another in his life, but something allowed his mind to override those feelings of love and affection for his family. Something allowed him to replace feelings of genuine affection with feelings of hatred and rage, thus leading him to do those things that were already in his heart. This is similar to what God told Cain in Genesis 4:7, *"If thou doest well, shalt thou not be accepted? And, if thou does not well, sin lieth at the door. And unto thee shall be his desire, and thou shalt rule over him."*

God knows that sin separates us from Him. Therefore, the enemy of our soul, the devil, always tries to tempt us into sin, because he also knows the Word of God. He knows that God has already said that the wages of sin is death, but the gift of God is eternal life. Make no mistake about it, the devil wants your soul, and he will do anything to get it. We must never yield into any temptation that allows us to sin. I know this now, but there was a time in my life, when I was blinded by sin, the devil, and my own stupidly. I am now led by the Spirit and the rest will take care of itself.

There are many other cases of people committing horrendous crimes against humanity. Some crimes are random, some are crimes of opportunity, some are crimes of passion, some are crimes of hatred, and some are planned. Whatever the reason, a lot of people have lost their lives as a result of crimes against humanity. The sad thing is that the very people, who are committing these awful crimes, act as though they will not be held accountable for their actions by Almighty God. Jesus, the Good Shepherd, who gave His life for us, teaches us in John, 10:10-11, *"that the thief,* (which is the devil) *cometh not, but for to kill, steal, and destroy: I am come that they might have life, and that they might have it more abundantly."* Therefore, when you see destruction like the Columbine High School Massacre, the Bath School disaster, the Virginia Tech massacres, and the University of Texas mass murders, know for sure that the devil has been involved in the situation. The Lord God warns us in 1 Peter chapter 5:8, *"Be sober, be vigilant; because your adversary the devil, as a roaring lion, walketh about, seeking whom he may devour."* The proof of his involvement is his trademark calling cards left at the scene of the crime - to kill, steal, and destroy. He leaves behind gruesome scenes of unimaginable atrocities against human life, dead bodies, mass destruction, and thievery on a grand scale. Major thefts similar to the collapse of the Wall Street financial district had a significant impact on the World Banking System.

Greed

Another example of one man's greed and covetousness is that of Bernard Lawrence "Bernie" Madoff. This man was an American businessman, a major investment advisor, a private financier, and a stockbroker. He was also an unscrupulous lawbreaker. Mr. Madoff, or Bernie as he was called by those who thought they knew him, was at one time Executive Chairman of the NASDAQ stock market. He was also discovered to be the main kingpin in charge of a Ponzi scheme operation. What is a Ponzi scheme? A Ponzi scheme is a fraudulent investment operation that pays returns to its investors from their own money or the money paid by subsequent investors, rather than from any actual profit earned by the individual or a legitimate organization running the business concern. It's like robbing Peter to pay Paul. Mr. Madoff cheated thousands of his investors out of their money and lined his pockets with billions of dollars. True, unchecked, greed does not set limitations. It can never have enough money. Greed and covetousness is a sin before the eyes of a Holy God. There are people with large resources of money who put their trust in their money; and not in God. Anything you put before God is a sin. Now, I don't know about you, but I am going to trust God, and listen to what He has to say and be obedient to His Word. He and he alone know that we are no match for the enemy of God, the enemy of our soul, which is the devil.

Allow me to share a bit of how God has blessed me and kept me from death or dying in my sins. God has been so good to me, that I sometimes cry for failing to realize, that at the time when I was living in sin, that had it not been for God's mercy and His grace, I would not be here today. I have made major mistakes in my life and I know that when sin has you blinded you cannot see how close you are to death's door. You cannot see that it is the hand of God that is restraining death from laying claim to your soul.

For some people, it's the love of money that has them blinded to the sins of this world. For others, it could be power, or drugs, (drug dealers) for some it's women, (the lust of the flesh), or Pride. Racial pride has caused many people to die at the hands of unjust and ungodly people. I have learned from studying the Word of God that whatever you put before God in your life that is not of God becomes the God that you worship. It can be your home, car, job, family, friends, or your love of sports. These are just a few. You tell yourself. "I would go to church, but I prefer to stay home to watch the football or basketball games on weekends". If that is your preference, then your god is sports. We cannot put anything or anyone before God.

God is the Center and Sustainer of my life and is the reason that I have life. I was not born to sit on my behind every weekend just to watch some guy, who is making millions, play a professional sport ,just to impress my buddies with my knowledge of the game. That same guy that you are spending valuable time with probably would probably not even give you his or her autograph if you asked. Many of the super-rich athletes are very conceited. They walk by you like you are not there, get in their limos and away they go.

■ ■ ■

Delivering on His Word

Chapter 16

This book is to please, to praise, and glorify God. I feel compelled to tell others about the hope that God gives and how He proves His promises as He walks with us daily. If I can cause one soul to rethink his or her life of sin and make a commitment to seek God with all their heart and all their soul, then my task will not have been in vain.

It is my hope that on the following four true examples, you will find hope for a soul that is lost in sin and desperately looking for a way out. The first example that I will tell you about I will just simply call it "God saved me from death". Here is what actually happened. I will let you judge for yourself.

Saved from Death

On December 27, 2008, my wife and I bought a used kitchen table set from a friend of mine that worked with me. He and his wife had just bought a new kitchen table set and no longer needed their old set. After he and I discussed the price I went to his home to look at the furniture. The kitchen set was in exceptionally good condition. I bought this furniture for my mother-in-law, who, at the time, needed a kitchen table and chairs. However, as it turned out, they ended up buying a new kitchen set before I could deliver the one I had just purchased for them. I gave the kitchen table and chairs to my older brother Larry since he also needed a kitchen table and set of chairs. Larry was excited about getting this furniture because he needed it, and the price was right - free. He and I agreed to move the furniture into his apartment shortly after Christmas.

My brother likes to frequent a place called the Oasis. The Oasis is a homeless shelter. At the Oasis, people who frequent the streets, some having no place to live, can get a hot cup of coffee, a shower, doughnuts and get out of the inclement weather. After Christmas, Larry went down to the Oasis to ask a friend who had a truck to come and haul the furniture to his home. Larry was to call me and let me know what time the truck would be coming. After waiting for over an hour and not hearing from Larry, I was about to leave and go over to the Oasis. I decided to call before I left. The call finally went through and Larry was called to the phone. Larry told me the guy had to go someplace first, and then he would come by my house to pick up the furniture. It was very cold that day, and Larry asked me if I would pick him up from the Oasis so we could go back to my house to load up the furniture to take to his apartment. I only lived about five minutes away and Larry said he would be waiting by the door when I pulled up. I pulled up and waited, and waited and waited, but no Larry.

The car I was driving was a 1999 four-door Cadillac Deville, which is a very large and heavy automobile. After waiting for about ten to fifteen minutes, I tried to blow my car horn, but the horn would not blow. The horn on my car had never refused to blow before, but now it seemed as dead as a door bell that won't ring. I couldn't imagine what would be wrong with the horn. I did not want to get out into the frigid cold weather and check because Larry knew that I was coming to pick him up so he should be ready to go. The Oasis faces a narrow two-lane street that runs east and west. I was in the north lane heading west on this cold and frigid morning. I had stopped my car directly in front of the Oasis with the motor running, trying to blow my car horn that, for some reason, now refused to blow. I decided to turn left and park directly in front of the Oasis building and to go inside to get my brother who was not by the door as I expected him to be. He was probably still in the Christmas spirit talking to some of his old friends, running his mouth and not looking for me like he was supposed to be doing. I began to turn the steering wheel to the left, and discovered that the steering wheel on my car was now locked. My steering wheel would not move an inch, either left or right. I tried to manhandle the steering wheel by using all of my human strength to turn the car wheels to the left, but the steering wheel would not budge an inch. It was like trying to move a building by hand. There was absolutely zero movement in the steering wheel in any direction. Now I am really getting upset! Why? Because it's freezing cold outside, my brother asked me to pick him up but he's nowhere to be found, my car horn all of a sudden has stopped working, and now my steering wheel does not work.

I put the car in park, and attempted to open my left door to get out and go get Larry to help me. I discovered that my left door would not open. I was really frustrated. I turned to my left door, trying to force it to open, when some guys in an old beat up mini–van flew past my car. They were going so fast, and were so close to the car that all I saw was a big blur as I looked up. They were traveling so fast as they passed my car that it caused my car to rock and move left and right. It takes a lot of speed to shake a parked 1999 Cadillac Deville. They were so close to my car, that if I had opened the door, they would have killed me instantly. My car probably would have burst into flames because of the high volume of speed that they were traveling.

After I regained my composure, I realized that I could have been killed. I did not think of God, I just assumed I was lucky that day. However, in retrospect, I now realize luck had nothing to do with it. It was God's mercy and His grace that kept me. After the van shot by me, I tried the horn, and it was working fine. The horn was now working as though it had never stopped. The power steering was working as though it had never stopped. I tried to open my left door; it now opened as though it was a work of art with no problem. I know that only the Providence of God and the will of God kept me that day. I know He told death, "not this time". For that, Lord I want to truly say thank You. I thank You for saving my life that day. I truly acknowledge and receive you as my Lord and Savior. I am so thankful for all my blessings!

The Wonderful Gift of Salvation

I remember the days I was not saved and not going to church. I was living a very sinful lifestyle. I had a good job; God was blessing me with stable employment, which led to some degree of financial stability. Yet, something was still missing in my life. My life was not complete and it used to bother me, that during the Easter holiday, I did not go to a church service. I would feel bad because something would kind of just gnaw at me all day.

I knew that I should be going to church with my family on a regular basis, not just on Easter Sunday.

I'm sure it is surprising the number of people who will buy new clothes, some women will get their hair fixed, and buy new Easter outfits for their entire family and go to church on Easter Sunday. Some of their kids will have already learned their Easter speeches, and parents will want their "little Johnny's" to participate in the Easter program. The sad thing is that after Easter, you won't see them again until the next Easter, or perhaps Christmas. This is the sad state of life for many young black and white families in America today. This was also true for me at one point in my life. I could find the time to do all the things I wanted to do except go to church. When it came time to go into any church, my flesh and my mind rebelled. Subconsciously, I perceived going to church as a waste of time. I would much rather spend my Sundays cleaning up my car, listening to music (usually jazz), or riding my motorcycle.

I had a lot of hobbies or excuses to fill my time rather than to go to a church and listen to a long and boring sermon. That was just my mindset at the time. But God had other plans for me. I thank God for not giving us what we deserve. I thank God for looking past my faults, and seeing my needs. I thank God for being the God of a first, a second, and a third, and many chances. I thank the Lord for saving me and not letting me die in my sins.

My true conversion began after the death of my only son on February 10, 2001. The pain that I felt over the death of my son was at times immeasurable. I mentally lost it for a while. My life began to spiral out of control. I began to stop taking care of myself, and I began to experiment with drugs - mostly a controlled substance. My new companion, cocaine, allowed me to meet and mingle with new people who did not have my best interests at heart. All these people wanted from me were money to buy more controlled substances, marijuana and alcohol. I found out the hard way that people will pretend to be your friend just as long as the friendship or relationship is beneficial to them. However, the moment you stop partying with them, they will quickly lose your number. They will forget your name and move on to the next victim.

It was during this time in my life that the Lord came to me in a dream. I had been out at a club, and had gotten home around 2:30 am on a Sunday morning. I went to bed and the Lord came to me in a dream. And to answer what might be one of your questions, no, I was not drunk or high.

When I went to sleep that night, I heard a voice saying, "what are you doing?" I gave an answer back, and the voice slightly elevated over my sorry and weak voice. The voice said. "Why are you doing this, and why are you and your family not in church? You were not raised like this." As I began to answer that question, I began to slowly wake up. I was agreeing with the voice in my dreams. When I woke up and looked at the clock directly beside my bed, it was only 4:45 am. I looked around my bedroom and there was no other person there; just me! It dawned on me that I had been talking to somebody. What had just happened were real and not my imagination running wild. I was having a conversation with someone! What I heard was not the result of a guilty conscience complex. Sinners usually don't have guilt complexes until they get caught. The voice that talked to me in my sleep was real.

The following Sunday, my wife, my daughter and I went to church. We ended up joining this church and after a year or so we left that church and joined a local holiness assembly. That is where the Lord began to develop me. He gave me an insatiable desire to study and learn more about Him. From 2002 to this date, that desire to study and meditate on God's Word has not changed. If anything it has gotten stronger. In 2006, I attended a church convocation in Memphis, Tennessee. This was the first time in my life that I had scheduled a week off from work to attend a religious convention. For me, this was a startling contrast to what I used to do on vacations.

I was completely amazed at the number of people from all walks of life coming together for one purpose - to worship and glorify God. For me, this was truly a sight to see. Thousands of people filled the FedEx Forum. To witness that many people singing and praising God was a moving and unforgettable experience. One experience happened the first night of the service which was a Sunday night prayer service that goes on all night. I had gone back home for the evening and I did not personally witness what I am about to share with you. I learned of this situation the following night during the Monday night main service. The main speaker was a Bishop and as he spoke, he brought it up. He told everyone in the audience what had happened during the prayer service the previous night. He shared that during the prayer service, a young black girl walked in off the streets. The Bishop's sister was on stage at the time and saw this young woman and asked her if she was alright or needed help.

The young lady said she did need some help. The Bishop's sister told her that she was in the right place, and invited her up on stage. She prayed for this young lady and using holy water, began to cast out demons. She said, "in the Name of Jesus, I command these demonic spirits to come out of this girl." One of the spirits talked back. The voice was not the voice of the young girl who had been talking to the speaker previously. The demon spirit said in a loud shrill voice, "you want me to come out, I will come out, but I am going to get in someone else." At this point the speaker forbade the demon from coming out of the girl. She said, "stop in the Name of Jesus, stop right there". She turned to a packed house of people sitting in the audience and said, "If there is anybody here who is not saved and absolutely sure about your salvation, please leave now." A lot of people got up and left. After they left, the speaker continued to cast the demon spirits out of the young girl. The lesson to learn here is that the power of God is real! The young girl came back the next day and she was a completely different and saved person. I often wonder what she is doing now. Hopefully, she has given her life to Christ Jesus and is still working for Him.

I gained a tremendous amount of knowledge at the convention. I learned the difference between having a heart for God, which is love for all mankind, and not having a heart of self-righteous perceived glory because of some religious affiliation. Religion alone cannot save you. Only God through the working of His Son, Jesus, through the indwelling of Holy Spirit will save you through faith.

God's Commands are Not Negotiable

Chapter 17

Christ sent out His twelve apostles, enabling them by His power to do miracles. His commandment is also for us today as well. Chapter 10 of Matthew deals with the mission of the disciples of Jesus Christ. If we are to be an effective witness for Jesus Christ, we need to know His charge to us. This is why I felt it appropriate to list them all. I know that some of you may not follow up and read them in the Bible, so I will list them all here. Study them and get familiar with them. As you read each verse, consider its application to your life today.

I am going to list all the verses of Chapter 10:1-42 from Matthew, because this chapter tells us how Christ sent out His twelve apostles. He lets them know what He expects from them and how they are to conduct themselves. Christ sent out His twelve apostles, enabling them by His power to do miracles. His commandment is also for us today as well. Chapter 10 deals with the mission of the disciples of Jesus Christ. If we are to be an effective witness for Jesus Christ, we need to know His charge to us. As you read each verse, consider its application to your life today. After you read the last verse of chapter 10, I will continue on with what God has put in my heart to share with you. Let's start with the 1st verse of chapter 10 of Matthew: ¹"*And when he had called unto him his twelve disciples, he gave them power against unclean spirits, to cast them out, and to heal all manner of sickness and all manner of disease. ²Now the names of the twelve apostles are these; the first, Simon, who is called Peter, and Andrew his brother; James the son of Zebedee, and John his brother; ³Philip, and Bartholomew; Thomas, and Matthew the publican; James the son of Alphaeus, and Lebbaeus, whose surname was Thaddaeus; ⁴Simon the Canaanite, and Judas Iscariot, who also betrayed him. (He commands them to preach and heal the sick) ⁵These twelve Jesus sent forth, and commanded them, saying, Go not into the way of the Gentiles, and into any city of the Samaritans enter ye not: ⁶But go rather to the lost sheep of the house of Israel. ⁷And as ye go, preach, saying, the kingdom of heaven is at hand. ⁸Heal the sick, cleanse the lepers, raise the dead, cast out devils: freely ye have received, freely give. ⁹Provide neither gold, nor silver, nor brass in your purses, ¹⁰Nor scrip for your journey, neither two coats, neither shoes, nor yet staves: for the workman is worthy of his meat. ¹¹And into whatsoever city or town ye shall enter, enquire who in it is worthy; and there abide till ye go thence. ¹²And when ye come into a house, salute it. ¹³And if the house be worthy, let your peace come upon it: but if it be not worthy, let your peace return to you. ¹⁴And whosoever shall not receive you, nor hear your words, when ye depart out of that house or city, shake off the dust of your feet. ¹⁵Verily I say unto you, it shall be more tolerable for the land of Sodom and Gomorra in the Day of Judgment, than for that city.* (He fortifies them against persecutions) *¹⁶Behold, I send you forth as sheep in the midst of wolves: be ye therefore wise as serpents, and harmless as doves. ¹⁷But beware of men: for they will deliver you up to the councils, and they will scourge you in their synagogues; ¹⁸And ye shall be brought before governors and kings for my sake, for a testimony against them and the Gentiles. ¹⁹But when they deliver you up, take no thought how or what ye shall speak: for it shall be given you in that same hour what ye shall speak. ²⁰For it is not ye that speak, but the Spirit of your Father which speaketh in you. ²¹And the brother shall deliver up the brother to death, and the father the child: and the children shall rise up against their parents, and cause them to be put to death. ²²And ye shall be hated of all men for my name's sake: but he that endureth to the end shall be saved. ²³But when they persecute you in this city, flee ye into another: for verily I say unto you, Ye shall not have gone over the cities of Israel, till the Son of man become. ²⁴The disciple is not above his master, nor the servant above his lord. ²⁵It is enough for the disciple that he be as his master, and the servant as his lord. If they have called the master of the house Beelzebub, how much more shall they call them of his household? ²⁶Fear them not therefore: for there is nothing covered, that shall not be revealed; and hid, that shall not be known. ²⁷What I tell you in darkness, that speak ye in light: and what ye hear in the ear, that preach ye upon the housetops. ²⁸And fear not them which kill the body, but are not able to kill the soul: but rather fear him which is able to destroy both soul and body in hell. ²⁹Are not two sparrows sold for a farthing? And one of them shall not fall on the ground without your Father.*

30But the very hairs of your head are all numbered. 31Fear ye not therefore, ye are of more value than many sparrows. 32Whosoever therefore shall confess me before men, him will I confess also before my Father which is in heaven. 33But whosoever shall deny me before men, him will I also deny before my Father which is in heaven. 34Think not that I am come to send peace on earth: I came not to send peace, but a sword. 35For I am come to set a man at variance against his father, and the daughter against her mother, and the daughter in law against her mother in law. 36And a man's foes shall be they of his own household. 37He that loveth father or mother more than me is not worthy of me: and he that loveth son or daughter more than me is not worthy of me.38And he that taketh not his cross, and followeth after me, is not worthy of me. 39He that findeth his life shall lose it: and he that loseth his life for my sake shall find it. 40He that receiveth you receiveth me, and he that receiveth me receiveth him that sent me. 41He that receiveth a prophet in the name of a prophet shall receive a prophet's reward; and he that receiveth a righteous man in the name of a righteous man shall receive a righteous man's reward. 42And whosoever shall give to drink unto one of these little ones a cup of cold water only in the name of a disciple, verily I say unto you, he shall in no wise lose his reward."

The Commandments that Jesus gave to His disciples in Matthew 10:1-42, are still active commandments (assignments) for those who love the Lord and are called according to Hs purpose.

In Mark 6:7, we learn that Jesus is an excellent Leader of His people. This verse states, *"And he called unto him the twelve, and began to send them forth by two and two; and gave them power over unclean spirits."* This verse tells us about how Jesus commands His army of disciples. He sends them out two by two. We learn from Ecclesiastes 4:9-12, starting with verse 9, *"Two are better than one; because they have a good reward for their labor. 10For if they fall, the one will lift up his fellow: but woe to him that is alone when he falleth; for he hath not another to help him up. 11Again, if two lie together, then they have heat: but how can one be warm alone? 12And if one prevails against him, two shall withstand him; and a threefold cord is not quickly broken."*

There are advantages of two being one in Christ. Two can withstand more of the troubles of this world when it comes, than one person acting alone. Two can withstand more pressure from this world (witnessing) than one person acting alone. The same is true when you go out witnessing for the Lord. The Lord allowed me to learn a very valuable lesson early in the development of my spiritual character in Him. What He taught me is that whenever He sends people out to work for Him, He equips them with whatever they need to be successful. If you go out on your own, you're going to fail. That happened to me. After I began to study and learn more about God, my inner strength began to grow. Over time, I became very zealous for the Word of God. I would find myself trying to prophesy the Word of God to anybody who would listen, without realizing that God had not called me, or sent me out to do this. I was a one-man savior of the world, or so I thought.

However, the truth of the matter is the only true one-man Savior of the world is Jesus, Christ. And there will never be another. People may have good intentions and some may even accomplish great things in the Name of Jesus and for Jesus, but they are still copies of the original. There is only one Master, and His Name is Jesus! People, like great works of art, though beautiful and elegant, are just duplicate copies of the original when placed before the Master's eye. It's perfectly okay to center our lives on trying to be like Jesus. That is a very worthy endeavor just as long as we do not forget to remember that no human being will ever duplicate Jesus.

I don't care how much of the Word you know, or you think you know, or how long you have been saved or your church affiliation. It does not matter your position in the church. None of us will ever achieve in this life what Jesus did for us. God had to teach me this, because in my own way, I was becoming spiritually arrogant. Unconsciously, I was beginning to see the world as we/saved vs. them/ unsaved.

This was one of the reasons I left a particular church in our community. The pastor and some of the more seasoned members of this particular church congregation loved to quote this saying: "We don't smoke, and we don't chew, and we don't run with those who do." Well, I am not sure that is the right thing to tell a sinner who has just come in out of the world and is struggling to overcome an addiction to smoking, drinking, chewing, or a drug habit. People who have been injured by the devil and the sins of this world need to hear encouragement, not more rejection. They seriously are looking for a way out of their addictions, not a reminder of what they are not, which is an immature Christian. What that person needs to hear is that God is able to help him/her overcome addictions and limitations, and welcomed into the house of the Lord. Not offering help to those struggling with addictions is not like Christ. These holier than thou people will try to hide their addictions, especially if they believe that they are holier than all the other churches.

Please allow me to make something perfectly clear. I have nothing against this holiness church. As a group, their organization is a strong church of righteousness for the Lord. But when the Lord placed this writing assignment on my heart, I made a vow not to hold back the truth of my feelings. As with most assignments, you will find people in leadership positions that sometimes, not intentionally, injure people. They assume that their view of the world is somehow superior to those who do not share their perceived sanctified upbringing. It's this attitude that comes across in their dealings with new converts. The average sinner with very little or no proper religious schooling detests this attitude. It's a spirit that is similar to the spirit that Jesus himself faced when He dealt with the Pharisee and Sadducees when He quoted the prophet Isaiah 29: 13 which says: *"Wherefore the Lord said, Forasmuch as this people draw near me with their mouth, and with their lips do honor me, but have removed their heart far from me, and their fear toward me is taught by the precept of men."*

I have learned that having a heart for the things of God will take you out of your comfort zone. Jesus did not look down on sinners. He came to save them from their sins; he talked to tax-collectors, Jews, Gentiles, beggars, prostitutes, and leprous people. He talked to everyone. My point is if Jesus did not discriminate or looked down on us struggling sinners, how can we who claim to be holy, filled with the Holy Spirit and speaking in tongues, look down on a struggling brother or sister trying to genuinely come in out of the world? More sinners go back into the world and don't venture into the church again, because of fear that they will not be accepted. The sad truth of this is they're right!

Allow me to give you a real life example. The last year of my membership at this local sanctified church, the church was having a revival meeting. I had finally talked my older brother, who has some serious issues with substance abuse, into attending one night. He went, but never returned. It was only after my repeatedly asking him why he would not come back to our church again that he told me "The people at my church made him feel as if he had a disease like A.I.D.S. or something". I asked him why he said that and he said, "Do you remember when the pastor asked the church congregation to shake hands with the visitors? Well, I went to shake hands with this one lady; she kind of withdrew her hands from me as though I was nasty". He said her hand shake was weak and empty with no feeling or compassion. I understood his refusal to never return to our church. His refusal to return was not a rejection of Jesus, or the church itself, it was because he did not want to be made to feel contempt. And the lady in question was our main missionary who held a high position in the church. "Good morning saints" was one of her favorite greetings.

How can we ever grow as a church if we continue to see people as saved vs. unsaved? We need to see people as God sees them; all people are His creation. If God allows His sun to shine on the just and the unjust, who am I to cause a cloud or stumbling to fall on the attempts of any human struggling to get right with my God? It is my belief that our duty in this life is to seek and save those who are lost through the ministry of repentance under the guidance of the Holy Spirit.

As a new member of this particular church, I hid my addictions. I did one day confess to the Bishop of the local church that I had an issue with cigarettes. This Bishop had the heart of God. He did not put me down, or make me feel inferior. What he said to me was, "in time you will overcome it, just stay with the Lord." To this day I am grateful to this "wise" Bishop for telling me that. It was God who allowed me to, over time, break through my addictions.

After I was saved, I had an urge to witness about the goodness of God and what He had done for me. One day I found myself over at the home of a friend. There is nothing wrong in testifying about the goodness of God and His mercy if you're called to do so. The Holy Spirit leads and guides in truth, so you will know who to witness with and what to say. I had to learn that not everybody wants to hear about the goodness of Jesus, and as unfortunate for them as this is, it is the truth. Some people, who are blinded by sin and under the control of some demonic spirit, will take offense and go on the attack when the truth of Jesus is revealed to them.

This happened to me that day at my friend's house. I had to learn that if you are not completely saturated in the Word, you can become a victim. God allowed me to experience for my own good this painful lesson. When I began to tell my friend and his girlfriend of the goodness of God and of how he saved me from smoking, and drug addiction, the girlfriend of my friend told me that she did not want to hear any more about what I was talking about. She asked me what church I attended and after I told her it was a sanctified church, she laughed at me, and said she grew up in a sanctified church and that she knew more about the Bible and the particular church I had attended, than I did. She went on to say that she and my boyfriend were happy. She said they liked getting high and smoking crack cocaine, and that they did not plan to stop. She told me if all I wanted to do was to talk about Jesus, then I could leave their house and not come back.

I admit I was completely hurt by her words, her cold words, her words of rejection. To make it more hurtful to me so this lesson would never be forgotten, the Holy Spirit had completely closed my mouth. I could not speak a word in my defense. I was struck dumb, and could not say anything. I sat there and continued to listen to this woman tell me how she was not going to change her life. I was immediately made speechless by the Spirit. I did not realize that it was the Spirit who had taken control of my tongue.

The Lord had just taught me four very valuable lessons: 1) when you embark upon a witnessing assignment, you better be ready; 2) if God does not send you, don't you go on your own; 3) if God sends you on a witnessing mission assignment, He will equip you for the task; and 4) I don't care how zealous you are for God, always allow yourself to be led by the Spirit. Do not try to lead Him. It does not work that way._

I do thank the Lord for the painful, yet valuable, lesson He taught me.

God Will Prove Himself

Chapter 18

I have a desire to see the hearts and minds of unbelievers turn to Jesus Christ. It is my sincere hope that all who read this book and do not know the Lord will give serious thought to seeking Jesus as their Lord and Savior.

As I continue to share some personal situations and experiences with you, please keep in mind these situations and experiences are real. I hope that you keep this in mind as you read and take to heart what I am saying. God is real. Jesus is real. The Holy Spirit is real. I hope and pray that some lost soul who does not know Jesus in the pardoning of their sins, will get a spiritual jolt that will enable him or her to rethink their position as a non-believer, and become converted to the truth of the Living God.

In the whole world of knowledge, there never has been a book like the Bible. The Bible is the Living Word of God. What are the convictions and arguments that would make a non-believer sure that God and the Holy Scriptures are not real? Are non-believers so wise that they can just rationalize away centuries of proven prophecy? Why would anyone choose to maintain a position that is non-defendable? Just saying something is not true because you don't believe it does not make that truth any less real.

Take for example energy. If we turn on a light switch, we expect to have electricity to light our homes at night. Very few of us have actually seen electricity in its natural state. However, we know that if we stick a finger in an electrical light socket, something that we cannot see, (electricity) will immediately shock us back into reality and get our attention.

Consider a major thunderstorm. A person would be foolish to rationalize away the power that Mother Nature has in any weather-related situation. If you are truly a non- believer, you should be able to reject that tornado's siren going off, or the weather bulletin warning people to take immediate cover. You may say that my argument is foolish because Mother Nature must be respected by all people; therefore, prudence says take cover. What man do you know who can order a tornado to go away, or tell a major hurricane to not come against his community? What man do you know who can tell the sun not to shine or the moon not to glow at night? What man do you know who can live on indefinitely and look death in the face and say, "not my family, I have money and power. Go down the street to that poor man's house; I have unfinished important business to take care of?" What man do you know who can tell the rain not to fall, or the wind not to blow? What man do you know who can tell the mighty ocean that when it reaches land, it must stop and return back to sea?

These are but a few of the things man has no control over, yet the non-believer thinks it is just nature, or some big bang theory that controls the elements that surround life. I have heard some people say, "I don't believe in God; I believe in a supreme being." Supreme Being – what is that? I also have heard others mention a new theory of intelligent design as a reason for choosing not to believe in God. There are many religions, and therefore many "gods" (small-g). Some may argue, "How do I know that the God that I serve is the real God?" My answer is this, "The indwelling of the Holy Spirit that lives in me, confirms that my God is real." My God is more than a book about a religion. He is the religion of life and any life lived without Him is a dead life. I know my Redeemer lives, because of what He has done for me in my times of crisis.

My God was with me when I was just like some of you - churchy; going to church but not really knowing Jesus. He was with me when I was living in a world of sin, and He revealed to me His blessings. I cannot say this enough. The events that I am sharing with you are not fabricated. They have actually happened, and I am a living witness and a living testimony to their authenticity.

I felt compelled to write this book. I have never had a strong desire to write a book before, but the words I am compelled to say, must be told. I am not trying to brag on myself or to give myself a standing ovation; I have nothing to brag about. My life now, and all that I cherish, comes from the Father, Son and Holy Spirit. I no longer have to wonder if He's real; I know He's real! God has made a believer out of me; He has allowed me to have my own "Damascus Road" experience. Now I am going to shout it to the entire world and to anybody that will listen!

On December 31, 2011, I was at home on New Year's Eve, waiting to go to our church "Watch Service." About 9:30 pm, I turned on the television, just to see how people were celebrating the birth of the New Year. As I flipped through the channels, the New York celebration got my attention. I was amazed at the thousands of people who were lined up to watch the dropping of an apple indicating the start of a new year. But what really got my attention, was the volume of people that were gathered to watch the performer Lady Gaga. She had on this huge black costume. The wearing of strange costumes is part of her genre, and this one was no exception. It was undoubtedly strange looking. As she was performing, a voice spoke in my mind and said, "How many of the thousands of people that you see watching this performer, will go to church tomorrow and tell God thanks that they were blessed to even be here and see the year end and a new year begin?"

As the cameras scanned the crowds and the many people, some appeared to be suggestively dressed. Men with men, and some women were seen holding hands; therefore, I assumed they were more than just casual friends. I was saddened by the situation and turned off the television. The scene reminded me of Sodom and Gomorrah. I am not suggesting the city of New York is indicative of Sodom and Gomorrah, but I will say that with the recent passage of laws that makes marriage between same sex individuals legal. I wonder what the people of Sodom and Gomorrah's generation were doing when God destroyed their city. I just could not shake this feeling, seeing all those people partying and celebrating. I, too, wondered how many of the thousands of people that I saw on television were of God. Only God knows that answer.

Sometimes when I am alone, I let my thoughts wander. I think about what would make a person, any person, not believe in God. They want to believe that God is a myth. Their reality is this, as long as God is a myth, I am free to continue living my life any way that I choose. Some non-believers will one day come to the realization that God is not a myth and is in fact, a reality. Hopefully, many will have a change of heart and repent, when they learn that God is going to hold them accountable for how they live their life. Imagine if God would allow a true unbeliever to get a good dose of His spiritual reality, that unbeliever would be forever changed! That unbeliever would probably develop an insatiable zeal for the work of the kingdom of God. This is exactly what happened to Saul of Tarsus, who we know as Paul. Paul had his mind and priorities changed when he had his encounter with Jesus on the road to Damascus. As a matter of fact, Paul said that he was the king of sinners. Consider the conversion of this great warrior for God. I will not paraphrase the whole story, only the part that is relevant to this topic.

If you have never read the book of Acts, I encourage you to do so. It will encourage your heart to see how God converted a man who was successfully working **against** Him, into a man with an insatiable zeal to work **for** Him.

The book of Acts: Chapter 9:1-9, *[1]"And Saul, yet breathing out threatening and slaughter against the disciples of the Lord, went unto the high priest, [2]And desired of him letters to Damascus to the synagogues, that if he found any of this way, whether they were men or women, he might bring them bound unto Jerusalem. [3]And as he journeyed, he came near Damascus: and suddenly there shined round about him a light from heaven: [4]And he fell to the earth, and heard a voice saying unto him, Saul, Saul, why persecutest thou me? [5]And he said, who art thou, Lord? And the Lord said I am Jesus whom thou persecute: it is hard for thee to kick against the pricks. [6]And he trembling and astonished said, Lord, what wilt thou have me to do? And the Lord said unto him, Arise, and go into the city, and it shall be told thee what thou must do. [7]And the men which journeyed with him stood speechless, hearing a voice, but seeing no man. [8]And Saul arose from the earth; and when his eyes were opened, he saw no man: but they led him by the hand, and brought him into Damascus. [9]And he was three days without sight, and neither did eat nor drink."*

Think for a moment about this big and powerful non-believer named Saul. He was a serious non-believer in Jesus. This man had powerful friends in high places and they had his back. He had made agreements with the leaders of the Jews who allowed Saul to wage war on the people who were called the disciples of God. Here is an example of a hard-hearted man who was convinced that his belief was correct. Saul was merciless in his attacks on the people of God, much like the "anti-God' rhetoric that non-believers publish today. When Saul had a head-on collision with the Almighty God, he was immediately converted. Gone was his rock-solid belief that he was right and the disciples of God were wrong. Saul's name was changed to Paul, and like me, he had to learn things the hard way. Lesson learned here is from Hebrews 10:31, "It is a fearful thing to fall into the hands of a living God."

When the God of Creation decides it is time to get your attention, you are in for a rude awakening. It will not matter to Him how long you've been an established non-believer. It will not matter to Him how many degrees you have. You may have your Associate's, Bachelor's, Master's and your Doctor's degree (doctorate) all framed and hanging on the wall behind you, but non-believer, today your "PHD" will not help you. Today you will meet the one who is all knowing.

I would like to be there when a federal judge for example, tries to show God his mastery of the legal profession. He points to his Juris Doctor credentials and proceeds to explain to God why he single-handedly passed a law in his home state. It was a law that made civil unions a legal and binding certificate of marriage. He used his power to authorize an alternative lifestyle which granted permission to allow marriage of two men or two women. I would like to see what words he will use as he proceeds to justify to God why he took it upon himself to override God's decree which is clearly stated in Leviticus 18:22, "*Thou shalt not lie with mankind, as with womankind: it is abomination.*" This judge will regret his decision. He will come to know that his membership in the prestigious club of non–believers, which was a source of financial support, will mean nothing to God. His years of study, which allowed him to publish his dissertation on the non-credibility of God, will be a confirmation of his intellectual ignorance. When he comes face-to-face with a Holy God, all that fake bravo and cock-sureness will evaporate like the smoke off the tip of a cigarette.

Consider this short story of Big Bad un-believing John. Big Bad John stood six feet, five inches tall and weighed 290 lbs. He was a coal miner and known throughout the south as a man of tremendous strength. He was known as someone not to mess with. He was absolutely fearless. Big John, as he was called, would walk the roads in the dead of night without fear of anything or anybody. When his poor wife and kids went to church on

Sunday, he would curse and mock them for believing in an invisible God. Furthermore, just as soon as his family left for church, John would continue his drinking from the previous night and walk over to his girlfriend's house. He might leave a note for his wife that said "I might come back home later if I am sober enough, if not, I will see you in a couple of days as soon as my shift is over." John only cared about John. If anyone tried to or found the nerve to confront him, it might be the last time that they drew a breath.

On a late Sunday evening, John was heading back home after gambling with his buddies. He had a pocket full of money and a pint of homemade corn whiskey in his back pocket. As he walked along the large and open corn field, the winds began to pick up. He cursed to himself and continued walking, vowing to get his old pickup truck fixed. The wind and the rain began to fall, but this did not even faze Big John. He just took a big swig out of his corn whiskey and continued to walk into the driving rain and lightning. As he walked he thought he heard the roar of a big train. He said to himself, "I am not close to any (blank, blank) train track; where is this (blank blank) noise coming from?" As he continued to walk, the noise only intensified. Big John stopped to take another drag out of his corn whiskey, but the whiskey bottle miraculously and suddenly flew out of his hands. When he turned around to see where the whiskey bottle had gone, he saw a huge tornado, about a half mile wide, coming in his direction. John was too drunk to say, "Lord, forgive me." To this day, no one has ever found his body.

The moral of this example is: No one is ever too big and bad that God cannot deal with them. Do not live your life like Big John, a life of continued unbelief in God Almighty. He lived a life that frowned on and mocked all believers as foolish dreamers and as weak people who worshipped an unreal and invisible God. Big John was so sure that God was a myth, that when his own ears heard the sounds of a noise similar to the rumble of a huge freight train he still remained unrepentant and unconvinced that God was near him. He was so brazen in his false beliefs and wrong attitude about God that he was spiritually blinded to God's presence. Spiritual considerations meant nothing to John. When he actually faced the manifestations of the reality of God's presence through the mist of the horrendous downpour and the mighty winds, Big John failed to say, "Lord, forgive me for my foolish beliefs. Lord I repent now and please, I pray thee, have mercy on my soul." Those were the words that Big John should have said before the tornado consumed him. His family, his friends and other people searched for him, but his body was never found.

Non-believers think and convince themselves and others that God is not real. However, just because they say and believe that He is not real does not deviate from the reality that God is very real! When you meet Him face-to-face, your unbelief will not save you. You cannot say on judgment day "Lord, I was deceived, I will now start believing." That might be a little too late. However in the case of Saul who was Paul the Apostle, that is exactly what happened. God gave Paul a second chance to change his mind.

Let's review Paul's conversion again. Saul ran into a powerful God on the road to Damascus, Syria, when suddenly there shone round about him a light from heaven. Saul heard a voice from heaven that said *"Saul, Saul, why persecutes thou me?"* (Acts 9:4) I don't think at this point Saul was very proud of wearing his badge of unbelief and of being overly zealous for his pious Jewish religious leaders. Paul's conversion resulted in his correct response to the Lord by asking in Acts 9:5-6, *"Who art thou, Lord?" And the Lord said "I am Jesus whom thou persecutes: it is hard for thee to kick against the pricks." Saul said, "What will thou have me to do?"* He did not say, "Lord, I still don't recognize your power over me. I will continue to disrespect you and there is nothing you can do about it." That would have been the wrong answer! You should read the book of Hebrews Chapter 10:30-31, because it warns us, *"For we know him that hath said, Vengeance belongeth unto me, I will recompense, saith the Lord. And again, The Lord shall judge his people. It is a fearful thing to fall into the hands of the living God."*

If you think that you are going to intimidate God just because you are a non-believer, you are dead wrong! You will end up like the captain of the Titanic, Edward John Smith, who will forever be remembered as the captain of one of the worst ship disasters in world history. Just like that great ship that sunk in the freezing north Atlantic sea, your life, which is your personal ship with you as the captain, will sink without Jesus guiding you through life's treacherous waters. Every non-believer needs to reexamine their own thoughts. (Please note: The writer of this book is not in any way shape or form implying that Captain Edward John Smith was a non-believer in Jesus Christ.)

You might want to start by asking yourself the question, "What is the basis of my beliefs that support the position there is not a God?" In other words, what proof can I find that will give me 100 % confirmation that God is not real? You will find what you want to find, and you will believe what you want to believe, but you will not find anything to confirm that God is not real. Yes, you will find tons of atheist books that are written by men who may be like you, men who possibly think like you, men who say God is not real. They are deceivers and are being deceived by the spirit of the devil. Remember, the devil comes but to steal, kill and destroy. If he can convince you that God is not real, he has claimed your soul and in hell you will one day open your eyes. If this is your position, repent and ask for God's forgiveness. Seek God with a pure heart and broken and contrite spirit, and you will find Him.

The non–believer says to himself or herself, "God is not real!" Some non-believers go to great lengths trying to convince themselves and others that God is a myth. If God is not real, we would not be discussing that He is not real. There would be no need to discuss something that is not in existence. Therefore, the non-believer's own argument is a testimony against them and is a confirmation for the reality of an almighty God. The non- believer ideology that God is not real confirms that God is real. It is the non–believer's anti-God position that is revealed. Kind of like the old expression, "when you point a finger at someone else, you have three fingers pointing back at you."

It is simply mind boggling to hear the different mindsets of some of our young people. Some of them have already made up their minds that going to church and belief in God is a waste of time. Some of them will even tell you, "I do not believe and I do not go to church", and they do not want to have a discussion about it. I see they have already discarded the values on which this country was built. They have discarded the deep convictions of their forefathers, who generations ago, built a nation on the belief in the Bible and what it meant to be a Christian. Anything else was not even considered.

I often wonder what makes people so sure that God is not real. Some will say, "If He's real then show me. Show me where He is so that I can see Him. Show me where He lives so that I can visit his home and see this God that you say exists." Well, non-believer, all you have to do is get up, walk outside, and look up, and name one thing that you see as you are looking up into the heavens that is man-made. Additionally, when you look on another human being, you are seeing His creation manifested before your very eyes. We learn in Genesis 1:27 that *"God created man in his own image, in the image of God created he him; male and female created he them."* Therefore, when you look at another human, not only are you seeing another unique creation of God, you are also seeing the expressed image of God Himself. The non-believer's argument that if he could see God, he would believe is incorrect. Jesus has already proved this to us. Jesus walked this earth and stood before the leading authority figures of His day and they still refused to believe and they crucified Him. Consider what the Apostle John told us in John 1: 1-13. John walked with Jesus; he had firsthand knowledge of what it was like to be in the presence of God. John says and I will quote him verbatim as follows: *[1]"In the beginning was the Word, and the Word was with God, and the Word was God. [2]The same was in the beginning with God. [3]All things were made by him; and without him was not anything made that was made. [4]In him was life; and the life was the light of men. [5]And the light shineth in darkness; and the darkness comprehended it not. [6] There was a man sent from God, whose name was John. [7]The same came for a witness, to bear witness of the Light that all men through him might believe. [8]He was not that Light, but was sent to bear witness of that Light.[9]That was the true Light, which lighteth every man that cometh into the world. [10]He was in the world, and the world was made by him, and the world knew him not. [11]He came unto his own, and his own received him not. [12]But as many as received him, to them gave the power to become the sons of God, even to them that believe on his name: [13]Which were born, not of blood, nor of the will of the flesh, nor of the will of man, but of God. [14]And the Word was made flesh, and dwelt among us, (and we beheld his glory, the glory as of the only begotten of the Father,) full of grace and truth."*

John tells us that Jesus came unto His own and His own did not receive Him. But they (the world) chose not to believe, which is the same thing that people are doing today. Some say this because they have no faith in an invisible God. Let me tell you from first-hand experience, even cancer is an invisible killer in your body until it's detected. If cancer is not discovered, it quietly goes about its business destroying good cells and its mission of killing you as its primary goal. Sin is like cancer, it can be a silent killer. Sin will completely destroy you in time and the only way to rid your life from sin is surrender to Jesus Christ. You cannot see cancer at work within your body without the help of tests and x-rays. You cannot see the effects of sin and the devil in your life without Jesus Christ. Jesus is the only filter that can cleanse and change your life before it's too late. The devil does not want you to see Him at work in your life; he wants you to focus on the things that take your mind off Christ. The devil wants people to worship him and not Jesus. Remember in Matthew 4: 8–10 when the devil tempted Jesus? Hear what he said to Jesus: *8 "Again, the devil taketh him up into an exceeding high mountain, and sheweth him all the kingdoms of the world, and the glory of them; 9And saith unto him, All these things will I give thee, if thou wilt fall down and worship me. 10Then saith Jesus unto him, Get thee hence, Satan: for it is written, Thou shalt worship the Lord thy God, and him only shalt thou serve."*

People who boast that they do not believe in God are by default saying that they believe in Satan. That is a scary position to take; to willfully continue living your life behind the big Black Door, and then die and be eternally labeled as a Satan worshiper by default. Think about it, you thought you were just exercising your God-given right to be a non-believer; therefore, you never changed. The Bible says, after death come the judgment. And at that point, I really think it will be too late to say I want to change and start believing. That is why we need to make our election sure, because one day we are all going to be held accountable for our actions in this life.

Sowing and Reaping

Chapter 19

The Holy Bible gives numerous examples as to the reality of God as the Divine Ruler of the universe and creation. As the Divine Ruler and Source of all, we need to study and learn as much as we can about our all-powerful, all-knowing, and all-present God. Allow me to pick just one of the many attributes of God - His principle of sowing and reaping. Why is this principle so important to know? Because God's Word will not return to Him void. If God said it, it will happen just as He said it would.

In the book of Galatians 6:7-10 we learn, *7"Be not deceived; God is not mocked: for whatsoever a man soweth, that shall he also reap. 8For he that soweth to his flesh shall of the flesh reap corruption; but he that soweth to the Spirit shall of the Spirit reap life everlasting. 9And let us not be weary in well doing: for in due season we shall reap, if we faint not. 10As we have therefore opportunity, let us do well unto all men, especially unto them who are of the household of faith."* God is telling us through the Apostle Paul, who at the time was speaking directly to the church in Galatia, "you will reap what you sow". For example, if you are living a life of pleasure, or living a life that does not recognize Jesus Christ as your Lord and Savior, then you are sowing into the ways of the world as a non-believer. If you put your career, race, family, or your sexual identity above God, you are sowing into things of the flesh and things of this world. People who year after year abuse their bodies with drugs, alcohol, tobacco, and sex will one day begin to reap in their flesh the sins of a life spent satisfying their fleshly cravings. Some may wake up one day with cancer; some will wake up to find out that they have a sexually transmitted disease such as HIV or AIDS. And because they have had many lovers, they will not know where they got the disease.

■ ■ ■

What is HIV? HIV stands for human immunodeficiency virus and is the virus that causes AIDS. This virus is passed from one person to another through blood-to-blood and sexual contact. In addition, infected pregnant women can pass HIV to their baby during pregnancy or delivery, as well as through breast-feeding. People with HIV have what is called HIV infection. Most people will develop AIDS as a result of their HIV infection.

Don't take my warning as a holier-than-thou attitude. Oh no, quite the opposite. I am not passing judgment on anybody; nor can I, because I was just as guilty as the next sinner living a life of sin, and at one time living to please the flesh. It was the mercy and grace of God that saved me and changed my life from being a slave to the flesh. He changed me from being a slave to sin to becoming a slave to His righteousness. I thank the Lord for allowing me to see my sins which were great in the flesh and to repent and change to a life of service to Christ.

The godly principle of sowing and reaping is just one of many confirmations of the reality of God. This principle is just one of many of the irrefutable and immutable laws of God that are embedded in the spiritual scheme of things of His creation. The process of sowing and reaping is what the Lord told Adam in the Garden of Eden after he and Eve had sinned. Genesis 3: 17-19, [17]*"And unto Adam he said, Because thou hast hearkened unto the voice of thy wife, and hast eaten of the tree, of which I commanded thee, saying, Thou shalt not eat of it: cursed is the ground for thy sake; in sorrow shalt thou eat of it all the days of thy life; [18]Thorns also and thistles shall it bring forth to thee; and thou shalt eat the herb of the field; [19]In the sweat of thy face shalt thou eat bread, till thou return unto the ground; for out of it wast thou taken: for dust thou art, and unto dust shalt thou return."*

God is letting Adam know that because of his sin of disobedience in eating of the tree of knowledge of good and evil (Genesis 2:16-17), that the earth is now cursed. As a result of that curse, Adam, and all his descendants after him, would have to work (till) the ground for food. Man would have to sow his seeds and reap the harvest if he wanted to eat bread. The process of sowing and reaping was true then and it is also true today. If a farmer does not plant his seeds in the ground in the spring, he will not have a crop to harvest in the fall to feed is family or to sell to the market. The farmer knows that if he is to reap a good harvest, he needs to plant good seeds.

This process of sowing and reaping also applies to spiritual things as well. Therefore, if you spend all your time in this life sowing into unrighteousness, you will one day reap unrighteousness. Moreover, if you sow into the things of God and His righteousness, you will one day reap the righteousness of His blessings.

Life Behind the White Door

Chapter 20

The key that opens the door and allows one to start living a lifestyle of faith in Jesus Christ, is a requirement for each resident. Life behind the white door comes at a cost. That cost was paid by Jesus who shed His precious blood for all mankind. Life behind the white door begins with the fear of the Lord. As pointed out in Proverb 1: 7, *"The fear of the LORD is the beginning of knowledge: but fools despise wisdom and instruction."*

When you open and walk through the small white door, you will immediately see the evidence and feel the presence of the fruit of the spirit. Yes, this is His home.

1. The spirit of love is there. Love for one another is found everywhere. Racial hatred does not exist here.

2. You will find peace behind this door. Peace that surpasses all understanding is everywhere present.

3. Joy is here. He boldly walks up to you and embraces you and wipes away all your tears as He calmly welcomes you into your new home.

4. Longsuffering is also here. He reassures you that He will walk with you through your pain and suffering. To make you feel at home with this new understanding, He introduces you to Lazarus, to Job, to Daniel and others who suffered for their belief in Jesus but refused to give in to the world demands.

5. Gentleness politely walks up and takes your hand and very softly and gently leads you into your first worship service of God Almighty.

6. As you take your seat in preparation to sing holy praises to the three on the throne - The Father, Son, and Holy Spirit, you feel the presence of Goodness all around you. He just smiles and says "Welcome home".

7. Just as you are beginning to really appreciate all that you are seeing, faith magically appears from nowhere and says, "Through Me is your life-line to God. All things are possible for those who believe, welcome home".

When we seriously study the word of God and begin to labor for Him, we notice a strange transformation that begins to develop. We begin to be more at ease within ourselves, we begin to see the world differently, and we begin to feel His presence. Although we are far from perfect, we begin to be content with our lot.

We will sometimes have days of tremendous doubt regarding our new position in Christ Jesus. We may not feel that God is near us or watching over us as we experience the many trials and tribulations in this life. If we continue to trust Him and to put Him first in our lives, God will give us the strength we need to persevere through the crisis, and we will emerge on the other side stronger for having gone through the situation. That is why it is so important for believers to maintain focus on Jesus.

Please understand this about God. He works in mysterious ways. I do not have all the answers as to how God manifests Himself to all people. I can only say HE IS A MIRACLE WORKER! Nothing escapes Him, no matter how small or insignificant it may seem to you. God knows what you are going through. You just have to believe and trust in Him to see you through the situation. In 2 Chronicles 7:14, the Lord God tells us, *"If my people, which are called by my name, shall humble themselves, and pray, and seek my face, and turn from their wicked ways; then will I hear from heaven, and will forgive their sin, and will heal their land."*

This is the preamble for living life in this world behind the small white door. We are to know who we are! We are not to indulge in anything that is not becoming of a true child of God. We are called to a different standard. Yes, we can live a saved life in a sin-infested world. How do I know this? Because Jesus Christ is our Standard Bearer! He, who was sinless in this world, became sin for us that through His birth, death, resurrection and ascension into heaven, that we, through faith in Him, are redeemed and eternally saved.

Prayer, Study and Meditation

Life behind the small white door is a life of prayer, a life of studying and meditating on the Word of God. It is a life that has been converted and now committed to obedience and keeping the commandments of God. It is a life spent seeking to know and please God. It is a life that is dedicated through faith in Jesus Christ, a life that is based in righteousness and a complete rejection of the things of this world.

Let's discuss a few of the requirements for living life behind the small white door, starting with a life of prayer.

God has established the method of prayer as the way to communicate with Him. Prayer, in the words of the old saints from my child-hood, is the key to Heaven, but it's faith that unlocks the door. Prayer is dialogue between God Almighty and people, especially His people who are called by His Name. Prayer is that invisible substance that makes things unseen, real. Show me a person who is really saved, and I will show you a man or woman that has a mature and very developed prayer life.

When you study the heroes of faith that are found in the Holy Bible, all of them were prayer warriors. In the Old Testament there was Abraham, Isaac, Jacob, Joseph, Moses, Elijah and Elisha, Daniel, David and Solomon. There are many more prayer warriors that I did not mention. In the New Testament, prayer warriors included John the Baptist up to and including Jesus, who prayed all the time. The point I am making here is that all the saints of old had one thing in common; they understood the meaning and value of prayer.

Prayer may be oral or mental, occasional, constant, or formal. Prayer is a "beseeching of the Lord" in Exodus 32:11; "pouring out the soul before the Lord" in 1 Samuel 1:15; "praying and crying to heaven" in 2 Chronicles 32:20; "seeking unto God and making supplication" in Job 8:5; "drawing near to God" in Psalm 73:28; and "bowing the knees" in Ephesians 3:14. Prayer is a belief in the personality of God, His ability and willingness to hold conversation with us, his personal control of all things. There are different kinds of prayers: secret (Matthew 6:6); social, as family prayers, and in social worship; and public, in the service of the sanctuary. Intercessory prayer is encouraged in Numbers 6:23, Job 42:8, Isaiah 62:6, Psalm 122:6, 1 Timothy 2:1, and James 5:14. There are many instances of answered prayer in God's Word.

God has not given us a specific way to pray. As a matter of fact, there are no rules that I could find anywhere in Scripture that mandate exactly when and how to pray. There is reference made to kneeling in prayer, of bowing and falling prostrate in prayer, and the spreading out the hands, or of standing. Our Lord and Savior Jesus Christ taught His disciples to pray in Matthew 6:9-13 this way: *"After this manner therefore pray ye: Our Father which art in heaven, Hallowed be thy name. ¹⁰Thy kingdom come. Thy will be done in earth, as it is in heaven. ¹¹Give us this day our daily bread. ¹²And forgive us our debts, as we forgive our debtors. ¹³And lead us not into temptation, but deliver us from evil: For thine is the kingdom, and the power, and the glory, forever."* Amen

If we accept the "Lord's Prayer", which is rather a model or pattern of prayer to be offered up, we have no special form of prayer for general use given us in scripture. The following lists of people are but a few examples of God's people who prayed their own unique prayer to God. Not only did God hear their prayer, He answered them.

- Abraham's servant prayed to God, and God directed him to the person who should be a wife to his master's son and heir. (Genesis 24:10-20)

- Jacob prayed to God and God inclined the heart of his irritated brother so that they met in peace and friendship. (Genesis 32:24-30; Genesis 33:1-4)

- Samson prayed and God showed him a well where he quenched his burning thirst, and lived to judge Israel. (Judges 15:18-20)

- David prayed, and God defeated the counsel of Ahithophel. (2 Samuel 15:31; 2 Samuel 16:20-23; 2 Samuel 17:14-23).

- Daniel prayed and God enabled him both to tell Nebuchadnezzar his dream and to give the interpretation of it. (Daniel 2:16-23)

- Nehemiah prayed, and God inclined the heart of the king of Persia to grant him leave of absence to visit and rebuild Jerusalem. (Nehemiah 1:11; Nehemiah 2:1-6)

- Esther and Mordecai prayed, and God defeated the purpose of Haman, and saved the Jews from destruction. (Esther 4:15-17; Esther 6:7, 8)

- The believers in Jerusalem prayed and God opened the prison doors and set Peter at liberty, when Herod had resolved upon his death. (Acts 12:1-12)

- Paul prayed that the thorn in his flesh might be removed, and his prayer brought a large increase of spiritual strength, while the thorn remained. (2 Corinthians 12:7-10)

"Prayer is like the dove that Noah sent forth, which blessed him not only when it returned with an olive-leaf in its mouth, but when it never returned at all"—Easton's Illustrated Dictionary

There is a lesson to learn about prayer. If you want to get closer to God, you must learn to bend the knees, humble yourself, and from an honest and contrite spirit, seek Him. Pour out your spirit to Him; tell Him you love Him and value His control over your life. Always remember, when you pray sincerely to the God of creation, He hears your prayers. Therefore when you pray to Him, mean what you are saying because as mentioned in Proverbs 15:8, *"The sacrifice of the wicked is an abomination to the Lord: but the prayer of the upright is his delight."* The God to whom you are praying can discern the difference between prayers from the just, and those who are just going through the motion.

Why is it important for a disciple and child of God to study and meditate on the Word of God? The Bible is full of reasons, and gives many examples as to the why we are to labor in the Word. Allow me to share with you a few of the Biblical references that are my favorites. These help to keep me focused on what "thus said the Lord":

2 Timothy 2:15, *"Study to shew thyself approved unto God, a workman that needeth not to be ashamed, rightly dividing the word of truth."* I love this verse! How can we know what "thus saith the Lord", if we do not take the time to study and meditate on His Word? Just going to church on Sunday, and listening to your pastor alone will not help you to grow in the Word. You must develop good study habits daily.

James 1:22-25, *[22]But be ye doers of the word, and not hearers only, deceiving your own selves. [23]For if any be a hearer of the word, and not a doer, he is like unto a man beholding his natural face in a glass: [24]For he beholdeth himself, and goeth his way, and straightway forgetteth what manner of man he was. [25]But whoso looketh into the perfect law of liberty, and continueth therein, he being not a forgetful hearer, but a doer of the work, this man shall be blessed in his deed."*

These verses help me to know that talk is cheap. If you are saved, you will not be a hearer of the Word only on Sunday and then the rest of the week return to your old sinful nature. If the only time you can live a saved life is the few hours you are at church, you need to get busy getting to know Jesus. You start by repenting of all your sins through faith in Jesus and ask Jesus to come into your life. Make a commitment to seek Him through prayer, study and meditation.

I love to quote some of the older saints from my youth, especially my mother. She always said; "If you are saved, you will not have to waste your time trying to convince other people that you are saved. They will see it for themselves." Being saved will manifest itself in a changed lifestyle. You will become less self-centered and more centered on the things of God. I have found this to be a reality in my life. Psalm 119:105 says, *"Your word is a lamp to my feet and a light to my path."* Not only is the Word of God a shelter in the storm of life, it is a light unto our path. If we follow His Word, it will lead us and teach us the correct way to go. What a joy it is to trust and follow in Him!

We read in 2 Timothy 3:16-17, *"All Scripture is breathed out by God and profitable for teaching, for reproof, for correction, and for training in righteousness, that the man of God may be competent, equipped for every good work."* The Word of God is our instruction book in righteous training. How can we say that we value the things of God without first studying and learning and then actually doing those things that God loves? How can we be an effective witness for Jesus Christ unless we are thoroughly grounded in Him and His Word? Matthew 4:4 tells us, *"But he answered, it is written, Man shall not live by bread alone, but by every word that comes from the mouth of God."*

There is more to this life than having a full belly of food while being starved spiritually. Actually, it is more profitable for man to crave the spiritual food and the things of God than to focus only on satisfying the body's physical need for food. We read in1 Peter 2:2, *"Like newborn infants, long for the pure spiritual milk, that* by *it you may grow up into salvation"*. Another passage in Job says, Job 23:12, *"I have not departed from the commandment of his lips; I have treasured the words of his mouth more than my portion of food."*

The first chapter of Revelation shares the importance of reading and studying the Word, *"Blessed is the one who reads aloud the words of this prophecy, and blessed are those who hear, and who keep what is written in it, for the time is near."* He who has ears let him hear what the Lord has spoken. The day of the Lord will come. The Bible says it will come like a thief in the night. To be foretold is to be forewarned. Don't let God catch you with your work undone. God's Word will come to pass, and no man will know the hour or the day of the fulfillment of this prophecy as outlined in the book of Revelation. Hear the Word of the Lord in the scriptures below:

2 Peter 1:5 - *"For this very reason, make every effort to supplement your faith with virtue, and virtue with knowledge."* Psalm 119:1- **1** Blessed *are* the undefiled in the way, who walk in the law of the LORD. **2** Blessed *are* they that keep his testimonies, *and that* seek him with the whole heart. **3** They also do no iniquity: they walk in his ways

Ephesians 6:10-17 - *"Finally, be strong in the Lord and in the strength of his might. Put on the whole armor of God that you may be able to stand against the schemes of the devil. For we do not wrestle against flesh and blood, but against the rulers, against the authorities, against the cosmic powers over this present darkness, against the spiritual forces of evil in the heavenly places. Therefore take up the whole armor of God that you may be able to withstand in the evil day, and having done all, to stand firm. Stand therefore, having fastened on the belt of truth, and having put on the breastplate of righteousness.*"

The Enemy of our Soul

Chapter 21

This book is not about the devil. It is a book about the glory of our Risen Savior, the Lord Jesus Christ, the Anointed of God, and His Holy Spirit. However, it would be unwise and incomplete to not discuss how the enemy of our soul operates. Oh yes, make no mistake about it, the devil is our enemy. The devil hates God. Not only does he hate God, he hates what God loves – us! We are God's creation and the devil wants to destroy us because he knows how much God loves us. The devil knows that God loves us so much that He sent His only Son, Jesus to die for us.

If people would take the time to reflect and truly understand the spiritual significance of Jesus dying on the cross to save a sinful soul like me and you, we would drop our heads in complete shame. People listen, do not ever entertain the idea or play around with the notion that the devil and his demons are not real. They are very real. The Bible lists many instances of demons and people who are possessed by evil spirits. One question might be asked, "Where do these evil demons come from?" The best answer that I believe is that the demons are really fallen angels or created beings. This is pointed out in Jude 1:6 which states: *"And the angels which kept not their first estate, but left their own habitation, he hath reserved in everlasting chains under darkness unto the judgment of the great day."* It is my belief and understanding that these angels were turned into demonic spirits when they rebelled against God and followed the evil one – the devil. This spiritual event was recorded and revealed to us in Revelation: 12:3-14, *3"And there appeared another wonder in heaven; and behold a great red dragon, having seven heads and ten horns, and seven crowns upon his heads. 4And his tail drew the third part of the stars of heaven, and did cast them to the earth: and the dragon stood before the woman which was ready to be delivered, for to devour her child as soon as it was born. 5And she brought forth a man child, who was to rule all nations with a rod of iron:*

and her child was caught up unto God, and to his throne. [6]And the woman fled into the wilderness, where she hath a place prepared of God that they should feed her there a thousand two hundred and threescore days. [7]And there was war in heaven: Michael and his angels fought against the dragon; and the dragon fought and his angels, [8]And prevailed not; neither was their place found any more in heaven. [9]And the great dragon was cast out, that old serpent, called the Devil, and Satan, which deceiveth the whole world: he was cast out into the earth, and his angels were cast out with him. [10]And I heard a loud voice saying in heaven, now is come salvation, and strength, and the kingdom of our God, and the power of his Christ: for the accuser of our brethren is cast down, which accused them before our God day and night. [11]And they overcame him by the blood of the Lamb, and by the word of their testimony; and they loved not their lives unto the death".

The great dragon is a reference to Lucifer, the shining one, or as some say, the morning star. However, God called him the "anointed cherub that covereth." This angel that later became the devil through his pride, rebellion and disobedience was, at one time, a powerful angelic being until iniquity was found in him (Ezekiel 28:11-17).

God tells us through His prophet, Ezekiel, that this powerful angel named Lucifer was not only powerful, he was also beautiful. It was his beauty that, according to the prophet Isaiah, found in chapter 14:12-17, that got him into trouble: [12]*"How art thou fallen from heaven, O Lucifer, son of the morning? How art thou cut down to the ground, which didst weaken the nations! [13]For thou hast said in thine heart, I will ascend into heaven, and I will exalt my throne above the stars of God: I will sit also upon the mount of the congregation, in the sides of the north: [14]I will ascend above the heights of the clouds; I will be like the most High. [15]Yet thou shalt be brought down to hell, to the sides of the pit. [16]They that see thee shall narrowly look upon thee, and consider thee, saying, is this the man that made the earth to tremble, that did shake kingdoms."*

It was pride and arrogance of Lucifer that caused him to become lifted in pride which corrupted his wisdom to the point that he thought that he should receive the same glory that was due Almighty God. That was a big mistake! God is God all by himself, and He says all through bible scripture that he will not share His Glory with another. The devil was a powerful and beautiful angelic being, but he lost sight of one thing. He is a created being just like the rest of God's creation. He forgot to see and to respect his creator as the "all power" behind his limited power. Therefore God told him, *"I will destroy thee, O covering cherub, from the midst on the stones of fire."*

The enemy that we face is real. We cannot defeat him or his demons in our own strength. We need to know how to fight and win each and every confrontation that is brought to us. We fight and overcome them with the Word of God and utilizing the armor that He gives us. Make no mistake, our enemy, Satan, and his demons, are real and they will and can do you harm if you take them on in your own strength.

The first thing one must understand is we cannot fight a spiritual war by using natural or materialist weapons. We are doomed to fail each and every time and the devil knows this and laughs at us for trying. Trying to fight the devil in our own strength is like going into a gunfight with a pocket knife. It is like fighting a war with a pellet gun and the enemies are using AK47s. The point is you are going to die! God tells us through the prophet Paul that we are to use spiritual weapons to fight a spiritual battle. We are to put on the full armor of God as explained to us in Ephesians 6: 11-18. Paul tells us to: *"Put on the whole armor of God, which ye may be able to stand against the wiles of the devil. [12]For we wrestle not against flesh and blood, but against principalities, against powers, against the rulers of the darkness of this world, against spiritual wickedness in high places. [13]Wherefore take unto you the whole armor of God that ye may be able to withstand in the evil day, and having done all, to stand. [14]Stand therefore, having your loins girt about with truth, and having on the breastplate of righteousness; [15]And your feet shod with the preparation of the gospel of peace; [16]Above all, taking the shield of faith, wherewith ye shall be able to quench all the fiery darts of the wicked. [17]And take the helmet of salvation, and the sword of the Spirit, which is the word of God: [18]praying always with all prayer and supplication in the Spirit, and watching thereunto with all perseverance and supplication for all saints."*

Pay close attention to that one word that the devil hates in verse 18. Paul tells us to **pray** always in supplication in the Spirit. The devil hates it when we pray to God because he knows full well who we are praying too. He also knows that God hears the prayers of the righteous, and that the footsteps of a righteous man are ordered by God. The devil knows that prayer changes things. Yes, the devil hates it when we pray, because he knows there is nothing that he can do to stop God from responding to our prayers, especially if we are following God in spirit and truth. The devil hates prayer!

One lesson in particular teaches us just how much power the devil has and what he will do to discourage us from praying. In Daniel 10:11-14, we learn that the devil hindered the response to Daniel prayers for twenty-one days. The angel, Gabriel, was in a battle with the devil and his demons, and the Archangel, Michael, had to come and help. This is a powerful story of the "unseen spiritual" war that is taking place every day around us. We should take stock of this clash and stay close to God; otherwise, we could end up becoming an easy casualty or pawn in this war. The devil's plans are unmistakable. He wants to destroy us because we choose to worship and serve God and not him. *11 "And he said unto me, O Daniel, a man greatly beloved, understand the words that I speak unto thee, and stand upright: for unto thee am I now sent. And when he had spoken this word unto me, I stood trembling. 12Then said he unto me, Fear not, Daniel: for from the first day that thou didst set thine heart to understand, and to chasten thyself before thy God, thy words were heard, and I am come for thy words. 13But the prince of the kingdom of Persia withstood me one and twenty days: but, lo, Michael, one of the chief princes, came to help me; and I remained there with the kings of Persia. 14Now I am come to make thee understand what shall befall thy people in the latter days: for yet the vision is for many days. "*

The devil comes but to steal, kill and destroy. But he also oppresses us. Another word for oppression is "to be vexed". The devil seeks to oppress the people of God to control us. In 1 Peter 5:8 we learn the devil's agenda is that of a roaring lion. *"Be sober, be vigilant; because your adversary the devil, as a roaring lion, walketh about, seeking whom he may devour."* The devil knows that if we allow him to oppress us, he can cause us to take our focus off Jesus and put it on him. We will begin to sink in the deep waters of despair and tribulation if we take our focus off of Jesus. This is what happened to Peter when he asked Jesus to bid him to come to Him by walking on the water. He was fine as long as he kept his focus on Jesus and did not doubt. The same is true for us today. It does not matter what we are going through, we are to remain focused on the Lord and obey Him.

The next tool that the devil uses to distract us is obsession. The definitions of the word obsession are: passion, allure, absorption, attraction, addiction, compulsion, craving, dependence and need. The devil knows that if he can hook us on the pleasures of life, the lust of the eyes, the lust of the flesh and things that are associated with the world's pride of life, he can entangle us and control us in a web-demonic deception. The devil knows what he is doing. He is skilled at his job and most people fail to realize that they are operating under the control of a demonic spirit by the name of obsession.

I smoked cigarettes for years and it seemed that I was powerless to stop this addiction. I made the mistake of telling Jesus one day that I was powerless to stop this habit. Not too long after I made my confession to Jesus, I discovered that I had prostate cancer. I immediately quit smoking cigarettes. I have now been cigarette-free for years. Don't tell God what you cannot do, because He knows how to make you do just that. You might not like how He gets your attention on the thing that you are allowing to control you. Just ask Jonah! Just ask me! I am in remission after having a lengthy forty-two-week radiation treatment and so far so good. The point: be careful when you tell God what you can and cannot do. I love my God because He showed me that He does answer prayer and that He rewards those who diligently seek Him. But never fail to forget, He is God!

There are many people who the devil controls through their obsession. The crack cocaine and drug users, people obsessed with power, money, sex, race, and politics. The list is endless. Whatever controls you and you can't live without, it is your god. The only solution or cure for that demonic obsession is the Blood of Jesus. The third tool that the devil uses to control us is possession. Another word for possession is control, ownership, and custody. In short, the devil wants to take possession of something that is not his. He wants to control and take ownership of God's creation – us! This is why the devil is called a thief. The devil comes but to steal, and if he can't steal you, then he wants to kill you, and if God does not allow him to take your life, he wants to destroy your life.

When the devil takes possession over a person's life, that person is no longer responding to what is righteous in God's eyes. One clear example of demonic possession is found in one of Jesus disciples, Judas Iscariot.

We learn of this possession from the Apostle John 13, verses 18-27 which occurred during Jesus' Last Supper. Now consider this, if the devil can take possession of one of Jesus' disciples, what would stop him from taking possession over us? One word answer: The Holy Spirit! Judas was never converted. He was a hypocrite, masquerading as a disciple. Lesson to learn: We better be careful trying to be something that we are not, especially in spiritual concerns. The devil is no match for the Holy Spirit and he knows it. The devil cannot move in and force the Holy Spirit of God to move out of the mind and body of a true believer. The devil does have power, but God has all power! God stands on His Word. He says that *"I will never leave you or forsake you"*. He also said that *"I will send you my Spirit that will lead and guide you in truth."* The devil will never lead and guide you in truth, because he is the Father of Lies!

John 13:18-27 says, *18"I speak not of you all: I know whom I have chosen: but that the scripture may be fulfilled, He that eateth bread with me hath lifted up his heel against me. 19Now I tell you before it come, that, when it is come to pass, ye may believe that I am he. 20Verily, verily, I say unto you, He that receiveth whomsoever I send receiveth me; and he that receiveth me receiveth him that sent me. 21When Jesus had thus said, he was troubled in spirit, and testified, and said, Verily, verily, I say unto you, that one of you shall betray me. 22Then the disciples looked one on another, doubting of whom he spake. 23Now there was leaning on Jesus' bosom one of his disciples, whom Jesus loved. 24Simon Peter therefore beckoned to him, that he should ask who it should be of whom he spake. 25He then lying on Jesus' breast saith unto him, Lord, who is it? 26Jesus answered, He it is, to whom I shall give a sop, when I have dipped it. And when he had dipped the sop, he gave it to Judas Iscariot, the son of Simon. 27And after the sop Satan entered into him. Then said Jesus unto him, what thou doest, do quickly"*.

One last thought in reference to demon possession. Who or what is getting the glory out of your life? A truthful answer to any to these questions below will indicate who we are serving.

- How much time to do you spend in reading the Word of God?

- How much time do you spend in humble church activities?

- How much time do you spend talking about Jesus to the members of your household, especially the younger members of your families?

- How much time to you spend witnessing to souls that do not know Jesus in the pardoning of their sins?

- How much time do you spend in prayer and fasting?

- How much time do you spend in activities that are designed to help the poor, the widows, orphans, seniors and those incarcerate?

Allow me to give one more observation of what I consider a case of demon possession that occurred recently. There is a case and a trial underway now in the city of Naperville, Illinois. This a case about a suburban Chicago, Illinois woman accused of repeatedly stabbing her seven-year old son and a five-year girl that she was babysitting. When questioned by police as to why she did what she did, her response was "that she was killing the devil and was saving the children from a poisoned world." This horrible crime took place in the city of Naperville October 30, 2012, a day before the celebration of the satanic holiday-Halloween. How sad is it for two innocent kids to die, but to die at the hands of a devil-controlled mind is hard to grasp. Unfortunately, there usually are one or more deaths reported around the pagan celebration of Halloween each year.

In the Naperville murder, a forty-one year old woman pleaded not guilty to the crimes. Police however, found the children in a blood–spattered bedroom where prosecutors say the woman forced them to kneel and pray before stabbing them dozens of times as they begged for their lives. Police documents the statement of the murderer as saying "that she saw the devil" that day and went crazy. An example of a lesson learned here is this invisible war between the enemy of our soul, the devil, and God's creation is real! However, if God is our Shield, we are not to be afraid. God is my portion and in Him will I put my trust. Psalm 1:2, "But his delight is in the law of the Lord, and on his law he meditates day and night".

Committed to Obedience

Chapter 22

The Apostle Paul's life is a good example of a man who God used to further the kingdom of God. Paul wrote thirteen epistles to the early church and his writings make up one-fourth of the books of the New Testament. Paul was one of the biggest non-believers of the way, as it was called in Jesus' day. Saul, as a Pharisee, believed in the God that Moses talked about in the first five books of the Bible. However, this same apostle was an agnostic when it came to understanding and accepting Jesus as God in the flesh. (An agnostic is a person who believes that nothing is known or can be known of the existence or nature of God; a person who claims neither faith nor disbelief in God.) It was not until Paul had an up-close and personal encounter with Jesus that he was converted.

After Paul's conversion, he became committed and was obedient even unto death to the calling of Jesus Christ on his life. This man went on several missionary journeys and experienced many hardships that would have caused a lesser dedicated man to change his occupation. Paul was a truly committed vessel unto the Lord. I highly encourage you to study the work of this great Apostle of God. He left us a great legacy to follow.

Honoring and Keeping our God's Commandments.

There are many examples of God-fearing men who dedicated their lives to keep the commandments of God. Moses is an example of a man who truly stands out to me. Moses was born into poverty during a time when the Pharaoh of Egypt wanted to kill all the newborn male babies in an insane attempt to control the population of the Jews that were living in bondage in their land. Pharaoh was afraid of the numbers and might of the growing Israelites. Therefore, he put the Jews under extreme bondage and slavery so they could not rebel against him. It was during the period of extreme cruelty to God's people that the Pharaoh of Egypt issued orders to have all of the male Israelite children killed that were being born. Moses was born during this time. However, the mother of Moses hid him for three months so he would not be found and killed by Pharaoh. After three months, his mother placed him in an ark made out of bulrushes, and placed him down by the reeds along the river banks hoping someone else would find him and raise him up safely. It was God who allowed the daughter of the Pharaoh to be the one who actually found him down by the river as she was getting ready to wash herself.

She found a Hebrew woman who was, in reality, the mother of Moses, and asked her to nurse him during the nursing stage. The story of Moses is a beautiful and inspiring story that reveals the power of God controlling the destiny of man.

Moses was educated in the wisdom of the Egyptians of his generation. He was a leader in the house of Pharaoh. One day he saw the abuse of his brethren, the Jews. He killed a soldier for cruelty to a Jew. After this was discovered, he fled Egypt and spent the next forty years in the desert. It was during this time that he had a personal encounter with God. God sent Moses on a journey back into the very country he had fled to deliver his people out of bondage.

Moses is credited with God's help in delivering the Ten Commandments to the people after they re-grouped in the desert at Mount Sinai. The people were disobedient and as a result of their murmuring and complaining and lack of faith, they were judged by God as being unfit to enter into the land that He had promised them. They endured forty years of living in the desert for their insubordination to Moses and to God. The majority of people who left Egypt died in the desert, not because God did not love them, but because of their disobedience. The older generation perished. Lesson learned from the Jews wandering forty years in the desert: Disobedience to God comes with a terrible price.

Seeking to Know and Please God

David is another example I want to look at as being the model of a man who is seeking to know and please God. I am not going to focus on David's mistakes, his life and the events surrounding the affair that he had with Bathsheba, or the death of her husband, Uriah. Yes, those are qualities that a man of God should not strive for, but what most intrigues me about David is what God said about him in Acts 13:22, *"And when he had removed him, he raised up unto them David to be their king; to whom also he gave testimony, and said, I have found David the son of Jesse, a man after mine own heart, which shall fulfill all my will."*

God sees past our faults. David had a heart to seek and to do God's will. David's life before God is truly awesome. At a young age, David learned to trust in God. It was this trust that allowed him to kill a lion and a bear. It was this faith in God that allowed him to defeat the Philistine giant, Goliath, in a battle using just five smooth stones. He only needed just one to kill the giant. David was the second King of Israel. Under his leadership, Israel was a united kingdom. David was a warrior, but he never tried to hurt Saul, the first King of Israel, even when Saul was trying to kill him at least 24 times. He never retaliated, but trusted God to deal with Saul.

In 2 Samuel 5:7, David captured and subdued the city of Jerusalem from the Jebusites and made it the capitol. David went on to subdue other nations who opposed him. He gained control of much of the land that God had promised his forefathers. David is mentioned as the greatest King of Israel; a King from whom the Son of God, Jesus, would come.

Dedicated through Faith in Jesus Christ.

John the Baptist fulfilled the description of one dedicated through faith in Jesus Christ. Many books have been written about him. This man was born to serve our Lord and Savior Jesus Christ. The one thing that I most admire about John the Baptist was his unselfish loyalty and devotion to Jesus Christ. John never tried to usurp Jesus' authority. He was never jealous; he never tried to hold people back from following him instead of Jesus. He always made it clear that he was not worthy to tie the shoes of our Master. In Matthew 3:11 John wrote, *"I indeed baptize you with water unto repentance: but he that cometh after me is mightier than I, whose shoes I am not worthy to bear: he shall baptize you with the Holy Ghost, and with fire."* John preached the message of repentance with fire and determination. His message never wavered or failed to convey whose side he was on. When he was challenged by the Jewish leaders of his day, he stood on the Word of God and was obedient even unto death.

The most important example of a life behind the small white door is our Lord and Savior, Jesus Christ. Jesus Christ set the standard for all mankind to follow regarding righteousness and seeking to do the will of His Father, God Almighty. Jesus paid the price for man's redemption. We belong to Him! I, for one, just want to say thank you, Lord. We can never repay Jesus for what He did for us! These words that were spoken through the Apostle Paul in 1 Corinthians 15:55–58, *"O death, where is thy sting? O grave, where is thy victory? 56The sting of death is sin; and the strength of sin is the law. 57But thanks be to God, which giveth us the victory through our Lord Jesus Christ. 58Therefore, my beloved brethren, be ye stedfast, unmoveable, always abounding in the work of the Lord, forasmuch as ye know that your labour is not in vain in the Lord."*

When we commit our lives to Jesus, we do not have to fear death. Yes, we all at some point in this life will die. Death does not discriminate. He cares nothing about your money or position in life. It does not matter to him what race you are, your gender, age, culture; it all means absolutely nothing to him. When it is your time to die the game is over. Or is it?

The Bible tells us in Ephesians 2:8-9 *"For by grace are ye saved through faith; and that not of yourselves: it is the gift of God: Not of works, lest any man should boast"*. This tells me that my faith in God through His Son Jesus, who lives in us through the indwelling power of the Holy Spirit, has sealed us unto the Day of Judgment. My life lived in Jesus Christ is not "wishful thinking" or daydreaming, but is based on the infallible Word of God. I will therefore, *"trust in the Lord and lean not to my own understanding. I will acknowledge him in all my ways and actions, and allow him to direct my path"*. (Proverb 3:5-6)

My cousin Essie, a retired Navy Lt. Commander, taught me to appreciate the beauty and spiritual truth of Proverbs 3:5-6. She is such a humble and bright child of God. She is just a treasure to be around, because she always focuses on the positive things in life. She is completely devoted to God and it shows in everything she does. She puts God first in her life. She is an example of a young lady who has learned the wisdom of putting God first in her life as she continues to live her life in spiritual order behind the small white door.

Jesus is our Role Model to follow. We are to strive and live a life that is pleasing to Him. We are to yield our bodies as living sacrifices unto Him. We are to live a holy life because He who created us is holy. We are to live a righteous life and completely reject the things of this world, and the things the world loves. We are to walk away from the sins of the flesh. Money, power, and sex are inherently neither bad nor evil. I am saying that if your life is controlled by them, and they have become an idol to you, then you are on the wrong side of the eternal life equation. As children of the Kingdom, we must always know who we are. Jesus paid for our salvation with His precious blood. Nothing can ever take precedence over Him in our life. He is our life! Most people are familiar with the scriptures of John 3:16-18. It says: *"For God so loved the world that he gave his only begotten Son, that whosoever believeth in him should not perish, but have everlasting life. [17]For God sent not his Son into the world to condemn the world; but that the world through him might be saved. [18]He that believeth on him is not condemned: but he that believeth not is condemned already, because he hath not believed in the name of the only begotten Son of God."*

These few verses sum up the reason for committing our life to Jesus. He paid our sin debt. A debt that He did not owe, yet willingly endured the cross, as was pointed out to us in Hebrews 12: 2, *"Looking unto Jesus the author and finisher of our faith; who for the joy that was set before him endured the cross, despising the shame, and is set down at the right hand of the throne of God"*.

I am completely ashamed of each and every sin that I have ever committed in my life. When I stop and consider what God actually did for me, it makes me want to hang my head in shame, at all the dumb things that I allowed myself to do. His Son died that I might live eternally with Him. How many people do you know that will die that you might live? I do not know of anyone. Some might say they will, but we all know "talk is cheap." Jesus' love for us is truly beyond human comprehension.

■ ■ ■

The Sin God Hates

Chapter 23

What is pride and why are we to guard against pride? Can pride actually hurt us? Some will tell you that having a sense of pride is a good thing and is part of the nature of man and is a requirement for successful living. However, it would behoove us to stop and take a closer look at the word "pride" and try to see it and understand it from the prospective of our Creator.

One Bible definition of pride is, "The undue confidence in and attention to one's own skill, accomplishment, state, possession, or position." Pride is easier to recognize than to define, easier to recognize in others than in oneself." (Holman Illustrated Bible Dictionary) Anything the Lord God Almighty hates, you can rest assured that we should hate it as well. Why? Who can provide better counsel than God Almighty? Take for example what He said in Proverbs 6: 16–19. He spoke through His servant Solomon and shared the following wisdom with us: *16"These six things doth the LORD hate: yea, seven are an abomination unto him: 17A proud look, a lying tongue, and hands that shed innocent blood, 18 An heart that deviseth wicked imaginations, feet that be swift in running to mischief, 19A false witness that speaketh lies, and he that soweth discord among brethren".* Notice the first of the six things that God hates is pride. Therefore, I should also hate it and do all that I can to make sure that pride does not rule or control my life. I will also look at the remaining negative human traits and do all that I can to not let any of them have dominion over my nature. The only way that I cannot be like any of the six things that God hates, is to be truly committed and stand on the Word of God.

Why do you think that God hates pride so much? Let me try to answer that spiritually with Bible references. Starting with the prophecy of Isaiah 14:12-16, we learn that pride was the downfall of Lucifer and the Babylon king who exalted himself as a god. These verses say: *12 "How art thou fallen from heaven, O Lucifer, son of the morning? How art thou cut down to the ground, which didst weaken the nations! 13For thou hast said in thine heart, I will ascend into heaven, I will exalt my throne above the stars of God: I will sit also upon the mount of the congregation, in the sides of the north: 14I will ascend above the heights of the clouds; I will be like the most High. 15Yet thou shalt be brought down to hell, to the sides of the pit. 16They that see thee shall narrowly look upon thee, and consider thee, saying, is this man that made the earth to tremble, that did shake kingdoms".* Jesus said in Luke 10:18, *"And he said unto them, I beheld Satan as lightning fall from heaven".*

Regarding pride, we learn from Ezekiel 28: 11–18, that God is talking to a human king that is under the control of Satan. God said to the devil through the man the following, *"Moreover the word of the LORD came unto me, saying, 12Son of man, take up a lamentation upon the king of Tyrus, and say unto him, Thus saith the Lord GOD; Thou sealest up the sum, full of wisdom, and perfect in beauty. 13Thou hast been in Eden the garden of God; every precious stone was thy covering, the sardius, topaz, and the diamond, the beryl, the onyx, and the jasper, the sapphire, the emerald, and the carbuncle, and gold: the workmanship of thy tabrets and of thy pipes was prepared in thee in the day that thou wast created. 14Thou art the anointed cherub that covereth; and I have set thee so: thou wast upon the holy mountain of God; thou hast walked up and down in the midst of the stones of fire. 15Thou wast perfect in thy ways from the day that thou wast created, till iniquity was found in thee. 16By the multitude of thy merchandise they have filled the midst of thee with violence, and thou hast sinned: therefore I will cast thee as profane out of the mountain of God: and I will destroy thee, O covering cherub, from the midst of the stones of fire. 17Thine heart was lifted up because of thy beauty, thou hast corrupted thy wisdom by reason of thy brightness: I will cast thee to the ground, I will lay thee before kings, that they may behold thee. 18Thou hast defiled thy sanctuaries by the multitude of thine iniquities, by the iniquity of thy traffick; therefore will I bring forth a fire from the midst of thee, it shall devour thee, and I will bring thee to ashes upon the earth in the sight of all them that behold thee".*

It was pride, the original sin, which led Adam and Eve to sin in the Garden of Eden (Genesis 3:6). It was the sin of pride in the form of jealousy that was the source of the first murder. (Genesis 4: 6–9) And yes, Satan had his hand in these events that directly led to the murder of Abel at the hands of his brother Cain.

Man is tested by the praise that he receives. Proverbs 27:21 says, *"As the fining pot for silver, and the furnace for gold; so is a man to his praise"*. In other words, the things that cause you to glory in are the things that you praise. For example, a millionaire or billionaire is someone who loves and praises money, wealth and power. There may be many other things that they praise, but having achieved vast wealth is the one thing that they most cherish. Unfortunately, large sums of money can work to create a kind of pride of spirit that blinds some people to the realities of life. They fail to understand the needs of the poor and depending on how prideful they are, many rich people simply do not care about the concerns of the poor and oppressed. The super-rich cannot see the poor as anything but an eyesore. Most of them think that the poor are lazy and don't want to work. They cringe when they are dressed up to go to some highly celebrated event and, by chance, if they actually meet a homeless man asking them for a hand. They will draw away as if the man or woman has leprosy. Heaven forbid if the beggar accidently touches the woman; she will hurry into the ladies room to freshen up to remove the filth from the homeless man's touch. All of these things do not go unnoticed by God.

Remember the story of Lazarus? He begged for crumbs from off the rich man's table? He was so poor that the dogs came to lick the wounds of his sore. But, in the end, when they both died, Lazarus went to heaven and the rich man went to hell. Ironically, the rich man who was in hell was still trying to give commands to Lazarus through Abraham. He asked Abraham to tell Lazarus what to do without addressing Lazarus. That pride of spirit can blind us and lead us straight into hell. The devil is an expert in using our own pride against us. For some, he will hide the sin of pride in racism. Racism is like cancer, if not removed from the body, it will spread and destroy the body. Jesus came to me in a dream one morning to show me how undetected racism destroys the soul of its host. In the vision that came to me on Sunday morning August 8, 2014. I was walking and talking with Jesus in the form of a man. However, at the time I did not know that this man, who I assumed was a normal person, was Jesus. As we went about our business discussing many things, we went into this famously expensive and very well-known department store.

As I looked around to observe my surroundings and looked back at my friend, I now became keenly aware that he had changed himself into a woman, a little old Jewish woman. As we continued to walk in this huge store, we came to a very elegantly dressed woman who appeared to be in her fifties. As Jesus watched this woman, when she came close to him He said in a very warm grandmother's voice. "Excuse me Miss. Could I trouble you to use your cell phone so that I can call store security? I think someone is about to have a heart attack."

The wealthy shopper took a step back, looked at Jesus, and then she looked at me his black friend, and said, "No. I don't want to get involved. I don't have time for that, find someone else." The lady walked off with her nose in the air. As Jesus and I turned to leave, I noticed that I did not see this woman anymore. On our way out of the store, we walked past her out in front of the department store waiting for her limo to come to pick her up. She was having a massive heart attack. As we passed by her lying on the sidewalk, she made eye contact with Jesus and me but it was too late. She died. Jesus was showing me how the sin of racism destroys the character and soul of its host.

Just like in the book of Proverb 15:27 "He that is greedy of gain troubleth his own house". The moral of this short story is that the wealthy woman in the store viewed the old Jewish woman and her black friend with contempt. She did not see them as children of the kingdom. Her racism had spread within her heart and affected her way of thinking. Her thoughts that day were, as long as it was one of them having the heart attack, it was not her concern. Little did she know that she was about to have an encounter with the King of Glory, similar to the "Saul of Tarsus" - Damascus road experience. She was judged according to the sins of her heart and the way she lived her life as a non-believer. He will convince the one race of people that they are superior and therefore are entitled to oppress the other race. This happens every day throughout the world.

Pride is like a snake in the grass. Most of the time it's right by you in the grass but you do not see it until it's too late. Then all of a sudden it will raise its ugly head and try to bite you. But if you are truly rooted and grounded in the Word of God, the bite is harmless. That snake in the grass did not go unnoticed by God. He sometimes will tell us where the snake is, and where to move before the snake strikes. That is the kind of God we serve. He is always with us, because He said: *"I will never leave you or forsake you"*. I have found this to be true, and I stand on His Word. 1 peter 5:8 tells us, *"Be sober, be vigilant; because your adversary the devil, as a roaring lion, walketh about, and seeking whom he may devour"*. I believe that man's pride will lead him to Jesus Christ or away from Christ. When you go away from Christ, you will go straight into the den of the devil. Self-pride tells us that it is okay to be a non-believer. This sin of pride tells us that we are the masters of our own destination. The sin of pride blinds us into not seeing the truth of scripture. The sin of pride blocks spiritual discernment. For example, a major difference between the devil and Jesus is that the devil deceives and destroys life in souls. Jesus quickens and brings dead souls to life.

Do not let self-pride rob and mislead you into a false sense of security by thinking as non–believers do. They incorrectly convince themselves that God is not real. Their large egos won't allow them to stop and look at pride for what it really is. Pride is a tool used by the devil to destroy self. At its core is the belief system that you are entitled and are of more value than the value of others.

Remember as a child growing up, when we accidentally hurt ourselves while playing outside, our parents would clean the wound, put medicine on it, and bandage it to protect the wound from dirt? At some point they would say "leave the bandage off to let some air get to it, and don't you pick at that wound." But just as soon as the wound developed a scab, we would take it off to see if the wound was healed. We just could not keep our hands off that wound. However, it was not until we left the wound alone, and the scab finally came off on its own, that we realized that the flesh was now healed and back to normal.

God heals us of pride and all our sins in a similar manner. When we commit our sinful lives to God, we all give Him an open wound of a "sin infested" life to heal. Our life will not be healed completely until we leave it totally in Jesus' hand, and continue to trust in His Word. As James said in Chapter 1:21-22 *"Wherefore lay apart all filthiness and superfluity of naughtiness, and receive with meekness the engrafted word, which is able to save your souls. But be ye doers of the word and not hearers only, deceive your own selves"*. We must be obedient to the Word of God, through study and learning the Word of God. As disciples of God through Jesus Christ and his Holy Spirit, we are to be more then hearers of the Word. As James told us in his book, we are to be "doers of the Word".

Question: If your church organization, the church that you attend on a regular basis, has more empty seats than full seats, what are you doing to get people to join your assembly? Who are you witnessing to? If you truly love the Lord, then you will be a witness for Him. If your local church assembly has more empty seats than full seats, what is that saying about your local congregation? Yes, we are to be at war against the enemy of God, and not sit back and assume it's the pastor's job to recruit membership and cause the church to grow. It is every Christian's responsibility to witness and invite people to come to know Jesus Christ, especially those who do not yet know Jesus in the pardoning of their sins. If you are walking around telling people of how saved you are, and you walk right past that sinner on the corner, the prostitute on the corner, or that young drug dealer who lives down the street, or you pass by him in your car, do you instinctively get that holier-than-thou attitude and turn your head to look the other way as you pass him?

Signs and Wonders

Chapter 24

As far back as the Old Testament, man has always had a problem believing in anything that he could not physically see. However, faith in God, or to say it another way, having real godly faith, is the ability to believe in spiritual and physical realities without seeing. Conversely, it is because of a saint's belief that God blesses them with the spiritual discernment to see the invisible.

When it comes to signs and wonders from God, seeing them is more often than not, still unbelievable. Why? It's because God makes the impossible – possible. Our human minds are not able to understand or accept all the ramifications of true God-initiated miracles. Ask Job what he learned from his brief conversation with Almighty God. He learned he was not worthy to question God about any of His decisions. This is true for all humanity.

God's signs and wonders are miracles. Notice I did not say magic. Magic is what men like David Copperfield do for a living. They create the illusion of miracles, but in truth, are fabrications and fakes that people pay money to be entertained. God is not in the entertainment business. When He uses a sign or wonder, it is real and truly an awe-inspiring event. It is usually once-in-a-lifetime experience.

Signs

Signs are miracles that have deep meaning or significance. One sign that comes to mind is when God allowed the sun to stand still for a whole day to allow His servant Joshua to defeat the five kings who warred against him at Gibeon. This most beautiful story takes place in Joshua 10:1-13, and demonstrates and provides encouragement for those on the battlefield for God to never give up and to have complete faith in Him. There is nothing He cannot do when you are called and working in your anointing according to

His will. Joshua 10:13 says, *"And the sun stood still, and the moon stayed, until the people had avenged themselves upon their enemies. Is not this written in the book of Joshua? So the sun stood still in the midst of heaven, and hasted not to go down about a whole day"*.

Wonders

Wonders are miracles that cause men to be amazed by their supernatural qualities. The Bible is full of examples of God-initiated wonders. From the ten plagues that God sent against Pharaoh, Jesus turning water into wine, Jesus feeding a multitude of people with just two fishes and a loaf of bread, or the raising of Lazarus from the dead, are just a few of the mighty wonders that God has allowed us to see.

God does the impossible! He is not limited to anything man does or says. He is God Almighty, and He is God all by himself! If you take a look at history, you will see how God has sometimes His sovereignty through signs and wonders. The Creator of the universe does not need man's permission to do this. He does whatever is His good pleasure.

I have discovered that God uses signs and wonders to not only reveal His sovereignty, but to get our attention. He uses signs and wonders to reflect His approval or disapproval of the actions of man. It is His way of showing man the right way to walk which leads to blessings if we follow His divine path or curses if we fail to obey His warning signs. Stop! Think about all the natural phenomena that recorded history can teach us and the marvelous and mysterious signs and wonders of the past that God has revealed to man. Do we ever stop and consider what each of them mean? God is all power. If He wanted to wipe man off the face of the earth, there is no one or any power on earth that could stop Him. But the God of Creation is a God of Love, not evil. We are His creation. That is why He loves us so much that He sent His only begotten Son to earth to die for us so that through faith in the resurrection of Jesus Christ, we can be redeemed and re-establish a right relationship with God the Father. It is this process of salvation that leads us to eternal life with God Almighty.

It is not what we have done. All our so-called man-made power, position, racial identity and ethnicity, means nothing to God. What matters to God is, "do you know my Son, Jesus Christ?" What you did in His name is what matters to God when that great and terrible day comes. I am speaking prophetically of the last day of life on this earth as man. The end of the Tribulation is revealed in Revelation, the Second Advent of our Lord and Savior, Jesus Christ. This will be a day unlike any other day. This day will be preceded by God's signs and wonders from heaven. God is not like man. He does not want anyone to perish and suffer eternal damnation; therefore, He uses signs and wonders to encourage man to change his ways and do what is righteous before God. Some men will see signs and wonders and change their lives. Others will reject them and continue their march like soldier ants following a blind leader straight into hell.

Let's look at some of the signs and wonders that God has used to guide man in the right direction.

1. Noah's Ark was a sign to man that God was about to make a complete end to all the sins of the world that was running rampant in the land during the days that God instructed Noah to begin building the Ark. I can just imagine all the mocking and abuse this great shepherd of the Lord had to endure the whole time he was at work on the most humongous assignment of his time. I can just see the people laughing at him and making fun of his work in progress. A boat out in the desert would give people the sad assurance that it would never be needed. But now we know how the story ended. The boat was needed, and as a result of Noah's obedience to God, he and his family, a total of eight people, were the only humans to survive the old world. There was Noah, his wife and his three sons, Shem, Ham, and Japheth and their wives. (Genesis 6:18-21) (1Peter 3:20 and 2 Peter 2:5)

2. God placed a mark or sign on Cain after he killed his brother Abel. Cain killed Abel because he was jealous of God's acceptance of Abel's sacrifice and rejected Cain's sacrifice. The Bible states in Genesis 4:2-4, that Abel brought fat portions from some of his first flock, and Cain brought some of his fruits (leftovers). God saw Abel's offering with favor because he gave God his best. Therefore, the first ever recorded murder in the world was over jealousy. Beware of the spirit of jealousy. If uncorrected, and removed from your spirit, it

can lead to serious consequences, even to murder. Pray to God to give you strength to overcome this spirit.

After Cain killed his brother Abel, God declared to Cain, *"Now you are under a curse and driven from the ground, which opened its mouth to receive your brother's blood from your hand. When you work the ground, it will no longer yield its crops for you. You will be a restless wanderer on the earth."* (Genesis 4:11-12) In response, Cain lamented, *"My punishment is more than I can bear. Today you are driving me from the land, and I will be hidden from your presence; I will be a restless wanderer on the earth, and whoever finds me will kill me"*. (Genesis 4:13-14) God responded, *"Not so; if anyone kills Cain, he will suffer vengeance seven times over"*. *Then the Lord put a mark on Cain so that no one who found him would kill him."* (Genesis 4:15-16) As far as I know, no one is completely sure what this sign was. We do know that God used this sign to protect the life of Cain, even though Cain took the life of his brother.

3. The great signs and wonders that God used to reveal to Pharaoh and the rest of the world that God Almighty has power over all creation, still mystifies and boggle the mind to this day. When Pharaoh refused to listen to the Word of God as presented to him out of the mouth of Moses, God used signs and wonders to teach Pharaoh and all unbelievers a lesson. That lesson is: God Almighty rules in the affairs of man!

The Bible tells us that as a result of Pharaoh's abuse of God's people in Egypt, they prayed to the Lord for deliverance from under bondage. The Lord heard their cries and sent His servant Moses to secure their release from Pharaoh, King of Egypt. When Pharaoh refused to listen to the God of the Hebrews, God sent ten plagues his way. The plagues are listed in order.

The Plague of Blood - All the water in the Nile River and in Egypt was turned into blood. This is significant because the Egyptians worshiped many gods and one of the gods they worshiped was the god of the Nile River.

The Plague of Frogs –Imagine thousands upon thousands of frogs everywhere. The more you kill them the more they continue to grow. There were frogs in your house, beds, your food pantries, your closets, bathrooms, everywhere you go or look you have to see and deal with slimy frogs. This would make the most hardened unbeliever rethink his or her position on the reality and the power of the God.

The Plague of Lice – Lice are a wingless parasitic insect that lives on the skin of mammals and birds. They can be very annoying. Lice, like the mosquito, are blood suckers. They are very small and hard to see with the naked eye. There are different kinds of lice.

The Plague of Wild Beasts – The hand of the Lord was on the cattle which were in the field, the horses, the asses, the camels, the oxen and the sheep. He told Pharaoh that all his livestock would perish at a set time if he did not do as Moses directed. Because Pharaoh failed to obey, he lost all his livestock. Only the Jews did not suffer the loss of any livestock.

The Plague of Pestilence – This plague is defined as a fatal epidemic disease, ESP. The bubonic plague is an example of a life-altering plague. Some consider the HIV virus and AIDS as a modern day human pestilence problem that has deathly causalities to all who are unfortunate enough to have this dreaded disease. The Bible does not list the specifics of the type of plague that struck Egypt, but it was severe enough to warrant Pharaoh to ask Moses to pray to his God to remove the plague.

The Plague of Skin Disease – In Exodus 8:9, *"The Lord told Moses to take handfuls of ashes of the furnace, and let Moses sprinkle it toward the heavens in the sight of Pharaoh. And it shall become small dust in all the land of Egypt, and shall be a boil breaking forth with blains (an inflamed swelling or sore on the skin) upon man, and upon beast, throughout all the land of Egypt".* Now I don't know of anyone to ever have a boil and think boils are okay. They are not okay! Boils can be very painful, and they are usually in places that people are shy to talk about.

The Plague of Hail – Because Pharaoh refused to obey the Word of God through his servant Moses, there was a very grievous plague. According to the book of Exodus 9:24, it states, *"So there was hail, and fire mingled with the hail, very previous, such as there was none like it in all the land of Egypt since it became a nation".* I think most people have seen hail at some point in their lifetime. However, I don't think many people have seen hail mixed with fire. This hail was very costly to the Egyptians as it killed and destroyed all servants and beasts that were left out in the field even after they were given a warning to not leave them in the field. Those who obeyed the Lord survived. Those who did not believe the warning perished.

The Plague of Locusts - A locust is small grasshopper-like insect with an enormous appetite. They do not seem to have a king, but they follow what looks like a military precision when they band together. When they develop into large swarms, they can do major damage to agricultural crops. This can and has contributed to famine and starvation to humans who must depend on their crops for food. The grievous plague of locusts that attacked Pharaoh's Egypt literally covered the face of the earth. All the trees as well as all the crops were affected. Yet, Pharaoh still refused to let God's people go.

The Plague of Darkness - After Pharaoh refused again to let God's people go, God told Moses to stretch out his hands toward heaven; and God sent a thick darkness into the land of Egypt. The darkness lasted three days and it was so thick that the people could not see each other. Yet, the Jews, God's chosen people, had light. That had to be scary to see. The Jews had the light of day but they could see the blackest of the black for three days over the Pharaoh Kingdom and the land of Egypt. Maybe this is where we get the expression, "it was so dark that you could cut it with a knife".

The Plague of Death - the Slaying of the Firstborn - It pays to listen to people who speak the Word of God with authority. This is especially true when you have seen demonstrated a proof of the power of God working in that person's life. Moses was not acting in his own power and authority. He was acting on the authority of God Almighty. God had given the people of Egypt nine mind-boggling miracles to demonstrate His power. Yet some of them refused to budge. God further hardened their hearts so that He could show His great power to them and the entire world. He told Moses in Exodus 11: 4-7 that He would send one more plague against Egypt. He said, *"And Moses said, Thus saith the LORD, About midnight will I go out into the midst of Egypt: ⁵And all the firstborn in the land of Egypt shall die, from the firstborn of Pharaoh that sitteth upon his throne, even unto the firstborn of the maidservant that is behind the mill; and all the firstborn of beasts. ⁶And there shall be a great cry throughout all the land of Egypt, such as there was none like it, nor shall be like it any more. ⁷But against any of the* *children of Israel shall not a dog move his tongue, against man or beast: that ye may know how that the LORD doth put a difference between the Egyptians and Israel.*

Verse 7 is so gripping to me because the power of the Holy Spirit was working mightily through the Jewish people. Not even a dog, which is considered a dumb animal by man, dared to even bark at the children. We all know how dogs bark and especially during the night they bark at anything that moves. Well, not this night; they mysteriously remained deathly silent. Talk about the power of God! Even animals are smarter than some people who refuse to believe in God. Exodus 12:29-33 describes what happened on this night of "Passover", in which the Lord caused the Death Angel to pass over the homes and lives of the Jewish people. They were spared the loss of the entire firstborn that died as a result of a curse that was placed on the land of Egypt for failing to obey the words of God that was sent to them through the Prophet Moses. God's message was clear, "Let my people go". It was Pharaoh's evil attitude towards God and His people that caused him to try and do battle with the God of Creation. That was and still is an awesome mistake that people continue to make. They let the Jews go and they gave to them so that they did not leave empty-handed. The power of God defies description! He says in Romans 8:31, *"If God be for us, who can be against us"*. This was confirmed in God's deliverance of His people out of the hands of the Egyptians and years of bondage to Pharaoh.

Exodus 12:29-33 reads, *29"And it came to pass, that at midnight the LORD smote all the firstborn in the land of Egypt, from the firstborn of Pharaoh that sat on his throne unto the firstborn of the captive that was in the dungeon; and all the firstborn of cattle. 30And Pharaoh rose up in the night, he, and all his servants, and all the Egyptians; and there was a great cry in Egypt; for there was not a house where there was not one dead. 31And he called for Moses and Aaron by night, and said, Rise up, and gets you forth from among my people, both ye and the children of Israel; and go, serve the LORD, as ye have said. 32 Also take your flocks and your herds, as ye have said, and be gone; and bless me also. 33And the Egyptians were urgent upon the people, that they might send them out of the land in haste; for they said, we be all dead men".*

God gave to the world and forever this will be the greatest sign and wonder. John 3:16-18 says all that needs to be said: *16"For God so loved the world that he gave his only begotten Son, that whosoever believeth in him should not perish, but have everlasting life. [17]For God sent not his Son into the world to condemn the world; but that the world through him might be saved. [18]He that believeth on him is not condemned: but he that believeth not is condemned already, because he hath not believed in the name of the only begotten Son of God".*

Jesus' precious birth was a sign that light had entered the world. Salvation had come to fallen man and a new dispensation was taking the place of the Law. Jesus was the Word of God made flesh and dwelt among us. Johns tells us that we (his disciples) beheld His Glory as the only begotten of the Father. Everything that Jesus did was awe-inspiring. Jesus gave His life for sinners like me, and others, who through faith, have been converted and have given their lives to Him. Jesus, the Son of God, lived as a man among us on earth. It was man that rejected Him and put the Son of God to a shameful death. Jesus, who knew no sin, became sin for the world to satisfy the righteous requirements of atonement for fallen man to be redeemed back to a Holy God.

The Bible is full of many signs and wonders that God gave to man to encourage him to walk in His ways. But man can be stubborn and refuse to obey the Word of God. That is a scary and unsafe place to be. Allow me to borrow a well-used cliché – "It does not matter how big and tough you think you are, your arms are too short to fight with God. You will lose that fight 100% of the time". Signs and wonders are found in many of the books of the Bible from the Old to New Testament. Some are done by the prophets of the Old Testament and some by the apostles of the New Testament. One thing that all the signs and wonders have in common is that they were done for the glory of God and that someone might repent and change his or her ways and serve the Lord. When God allowed a sign or wonder to happen, it was for a specific reason. It was never to impress man or brag about the power of God. It was done to save souls for the Lord. Other examples of what I call signs and wonders of God are: Daniel in the lion's den, David slaying of the giant Goliath, the parting the Red Sea, the strength of Samson, Jesus' Transfiguration and the Holy Ghost descending from heaven in the form of a dove. The list is endless. God has always given man signs and wonders before He did something major.

I need to make a point concerning the signs and wonders of God. On February 15, 2013, man was again reminded that he does not control the universe. On this date a large meteor entered the earth's atmosphere without any warning and landed in a field over Russia.

The report said a chunk of a meteor that exploded over Russia was found in a lake injuring about 1,100 people. The Russians were frightened and some thought the world was coming to an end. Many were injured by flying glass as they stood by their windows to see what was producing the blinding flash of light. The Russian Academy of Science said in a statement, the meteor was estimated to be about 10 tons and 49 feet wide and entered the Earth's atmosphere at a hypersonic speed of at least 33,000 mph and shattered into pieces about 18-32 miles above the ground. One expert said a 10-meter size object already packs the same energy as a nuclear bomb. Amateur video showed an object speeding across the sky about 9:20 a.m. local time, just after sunrise, leaving a thick white contrail and an intense flash. The meteor hit less than a day before Asteroid 2012 DA14 is to make the closest recorded pass of an asteroid to the Earth for a rock of its size -- about 17,150 miles. But the European Space Agency said its experts had determined there was no connection -- just cosmic coincidence. The meteor released several kilotons of energy above the region according to the Russian Science Academy. According to NASA, it was about 15 meters or 49 feet wide before it hit the atmosphere, about one-third the size of the passing asteroid.

Meteor vs. meteorite: What's the difference? Meteors are pieces of space rock, usually from larger comets or asteroids, which enter the Earth's atmosphere. Many burn up by the heat of the atmosphere; those that strike are called meteorites. They often hit the ground at tremendous speed -- up to 18,642 mph. That releases a huge amount of force.

This was how the world got a really up-close and personal look at the meteor as it passed over Russia that day. Thank God it did not land and kill a lot of people. This is why I know it was from the hand of Almighty, since no one was killed. It was a sign and a wonder to man, specifically Russia, that God is about to do something on a grand scale. This is just my opinion. I am not trying to speak for God. No man can speak for God! I am just giving my interpretation of what this sign and wonder might have been. God knows how to get our attention. The meteor that hit Russia means something, and we can know for sure that this sign and wonder was no accident.

We can dance around this all we want to by saying things like, "this was a freak of nature", or "this happens every 10 years or more". This is nothing but man's way of covering up the unknown. Man hates to admit there are things beyond his control because it frightens him to have to admit his lack of control. There are things beyond man's ability to control. The weather of 2011 and 2012 was plagued with a series of tornadoes that were very active for the majority of the year.

Tornadoes are just one of many tools God uses to get our attention. Tornadoes appear at anytime and anywhere and man can do nothing to stop them. All man can do is admire the awesome destruction that tornadoes leave in its wake. This country has had many big and powerful storms which have spawned F5 tornadoes. On May 20, 2013 in the city of Moore, Oklahoma, an F5 tornado struck the city of over 40,000 and completely destroyed it. Over 13,000 homes and two schools, plus area businesses were destroyed. This massive tornado killed thirty-four people and was only on the ground for seventeen minutes.

No one knows why a tornado hits a specific area and avoids another, only God knows that. I will say that when a tornado or any catastrophic event strikes, it is not a freak of nature, and it does not happen without God's knowledge. Nothing ever catches God off guard and surprises Him. He is all knowing. We need to examine our lives and how we live our lives when we see natural catastrophes happening in our land. Perhaps God is letting us know that He is not pleased with our lives. It is my opinion that when we see major natural catastrophes events such as Katrina, the hurricane that hit New Orleans, major droughts and famine anywhere in the world, hurricanes, and tornadoes, man would be wise to focus on what God is saying. It is a fact that He is speaking. Again, God works in mysterious ways, and we need to pray and ask for understanding and guidance.

We should not think that an F5 tornado with sustained winds of 200 miles per hour is just a freak of nature. We need to stop referring to major natural disasters as "Mother Nature having a bad day". The fact is Mother Nature can do nothing apart from the will of Almighty God. The use of the phrase "Mother Nature" is nothing but man's attempt to label something that He cannot control or understand.

In 2012, there was severe case of draught conditions across the United States of America. In the small community of Decatur, Illinois we were under water restrictions for most of the year and draught conditions continued into the 2013 season.   There is a large bridge that borders between the state of Missouri and the state of Tennessee. Since I am from the great state of Tennessee, every time I drive home from Decatur, IL, I must pass over this bridge. It was during the Labor Day holiday weekend of 2012 when we saw an almost dry river bed. Looking from the south to the north we could see nothing but large sand domes that was on the bottom river bed from east to west. The river was ninety percent dry in this section of the river. I had never seen the bottom of the mighty Mississippi River before in my life and I have crossed this bridge many times. Where did all the water go? I thought about that question a long time. Could this also be a sign that God is not pleased with man? The only answer that I can come up with is it appears likely to me that the drought conditions of 2012 caused the mighty Mississippi River to dry up in sections. And yes, I think the Lord is not pleased with man's sinful and rebellious ways. When you stop and consider the entire natural phenomenon that we have seen in this world during the last five to ten years, God is revealing to man that He rules His creation and that He and He alone does His good will at His pleasure. To put it straight to the point, it is God Almighty, not man, who controls the universe.

To use a biblical word "behold", look at all the tsunamis to hit this world recently. One hit in 2005 over India; or look at Hurricane Katrina. We have suffered major floods, earthquakes, tornadoes, and drought conditions. Hurricane Sandy which hit the East Coast in 2012 caused millions and millions of dollars in damage. Yes, the Lord is telling man something. We are seeing sink holes in the earth open up and swallow people as they sleep in their beds. For example, the sinkhole incident in the state of Florida which opened up and swallowed a man while he slept in his bedroom. It was a tragic story where a sinkhole opened up overnight underneath the bedroom of a 36 year old Florida man. The man was swallowed by the sinkhole pulling him down 20 feet. The man's brother tried to save him, but was not successful and had to be rescued himself. Local officials had geophysical surveys performed to determine the size of the sinkhole and evaluate the hazard posed to rescuers and other nearby houses. The sinkhole was determined to pose a serious risk, and some residents were required to leave their homes. Some were given only 30 minutes to clear out their belongings. Later they found out the sinkhole was fifty feet deep and thirty feet wide and was growing.

The Bible lists cases of the earth opening up and swallowing people as far back in the Old Testament in the book of Numbers. I will cite two examples. Both were the result of disobedience to God.

1. The Story of Korah in the Book of Numbers: 16: 23-33.

   Korah was a leader of a rebellious group against the leadership of Moses and Aaron while Israel was camped in the wilderness of Paran. At this time, Korah, Dathan, and Abiram led a conspiracy of two hundred fifty princes of the people against Aaron's claim to the priesthood and Moses' claim to authority in general. The rebels contended that the entire congregation was sanctified, and therefore qualified to perform priestly functions. As punishment for their insubordination, God caused the earth to open up and swallow the leaders and their property. Fire from the Lord came down from heaven and consumed all the followers and they all perished.

The story of the rebellion of Korah against Moses' leadership, and the example of how God dealt with that rebellion is confirmed in Psalms 105:15. This verse is clear and is a warning to all who seek to overthrow God's chosen people: *"Saying, Touch not mine anointed, and do my prophets no harm"*. I am so thankful that God does not need man's permission to do His good will. God picks and chooses who He wants, and His choice is never about money, race, or politics or any of the human traits that man uses to select a leader. Oh what a Mighty God we serve!

2. This is prophetic and will be fulfilled during the "Great Tribulation". This unveiling is revealed to us in Revelation 12:12-17. *12Therefore rejoice ye heavens, and ye that dwell in them. Woe to the inhibiters of the earth and of the sea! For the devil is come down unto you, having great wrath, because he knoweth that he hath but a short time. 13And when the dragon saw that he was cast unto the earth, he persecuted the woman which brought forth the man child. 14And to the woman were given two wings of a great eagle, which she might fly into the wilderness, into her place, where she is nourished for a time, and times, and half a time, from the face of the serpent. 15And the serpent cast out of his mouth water as a flood after the woman, that he might cause her to be carried away of the flood. 16And the earth helped the woman, and the earth opened her mouth,*

and swallowed up the flood which the dragon cast out of his mouth.
[17]And the dragon was wroth with the woman, and went to make war
with the remnant of her seed, which keep the commandments of God,
and have the testimony of Jesus Christ".

The Book of Revelation

We need to pay close attention to what God is saying in Revelation. There will be many signs and wonders that we will not be able to explain or we will dismiss as a freak of nature. Revelation is a book like no other. It explains in graphic detail what has been prophesized to take place on this earth. If man thinks that the meteor that passed over Russia was significant, He needs to read the book of Revelation. This book means "the unveiling", and is about the Second Coming of Jesus Christ. Before Jesus returns to this earth with all power, the earth will experience signs and wonders that have never before been seen by man, and will never be seen again. The book reveals the day of Lord, and the various great signs and wonders that are about to be unleashed on this world. You will learn about the Abomination of Desolations and the enemies of God – the devil, the beast, and the anti-Christ. You will learn about the millennium period, and the symbol 666 and what it means. Revelation tells about the Tribulation and the Great Tribulations. There are many things that the book of Revelation teaches. One thing I want to share with anyone who is a first-time study in the book is this: regardless of what you read in the book, remember God wins the battle. If you are on God's side you win.

Other interesting things that you will find as you read the book of Revelation:

- The messages to the seven churches
- You will meet John, the writer of the book of Revelation, as revealed by God to him.
- The four horsemen
- The seven seals
- The seven trumpets
- The seven bowls
- The woman and the dragon

- The sea beast
- The earth beast
- The 144,000
- The seven messages of Judgment
- The seven visions

In closing this chapter on the mighty signs and wonders of God, I just want to say, if you really want to know God, the only way to do that is through His Word. If you really want to know what is going to come into this world and what is going to happen to this world, you must study and become familiar with the book of Revelation.

The Divine Favor of God

Chapter 25

Let's look at the divine favor of God and see how His favor relates to the subject of this book. What is meant by the divine favor of God? It is God's unmerited grace and mercy that He provides for His people in spite of our sin and our daily transgressions. It is Agape love in the face of man's rejection of the Almighty God. It is Jesus' love for us in that He gave His life as a ransom for many to be free from the bondage of sin and shame. God's favor is like the sun light breaking through the clouds on a cold, wet, and dreary day, just so we can bask in His eternal love for us. How can mortal man repay such devotion?

There is only one way to repay God, and that is to have faith in His Son, Jesus. The only way we can be saved is by repenting of our sin and turning to Jesus. After we are saved, we must keep the commandments of God through His Son Jesus. We must strive to live a holy life because God Almighty is Holy. This is how we can start to say thanks to God for sending His Son into the world to die for us. Additionally, the divine favor of God as it relates to the number two and our choice of two directions or doors to open, can be found throughout the Bible. Remember the two doors we discussed earlier? God has made two doors of curses and blessings available to all people. Chapter 28 of Deuteronomy clearly explains in great detail God's divine plan for His people. There are blessings if we are obedient to His words and curses if we are disobedient.

I am going to copy the entire 28th Chapter of Deuteronomy for the readers of this book, because I want to clearly make known the fact that it is very important for us to understand that when God says something, He means it! He is not like man, because man will say one thing and turn right around and do another. God's Word stands the test of time and extends across generations. What He said to His people thousands and thousands of years ago, applies to us today. I am not indicating that we are still under the law. I am saying that God is Holy! The righteousness of His words was right when Moses gave the law, and they are still righteous today. The only difference is Jesus came into the world, He fulfilled the law, and we entered into the Dispensation of Grace. Just because we are under the Dispensation of Grace does not means that we have acquired a "carte blanche" or "get out of sin jail free" card to commit more sin. Under grace, we should work even harder not to sin, because we have a Mediator in heaven – Jesus Christ, our High Priest - who pleads our case for us.

Once we come into the knowledge of truth of the Lord Jesus Christ, we should be willing to do anything that will please Him; and resist those things that displease Him. Our walk should be in His righteousness, not our own. Please take the time to read, study, and meditate the entire 28th Chapter of Deuteronomy. You will see the two doors of life. One door leads to blessings, the other door leads to curses. One door leads to eternal salvation and continued joy in the Lord, the other door leads to eternal damnation and separation from the Lord. These two doors are still here for us to choose. The question becomes: Which side of the cross are you standing on? Are you standing on the side leading to Heaven or to Hell?

The Blessings for Obedience

Deuteronomy 28:1-68 (KJV)

1 "And it shall come to pass, if thou shalt hearken diligently unto the voice of the LORD thy God, to observe and to do all his commandments which I command thee this day, that the LORD thy God will set thee on high above all nations of the earth: 2And all these blessings shall come on thee, and overtake thee, if thou shalt hearken unto the voice of the LORD thy God. 3Blessed shalt thou be in the city, and blessed shalt thou be in the field. 4Blessed shall be the fruit of thy body, and the fruit of thy ground, and the fruit of thy cattle, the increase of thy kind, and the flocks of thy sheep. 5Blessed shall be thy basket and thy store. 6Blessed shalt thou be when thou comest in, and blessed shalt thou be when thou goest out. 7The LORD shall cause thine enemies that rise up against thee to be smitten before thy face: they shall come out against thee one way, and flee before thee seven ways. 8The LORD shall command the blessing upon thee in thy storehouses, and in all that thou settest thine hand unto; and he shall bless thee in the land which the LORD thy God giveth thee. ⁹The LORD shall establish thee an holy people unto himself, as he hath sworn unto thee, if thou shalt keep the commandments of the LORD thy God, and walk in his ways. ¹⁰And all people of the earth shall see that thou art called by the name of the LORD; and they shall be afraid of thee. ¹¹And the LORD shall make thee plenteous in goods, in the fruit of thy body, and in the fruit of thy cattle, and in the fruit of thy ground, in the land which the LORD sware unto thy fathers to give thee. ¹²The LORD shall open unto thee his good treasure, the heaven to give the rain unto thy land in his season, and to bless all the work of thine hand: and thou shalt lend unto many nations, and thou shalt not borrow. ¹³And the LORD shall make thee the head, and not the tail; and thou shalt be above only, and thou shalt not be beneath; if that thou hearken unto the commandments of the LORD thy God, which I command thee this day, to observe and to do them: ¹⁴And thou shalt not go aside from any of the words which I command thee this day, to the right hand, or to the left, to go after other gods to serve them."

The Curses for Disobedience

¹⁵"But it shall come to pass, if thou wilt not hearken unto the voice of the LORD thy God, to observe to do all his commandments and his statutes which I command thee this day; that all these curses shall come upon thee, and overtake thee: ¹⁶Cursed shalt thou be in the city, and cursed shalt thou be in the field. ¹⁷Cursed shall be thy basket and thy store. ¹⁸Cursed shall be the fruit of thy body, and the fruit of thy land, the increase of thy kind, and the flocks of thy sheep. ¹⁹Cursed shalt thou be when thou comest in, and cursed shalt thou be when thou goest out. ²⁰The LORD shall send upon thee cursing, vexation, and rebuke, in all that thou settest thine hand unto for to do, until thou be destroyed, and until thou perish quickly; because of the wickedness of thy doings, whereby thou hast forsaken me. ²¹The LORD shall make the pestilence cleave unto thee, until he have consumed thee from off the land, whither thou goest to possess it. ²²The LORD shall smite thee with a consumption, and with a fever, and with an inflammation, and with an extreme burning, and with the sword, and with blasting, and with mildew; and they shall pursue thee until thou perish. ²³And thy heaven that is over thy head shall be brass, and the earth that is under thee shall be iron. ²⁴The LORD shall make the rain of thy land powder and dust: from heaven

shall it come down upon thee, until thou be destroyed. *25The LORD shall cause thee to be smitten before thine enemies: thou shalt go out one way against them, and flee seven ways before them: and shalt be removed into all the kingdoms of the earth. 26And thy carcass shall be meat unto all fowls of the air, and unto the beasts of the earth, and no man shall fray them away. 27The LORD will smite thee with the botch of Egypt, and with the emerods, and with the scab, and with the itch, whereof thou canst not be healed. 28The LORD shall smite thee with madness, and blindness, and astonishment of heart: 29And thou shalt grope at noonday, as the blind gropeth in darkness, and thou shalt not prosper in thy ways: and thou shalt be only oppressed and spoiled evermore, and no man shall save thee. 30Thou shalt betroth a wife, and another man shall lie with her: thou shalt build an house, and thou shalt not dwell therein: thou shalt plant a vineyard, and shalt not gather the grapes thereof. 31Thine ox shall be slain before thine eyes, and thou shalt not eat thereof: thine ass shall be violently taken away from before thy face, and shall not be restored to thee: thy sheep shall be given unto thine enemies, and thou shalt have none to rescue them. 32Thy sons and thy daughters shall be given unto another people, and thine eyes shall look, and fail with longing for them all the day long: and there shall be no might in thine hand. 33The fruit of thy land, and all thy labours, shall a nation which thou knowest not eat up; and thou shalt be only oppressed and crushed always: 34So that thou shalt be mad for the sight of thine eyes which thou shalt see. 35The LORD shall smite thee in the knees, and in the legs, with a sore botch that cannot be healed, from the sole of thy foot unto the top of thy head. 36The LORD shall bring thee, and thy king which thou shalt set over thee, unto a nation which neither thou nor thy fathers have known; and there shalt thou serve other gods, wood and stone. 37And thou shalt become an astonishment, a proverb, and a byword, among all nations whither the LORD shall lead thee. 38Thou shalt carry much seed out into the field, and shalt gather but little in; for the locust shall consume it. 39Thou shalt plant vineyards, and dress them, but shalt neither drink of the wine, nor gather the grapes; for the worms shall eat them. 40Thou shalt have olive trees throughout all thy coasts, but thou shalt not anoint thyself with the oil; for thine olive shall cast his fruit. 41Thou shalt beget sons and daughters, but thou shalt not enjoy them; for they shall go into captivity. 42All thy trees and fruit of thy land shall the locust consume. 43The stranger that is within thee shall get up above thee very high; and thou shalt come down very low.*

44He shall lend to thee, and thou shalt not lend to him: he shall be the head, and thou shalt be the tail. 45Moreover all these curses shall come upon thee, and shall pursue thee, and overtake thee, till thou be destroyed; because thou hearkens not unto the voice of the LORD thy God, to keep his commandments and his statutes which he commanded thee: 46And they shall be upon thee for a sign and for a wonder, and upon thy seed forever. 47Because thou served not the LORD thy God with joyfulness, and with gladness of heart, for the abundance of all things; 48Therefore shalt thou serve thine enemies which the LORD shall send against thee, in hunger, and in thirst, and in nakedness, and in want of all things: and he shall put a yoke of iron upon thy neck, until he have destroyed thee. 49The LORD shall bring a nation against thee from far, from the end of the earth, as swift as the eagle flieth; a nation whose tongue thou shalt not understand; 50A nation of fierce countenance, which shall not regard the person of the old, nor shew favour to the young: 51And he shall eat the fruit of thy cattle, and the fruit of thy land, until thou be destroyed: which also shall not leave thee either corn, wine, or oil, or the increase of thy kind, or flocks of thy sheep, until he have destroyed thee. 52And he shall besiege thee in all thy gates, until thy high and fenced walls come down, wherein thou trustedst, throughout all thy land: and he shall besiege thee in all thy gates throughout all thy land, which the LORD thy God hath given thee. 53And thou shalt eat the fruit of thine own body, the flesh of thy sons and of thy daughters, which the LORD thy God hath given thee, in the siege, and in the straitness, wherewith thine enemies shall distress thee: 54So that the man that is tender among you, and very delicate, his eye shall be evil toward his brother, and toward the wife of his bosom, and toward the remnant of his children which he shall leave: 55So that he will not give to any of them of the flesh of his children whom he shall eat: because he hath nothing left him in the siege, and in the straitness, wherewith thine enemies shall distress thee in all thy gates. 56The tender and delicate woman among you, which would not adventure to set the sole of her foot upon the ground for delicateness and tenderness, her eye shall be evil toward the husband of her bosom, and toward her son, and toward her daughter, 57And toward her young one that cometh out from between her feet, and toward her children which she shall bear: for she shall eat them for want of all things secretly in the siege and straitness, wherewith thine enemy shall distress thee in thy gates. 58If thou wilt not observe to do all the words of this law that are written in this book, that thou mayest fear this glorious and fearful name, THE LORD THY GOD; ⁵⁹Then the LORD will make thy plagues wonderful, and the plagues of thy seed, even great plagues, and of long continuance, and sore sicknesses, and of long continuance. ⁶⁰Moreover he will bring upon thee all the diseases of Egypt, which thou wast afraid of; and they shall cleave unto thee. ⁶¹Also every sickness, and every plague, which is not written in the book of this law, them will the LORD bring upon thee, until thou be destroyed. ⁶²And ye shall be left few in number, whereas ye were as the stars of heaven for multitude; because thou wouldest not obey the voice of the LORD thy God. ⁶³And it shall come to pass, that as the LORD rejoiced over you to do you good, and to multiply you; so the LORD will rejoice over you to destroy you, and to bring you to nought; and ye shall be plucked from off the land whither thou goest to possess it. ⁶⁴And the LORD shall scatter thee among all people, from the one end of the earth even unto the other; and there thou shalt serve other gods, which neither thou nor thy fathers have known, even wood and stone. ⁶⁵And among these nations shalt thou find no ease, neither shall the sole of thy foot have rest: but the LORD shall give thee there a trembling heart, and failing of eyes, and sorrow of mind: ⁶⁶And thy life shall hang in doubt before thee; and thou shalt fear day and night, and shalt have none assurance of thy life: ⁶⁷In the morning thou shalt say, Would God it were even! And at even thou shalt say, Would God it were morning! For the fear of thine heart wherewith thou shalt fear, and for the sight of thine eyes which thou shalt see. ⁶⁸And the LORD shall bring thee into Egypt again with ships, by the way whereof I spake unto thee, Thou shalt see it no more again: and there ye shall be sold unto your enemies for bondmen and bondwomen, and no man shall buy you".

Choose Life

Chapter 26

I have been completely honest with what God has allowed me to see. Without a doubt, there will be some who will mock what I have communicated. There will be some who will reject as pure fabrication the things that God has shown me, but there will be some who will be drawn to the truth. I pray they move past the curiosity stage and go right into the "seek" and ye shall "find" stage of life, because His Second Coming is closer than we think. All who are the least bit curious and want to know about the risen God and what they must do to get to know Him, must "repent" and ask forgiveness for their sins through faith in Jesus Christ. To those people I say, "Run, don't walk, to a good church that has a pastor that will teach and preach the Word of truth with conviction". Find this church and get to know God. Do not let self-doubt, personal pride, family, job, money or anything get in your way of following the Risen Savior. God lives and He has done and is doing, and will continue to do all those things mentioned in the Bible from the first book of Genesis to the last book of Revelation.

People, don't let God catch you with your work undone. It is an absolute fact that one day we all are going to leave this place. We will go the way of departure from all life as planned by God. All men will die and return back to the earth from where we came. That is just a fact of life. Money, position, political party affiliation, family or whatever people love and hold dear, will not keep us here. Name me one human being that can boast of living forever, or who can say with confirmation, "I will stay young forever and die when I get ready". Who is this person, where does he live? Look all you want, I guarantee you on the Word of Jesus Christ, as revealed to us in Hebrews 9:27, *"And as it is appointed unto men once to die, but after this the judgment."* Death is not a guess, or a "maybe", it is a confirmed reality and a final act of the first natural life. How can any man have a mindset that this life on earth is all there is, or in a God who is the

Supreme Source of all life. And your nonbelief does nothing to keep you on this earth. It will; however, keep you eternally separated from your Creator.

The same God, who is the Source of all life, is the same God who determines when each life will end. Who, or what, can overrule His decree? If it were possible for man to position his case directly to Almighty God, and tell Him that in his unique case, this man wants to live forever, and wants to challenge God regarding life or death of all mankind, I say to such a person, "Really? Are you so arrogant that you would stand up and look into the face of Almighty God and tell Him what is best for you? Can anybody be that bold, and foolish? The sad truth of the matter is yes. There are people who think that they are qualified to bargain with an all-powerful, all-wisdom, and omnipresent God. This man vs God confrontation is not in the best interests for man. How are you going to match wits with He who has perfect wisdom? How can flesh and blood that is housed in a vessel of dirt do battle with an Eternal Spirit who has all power and lives forever? Allow me to try and make a comparison. This would be like a tiny flying gnat telling a mega 5 tornado that is 10 to 20 miles wide with sustained winds of between 300 to 375 miles per hour to go around it. . It would be like a tiny wooden one-man fishing boat caught in the middle of the Pacific Ocean during a monstrous hurricane with 50ft to 100ft giant swells and with wind speeds between 130 to 200 miles per hour. My point is you are going to lose that confrontation. When it comes to God, there is no room for doubt.

There are two doors of life! You have two choices.

Choice 1 -

> Through faith in his Son Jesus Christ, you "repent" of your sins and accept Him; this is complete acceptance of His son. This is your ticket to eternal salvation. Jesus has already paid the price with His blood on the Cross of Calvary. You cannot earn your way into heaven, salvation is a free gift from God to all based on faith in His Son.

■ ■ ■

Choice 2 -

You can reject Him based on your own superior knowledge that you know all there is to know about life and you want to live a life that is pleasing to you only. In so many words, your rejection of God is your proof that He does not exist. If that is your position, and you are not willing to change your mind, you are headed straight into eternal separation from God.

And that my friend is not a position you want to be in. One word: "Repent." Seek to know God, start reading your Bible, ask questions, and don't be left behind. This world is making foolish choices every day. Don't be like the world. It was the world that first rejected the Son of God who died for our sins. It was the world who mocked Him, spit on Him, and cruelly beat Him during His first coming. As matter of fact, He said in John 1:11, *"He came unto his own, and his own received him not"*.

Don't let the world fool you. The world does not want to accept that it killed the Son of the Most High God. The world wants to do its own will, independent of the Word of God. It's my opinion that there is a possible reason as to why we get all the natural disasters that are sure to continue to come on the world because of our rejection of its Creator. When I talk about the world, I am not talking about the natural world, the planets, the trees, the sun, the moon and the stars and so on. I am talking specifically about the world of man and his system of politics, religion, money, power, science, the arts, and so on. Anything that man puts before God is his idol. When you directly or indirectly worship an idol by default you are rejecting God. Idol worship is devil worship.

Allow me to give you a few examples. Look at all the football and basketball games that some people travel great distances to be a part of. This is a major human activity, and yes, people will spend good money on expensive tickets to see their favorite team play. Some fans will go to the extreme of painting their faces, and wearing or not wearing clothes to the game. Some will sit in below zero temperatures in the dead of winter freezing, just to see their team win a game. Yet, some of those same people will not walk a block to go to church and hear a sermon about the risen Savior.

Remember, an idol is anything that you value above God. It could be your car. People will spend countless hours washing and polishing and waxing their cars on the weekend, and are therefore too busy to go to church on Sunday. Additionally, they will spend their hard-earned money on expensive paint jobs, big tires with shiny mag rims; some of the tires and rim combinations cost more than the cars. They drive around the city showing off their cars. Try to get then to go to church with you on Sunday and they will find some excuse not to go.

There are also the pleasure-seeking people. These are people who have made "themselves" an idol to God. Their whole lifestyle is designed to please themselves. They choose drugs, sexual gratification, fornication, adultery, and any other shameless behavior as being a normal lifestyle for them. Their view is, "what harm is it to get high off of crack cocaine, or heroin, marijuana, or alcohol?" They see nothing wrong with having sexual relations with as many women or men as humanly possible. They tell themselves it's just sex, and as long as it feels good and I can find the right person, I am going to get high and spend my money on the things that I like.

This world is slowly but surely moving away from the fear of the Lord. This world seems to say, "We know what is best for us". This is a world that is leaning toward a complete rejection of sound Christian doctrine. One example of this rejection of sound, Christian doctrine again, is the rise of acceptance of same sex marriages. My focus right now is strictly on the United States of America. The current position of some states is to redefine marriage to include same sex marriage. Some states want to include same sex marriages as a legal and an acceptable alternative lifestyle. This is another example of the world system of man rejecting the sound doctrine of a Holy God. It is man telling his Creator that he knows what is best for him, and he (man) will, through the power of man's political system, make same sex marriage legal, even though the Bible says is an "abomination to God."

I have stated it before in this book, but it is so important I want to repeat it again and again. The proponents of same sex marriage are the same ones who opposed the civil rights movement of the black man during the turbulent times of the 1960's. Yet, some of these same people now want to claim the right of same sex marriage as a civil right. I have always had a problem with the man who wants another man to poke him in his rear, and says that his rights are violated when he does not get his way. In other words, the pervert says it is a violation of his civil rights not to live as he chooses. This lustful lifestyle has nothing to do with real civil rights legislation aimed at improving equal employment opportunities without discrimination, fair housing, and the right to vote and so on. The human civil rights of a nation have nothing to do with the freedom of deviant sexual preference. The right of two men or two women to engage in same sexual relations has nothing to do with civil rights. In one relationship, same sex relationships fail to produce any kind of life and are in reality, anti-life. There is nothing two men or two women can do together that will create the birth of a child. Same sex unions are nothing but lust of the flesh and the pride of life. There is nothing "civil" or "right" about it. Where I come from, there is an old saying called "he/she and she/he". A "he/she" is a man who wants to be a woman, and a "she/he" is a woman that wants to be a man. The key underlying word is they want to be something that they were not born into. So what do they do? They go to college, get educated, find other people with similar likes and dislikes, and they form committees. They get themselves elected, and over a period of time, become judges and politicians where they can directly redefine and change laws to meet or suit their deviant lifestyle. And some have the nerve to call themselves God- fearing. The point is if you really know God, you would not put same sex rights above the already established "sacred sanctity of marriage" as defined in the book of Genesis.

I cannot say it any better than what has already been said in the book of Galatians 6:7-8 *"Be not deceived; God is not mocked: for whatsoever a man soweth, that shall he also reap. For he that soweth to his flesh shall of the flesh reap corruption; but he that soweth to the Spirit shall of the Spirit reap life everlasting"*. This is a fact from a Holy God to all His creation. You will reap what you sow. Therefore, all those politicians and actors, who dance around and flaunt their deviate sexual lifestyle and thumb their noses in God's face, will have to give an account one day for their blatant disobedience. However small your contribution was to the passing of laws thereby making same sex marriage in this country legal, you will not get by. God knows exactly what you did and you cannot hide your involvement.

What our brother and great prophet of God, Isaiah, said many years ago still applies to us today. He said in his book, Isaiah 5: 20-21, *"Woe unto them that call evil good and good evil; that put darkness for light, and light for darkness; that put bitter for sweet, and sweet for bitter! Woe unto them that is wise in their own eyes, and prudent in their own sight!"* One thing man must come to know is this: God is still God! Your belief or unbelief will not change that.

Summary
Chapter 27

I want to begin to summarize some of the highlights we have talked about in this book. We know there are only two kinds of people, those who believe in Christ and those who do not. To believe or not to believe really is the eternal question and the point of my message to you. A question that each and every living soul that has ever lived, living now, or yet to be born in this world, will have to answer for themselves is if they are believers in Jesus Christ or non-believers. Specifically, believing in God means more than just giving lip service. What good does it do for sinners to say, "Yes we believe in God", but they continue to live in sin? On the one hand, they will tell you that they do believe in Jesus, but they never go to church or worship Him. They continue to commit fornication whenever the opportunity presents itself, and some commit adultery to their heart's content. Yet when you ask them a direct question, "do you believe in God?" most of them will automatically nod his or her head in agreement. But take a closer look at their lifestyle, and you will see there is nothing about these people that would make a serious child of God agree with what they are doing. Jesus tells us in 1 John 5:3-4, *"For this is the love of God, that we keep his commandment: and his commandments are not grievous; for whatsoever is born of God overcometh the world: and this victory that overcometh the world even our faith"*.

People who say they believe in God, but fail to keep God's commandments are deceiving themselves. God wants His believers to change from a love of this world to a love for Him by putting Him first in their lives. If we love God, we will keep His commandments. If we fail to keep and obey God's commandments, it means we are following the dictates of the prince of this world, the devil. The choice is truly ours to make and we will be held accountable for our decision. When our Lord and Savior returns to this earth to rule His Kingdom, all the non-believers will not be able to run and hide and say they made a mistake. Your position of power, race, color of your skin, private country club membership, your money, major real estate holdings, good looks, intellectual ability, and all that you can think of will not sway the decision of a righteous and Holy God. He will know all there is to know about you before you stand before His eternal throne room.

Jesus said to all who have lived their life in complete disobedience and non-belief in Jesus, "depart from me, I never knew you". In Matthew 7:21-23, he said, "Not everyone that saith unto me, Lord, Lord, shall enter into the kingdom of heaven; but he that doeth the will of my Father which is in heaven. 22Many will say to me in that day, Lord, Lord, have we not prophesied in thy name? And in thy name have cast out devils? And in thy name done many wonderful works? 23And then will I profess unto them, I never knew you: depart from me, ye that work iniquity".

When I die and meet our Lord and Savior, I want to hear Him say: "well done my good and faithful servant, welcome into the Kingdom of the Lord". That is my hope, and this is why I want to reach as many unsaved people as possible through this book and get them to reevaluate their non-believer ideology and repent. Our God is a forgiving God and is ready to forgive us for our sins.

Murderers will not enter into the Kingdom of heaven. Remember the Trayvon Martin case, and how it appears the guilty man went free. Many sent money to support George Zimmerman. You cannot buy God off, nor does He show favor to any race. God is a righteous Judge and He says that vengeance is His. If Zimmerman truly initiated, tracked, and killed without mercy this young, seventeen year old boy, he will have to answer to a higher court than the kangaroo court that gave him his freedom. He will not escape his appointed meeting with the Almighty God who will judge sin.

We have a society who wants to tell Almighty God that they know what is best for them. In other words, the clay wants to tell the potter how to create it. This is synonymous with a medical patient with brain cancer trying to advise or tell the surgeon how to operate and remove the cancer. It is like the infant child trying to convince its parents that a cold beer is better than milk. Woe to those who work behind the scene to make and pass laws that attempt to mock the Word of God. I am specifically talking about laws that call evil good and good evil. You will not escape the wrath of a Holy God. You can run, but you cannot hide your deeds. I am purposely talking about all the judges, politicians, leaders of major political parties, actors, and all people rich or poor, who are not only supportive of the gay rights movement, but they have actively assumed a leadership role in solidifying the legitimacy of homosexuality and gay rights. They are using their position of authority to thumb their nose in God's face by helping to lead this once great nation into immorality and moral decay. Remember Sodom and Gomorrah. God is still God and He hates the sin of homosexuality. It is immaterial what man says, either we believe in what our God says in His Word as presented to us in the Holy Bible, or we don't. If you are on the side of the non-believer, you have made the God of Creation your enemy. That's not a place I want to be. But if nothing I have said will get you to reevaluate your position, then in hell you will one day open your eyes.

We all have two choices: Heaven or Hell. Two positions in life: those who believe, and those who choose not to believe. It is hard not to run into the number two universal equation. We talked about this in another chapter, the "two" factor - male or female, young or old, either straight or gay, believer or non-believer, saved or unsaved, eternally blessed, or eternally cursed, prejudiced or respect for all people, God-centered or self–centered, righteous or unrighteous, rich or poor, educated or illiterate, married or unmarried. The list really seems to be endless. You can find the number two all over God's creation on the human body. Two eyes, ears, nostrils, one set of teeth, upper and lower body parts, two arms, two hands, two legs, and, two feet. You cannot escape His design of the human anatomy which utilized the number 2 in His creation.

The Concept of Time

The Good Lord put it in my spirit to close this book focusing on the concept of time. He wants me to tell all who will listen that time, as we humans know it, is running out. He wants us to know that God's concept of time is nothing like the system of time that man has created for himself. Man's concept of time is natural, temporal and finite. God's concept of time is eternal. He sits outside of man's knowledge and understanding of what time is.

God informs us through Apostle Peter in 2 Peter 3:8, not to be ignorant. He said, *"But, beloved, be not ignorant of this one thing, that one day is with the Lord as a thousand years, and a thousand years as one day."* People, there is coming a day of judgment! Don't allow the devil to blind you to this fact. God is going to judge the quick and the dead not only on how we lived our life, but more importantly, what we did with His Son, Jesus. He sent His Son, His only Son to die for our sins. Did we accept or did we reject His final offer of salvation? That question will need to be answered in the face of an all-knowing and all-powerful God. We need to prepare ourselves to stand before Him.

In the first book of the Bible, the book of Genesis 6:3, God told us, *"And the LORD said, my spirit shall not always strive with man, for that he also is flesh: yet his days shall be an hundred and twenty years"*. There is a limit as to what God will and will not tolerate from His creation. Yes, He is longsuffering, yes, He is merciful, yes, God is love and His agape love for man defies our understanding of love. However, man would be well advised to remember God is a Holy God who cannot overlook unrighteousness and sin. God will judge us for our transgressions and hold us accountable for our iniquity, unless we confess our sins and repent and turn from our wicked and evil self-destructive ways.

When it comes to time, man must be diligent, and not allow the enemy, Satan to blind us. The devil has many people thinking that it is okay to prolong not getting saved and not living a life that is pleasing to God. The devil wants man to live a sinful and pleasure-seeking lifestyle that has no limitations or boundaries. The phrase- "if it feels good do it" was very popular during the 60's and is still a very accepted worldly phrase that is still accepted in the minds of lost souls today. The enemy wants man to focus on life as a freedom of choice. Doesn't that look just like the devil, wanting to take credit for something that he did not create? God is the Creator and Source of all life. It is the devil who came to steal, kill or destroy life and to get God's creation to serve him. Make no mistake about it. The devil wants people to worship him and not God. If you need a reminder of this, let's do a quick review of how Satan tricked Eve to "usurp" the authority of Adam in the Garden of Eden. The devil used his plan to attack the woman first by getting her to doubt the Word of God. He said in Genesis 3:1-6, *"Now the serpent was more subtle than any beast of the field which the LORD God had made. And he said unto the woman, Yea, hath God said, ye shall not eat of every tree of the garden? 2And the woman said unto the serpent, we may eat of the fruit of the trees of the garden: 3But of the fruit of the tree which is in the midst of the garden, God hath said, ye shall not eat of it, neither shall ye touch it, lest ye die. 4And the serpent said unto the woman, ye shall not surely die: 5For God doth know that in the day ye eat thereof, then your eyes shall be opened, and ye shall be as gods, knowing good and evil. 6And when the woman saw that the tree was good for food, and that it was pleasant to the eyes, and a tree to be desired to make one wise, she took of the fruit thereof, and did eat, and gave also unto her husband with her; and he did eat. "*

Note: The devil's approach to the woman was he asked her a question. Most people will respond to a question even if it's from a stranger. That was Eve's first mistake, because by answering the devil's question, she had now entered into a conversation with him. People, we are no match for the devil, especially if we are dealing with him in our own strength. The Bible tells us in Genesis 3:1 that the devil is subtle. The *Webster's New Collegiate Dictionary* defines the word " subtle" as: "highly skilful, elusive, difficult to understand, of distinguish, perceptive, refined, marked by keen insight and ability to penetrate deeply and thoroughly, a scholar, very cunning, crafty, insidiously clever". We are no match for the devil. Do not be deceived!

Another example of how the devil wants people to fall down and worship him is given to us in the first four books of the New Testament: Matthew, Mark, Luke and John. Let's review Matthew 4:1-11's account of the devil's temptation of Jesus and his desire for Jesus to worship him. *"Then was Jesus led up of the Spirit into the wilderness to be tempted of the devil. ²And when he had fasted forty days and forty nights, he was afterward an hungred. ³And when the tempter came to him he said, if thou be the Son of God, command that these stones be made bread. ⁴But he answered and said, it is written, Man shall not live by bread alone, but by every word that proceedeth out of the mouth of God. ⁵Then the devil taketh him up into the holy city, and setteth him on a pinnacle of the temple, ⁶And saith unto him, If thou be the Son of God, cast thyself down: for it is written, He shall give his angels charge concerning thee: and in their hands they shall bear thee up, lest at any time thou dash thy foot against a stone. ⁷Jesus said unto him, it is written again, Thou shalt not tempt the Lord thy God. ⁸Again, the devil taketh him up into an exceeding high mountain, and sheweth him all the kingdoms of the world, and the glory of them; ⁹And saith unto him, All these things will I give thee, if thou wilt fall down and worship me. ¹⁰Then saith Jesus unto him, Get thee hence, Satan: for it is written, Thou shalt worship the Lord thy God, and him only shalt thou serve. ¹¹Then the devil leaveth him, and, behold, angels came and ministered unto him".*

In verse 9, we see the devil wanting the Son of God to worship him. The lesson learned, should be this: If the enemy has the nerve to try and connive and scheme his way into tricking Jesus to worship him, how about us? This verse confirms for me that the devil will use any trick in the book to deceive man into worshiping him and to abandon any worship of the True and Living God. In short, if the devil is not afraid of God, then rest assured he won't be afraid of you!

I see a countless number of people today who fail to consider that their time is running out. Each day as I read the daily paper I see in the obituary that death is an everyday occurrence. I see people who go to work every day, and work long hours which include weekends and, on many occasions, Sundays. They fail to see that they have time to do all the things in life that they want to do except give some time to Him that is the Source of all time. I see people pack football stadiums every Sunday to worship their favorite team. They bring the family, and have what the world calls tailgate parties where they cook on the grill, play music, and drink alcohol and even use this time to get high off illicit drugs. They see Sunday not as a day of worship to God, but as just another day to be enjoyed in the pursuit of self–pleasure. Since they don't seem to think about God, I wonder what they would say if God, just for one minute, stopped them from breathing His God-given air. What would they do? What if God was too busy to wake them up one morning, would they finally realize that nothing in this life is more important than having the correct understanding of who and what God is to us? There is nothing in this life that can ever compare to His Greatness. Any and all things fail when we try to compare it to God. What can match His greatness?

The correct answer is **nothing**! Not gold, silver, money, position, power, nor possessions. Nothing compares to God! Therefore, can you not see just how much of an insult it is to Him for His creation to not know this? It is similar in the Old Testament when the ancient people of God, the Israelites, began to worship idols that were made of wood or stone. These lifeless man-made objects could never take the place of God. Yet the people allowed themselves to be deceived into thinking that idols (a trick of the devil) could serve them. People today are making the same mistake. We fail to give proper respect to God and worship Him when we fail to study and learn about His ways and commandments. We fail Him by the use of our allotted time here on this earth; we fail Him by being too busy to go to a God-fearing church. We fail Him by not taking authority and being the head of our households and taking our family, especially our children, to church.

In Ephesians 5:15-16 we are told to redeem the time. *"See then that ye walk circumspectly, not as fools, but as wise, redeeming the time, because the days are evil"*. We are told not to walk as fools walk. How do fools walk? Allow me to try and give an answer to that question. When a person continues to live his or her life as if God does not exist, that person is living and walking as a fool. When people make laws that glorify wrong, laws that are in direct violation of the Word of God, they are walking as fools. When we allow our children to disrespect us we invite anarchy into our homes and into our society. It should not come as a surprise that our kids are showing signs of a mass apostasy from the church and are falling victims to witchcraft, which leads to devil worship. Some of our kids are so confused that they will fall for any new and anti-traditional religion. That is why it should not be surprising to see more and more of our kids in America joining forces with another faith. As parents, we do our kids a disservice when we fail to teach, train, and raise them in the fear of the Lord. This is nothing short of abandonment. To me, it's the same as leaving an unprotected child or baby alone in the wilderness, which would allow any animal that comes along to eagerly devour the helpless child. This is what I see happening today in this country. I see morality slowly diminishing into the days of old, when sin is the king and unrighteousness seems to prevail. I see people not having a love for God in their heart, in positions of authority making decisions that promote their own private agenda and not caring what the majority of people want.

As I write this summary, we as a nation are divided. The Republican Party is made up of predominantly white individuals. About 30% of them are controlled like puppets. They are controlled by a very ultra neo-conservative right wing group that call themselves the Tea Party. They have organized their party into political action committees, and their aim is to control the government or as they say, "take back our country". The Tea Party wants to control who gets into power and those who do not cater to their rules will pay a price. Right now, they have bullied the current Speaker of the House, John Boehner, into submission. Their strategy is to apply pressure on the G.O.P. into shutting down the government. Why? It's because their party and the Tea Party supporters do not want the Obama healthcare initiatives to become law.

It is God Almighty that they are really fighting against. It is God who raises up leaders and puts them into major leadership positions. They would disagree with me because, 1) They do not know scriptures, or 2) They have rejected the scriptures. Acts 23:5 says, *"Then said Paul, I wist not, brethren, that he was the high priest: for it is written, Thou shalt not speak evil of the ruler of thy people."* Their plan is to attack the first black president publicly with negative name calling, by demonizing the man, and convincing the public that he is bad. There is a God that sits high and looks low. Psalm 14:2 states, *"Nothing is hidden from his eyes, and he can discern thoughts of man a far off"*. To the members of the 2013 G.O.P. that have fallen under the sway of a devilish group of people, your deeds will not go unpunished!

Political disagreements are one thing, but using political gamesmanship to purposely sabotage the government under the guise of helping to control spending, shutting down the US Government, and effectively putting 800,000 plus people out of work just to prove a point is another thing Ok, let's cut to the chase. I believe the real issue is for the first time in America's history, the country elected a black man to be President. God wanted this particular black man to be in office and he won. Now you have a President who wants to be fair to all the people, and that "good old white boy" network can't seem to control him. They can rant and rave about the President's birth certificate; they can try to demonize him and call him all the ugly names they want, but let one of them get too close to God's anointed and see what happens. He clearly says in Psalm 105:15, *"Saying, Touch not mine anointed, and do my prophets no harm"*. Those are not just empty words, my friend. I do believe that God has angels encamped around the family of this first black President.

If they could talk with Pharaoh, the King of Egypt, I truly believe he would tell them to leave God's anointed alone. Pharaoh would tell them not to be led by the hardness of their hearts. If they could turn back the pages of history and ask Goliath why he was defeated by a Hebrew boy named David, I think Goliath would tell them not to lose their head in following the dreams of a mad Tea Party or political action committee. If they could somehow get a question back to King Nebuchadnezzar, the king of the Chaldean, (also known as the Neo-Babylonian) I am convinced this mighty King would tell them to stand down. This king would tell them this God is real!

Lastly, if they could somehow locate Noah, and ask him if they will prevail against God's anointed? I do believe Noah would tell them; only eight people survived the wrath of God of his generation. That means countless numbers of people were lost because they were on the wrong side of righteousness. I do believe Noah would tell them in the words of Balaam, "You cannot curse what God has blessed, so stand down".

Time as we know it is running out. Yes, we all have heard people of old say the same thing, and yes, I am saying it too. Man's time on God's earth is running on the downward spiral into a showdown with the Creator of all things. Which door will you pass through? There are only two doors.

Will it be the door that opens into eternal paradise and the full blessing of an Almighty God? Or will it be the door that opens into eternal damnation and eternal separation from God? The Day of the Lord is real and it will be a day that the likes of which will never be again. But before that day comes, God is giving all of us a chance to repent and to change our wicked ways. The Bible tells us that David's son, Solomon, was the wisest man to have ever lived. Now I know that some of you think that in this current generation of high speed internet, and mega-billionaires like Bill Gates, we could make a list of some of the smartest people to ever live. People like Albert Einstein, Leonardo Da Vinci, Sir Isaac Newton, Nikola Tesla, Galileo Galilei, Stephen Hawking, Charles Darwin, and Benjamin Franklin would be on the list. There are arguably more that could make this short list, but for the sake of pure genius, these are some of the top ones. However, they all pale when compared to Solomon. God blessed Solomon with divine wisdom and with great riches untold. If you could find the richest man in the world, he would not surpass the splendor of this third great king of Israel.

In 1 Kings 3:5-14, we learn of how the God of Heaven and Earth, the God of Creation, the God of Abraham, Isaac, and Jacob, blessed Solomon with wisdom, wealth, honor and long life if he remained obedient to the commandments of God and to walk in God's ways. Here is what the scriptures tell us: *"In Gibeon the LORD appeared to Solomon in a dream by night: and God said, ask what I shall give thee. 6And Solomon said, Thou hast shewed unto thy servant David my father great mercy, according as he walked before thee in truth, and in righteousness, and in uprightness of heart with thee; and thou hast kept for him this great kindness, that thou hast given him a son to sit on his throne, as it is this day. 7And now, O LORD my God, thou hast made thy servant king instead of David my father: and I am but a little child: I know not how to go out or come in. 8And thy servant is in the midst of thy people which thou hast chosen, a great people, that cannot be numbered nor counted for multitude. 9Give therefore thy servant an understanding heart to judge thy people that I may discern between good and bad: for who is able to judge this thy so great a people? 10And the speech pleased the Lord, that Solomon had asked this thing. 11And God said unto him, Because thou hast asked this thing, and hast not asked for thyself long life; neither hast asked riches for thyself, nor hast asked the life of thine enemies; but hast asked for thyself understanding to discern judgment; 12Behold, I have done according to thy words: lo, I have given thee a wise and an understanding heart; so that there was none like thee before thee, neither after thee shall any arise like unto thee. [13]And I have also given thee that which thou hast not asked, both riches, and honour: so that there shall not be any among the kings like unto thee all thy days. [14]And if thou wilt walk in my ways, to keep my statutes and my commandments, as thy father David did walk, then I will lengthen thy days".* If God says that Solomon was the wisest, the richest and the most honorable man to have ever lived, who am I to argue with Him? I accept it and will use God's confirmation to build my next point. My point is: Since Solomon was the wisest man to have ever lived, and there were none wiser before, during, or after his life time, (with one exception-Jesus Christ) I am going to clearly listen to and adhere to what this man had to say. In the conclusion of the book of Ecclesiastes 12:13-14, we are given a warning by this great and wise king. Solomon said that when it comes to God Almighty, *"Let us hear the conclusion of the whole matter: Fear God, and keep his commandments: for this is the whole duty of man. For God shall bring every work into judgment, with every secret thing, whether it be good, or whether it be evil."*

Solomon is telling us that in this thing we call life, the conclusion of the whole of man's existence, or the sum total of all life, as to why we are here, is, 1) To fear God and keep His commandments, and, 2) To do our duty, our whole duty and keep his commandments. Nothing else will have priority over this one commandment. He also warns us that if we fail to correctly honor God, which by the way, is our sole purpose for being here in the first place, God will hold us accountable for everything that we did that was contrary to the Word of God. Everything done in secret will be manifested and made known regardless of whether the deed was good or evil. Solomon's advice to us, and to all who are blessed to be born after us, is to fear God and keep His commandments. That is plain enough for me!

A Parable: The Lust of the Flesh, Lust of the Eyes, and the Pride of Life.

On board this plane, there are groups of lesbian lovers and men who are committed homosexuals. Both the lesbians and homosexual men have powerful positions in their personal lives and financially support same sex laws, and same sex marriage. Also on board this plane are people who are non-believers, people who are racists and do all kinds of devious things against the Jews of the world. They hate black people and women who fail to keep their place. There are also, lawyers, pedophiles, teachers, judges, politicians, movie stars, and others who are headed to a private beach area in the beautiful state of Honolulu, Hawaii. As the plane taxies to its final area to be given the final okay from the control tower for permission to take off, suddenly you hear the roar of four large twin turbo buster engines, being raised to maximum PRM. The pilot releases the brakes and the big 747 effortlessly takes off.

This is symbolic in that we have people who are on a collision course straight into hell and they do not even know it. The reason they do not know that they are headed straight to hell is: 1) they either don't know or believe that the devil exists or therefore are unaware of his schemes, and, 2) They over-estimate their own unique strengths and under-estimate the power of the god of this world. When we face Satan in our own strength, we lose. For example, people who have been tricked or hoodwinked by the tricks of the devil are similar to passengers that board the 747 airplane for a summer trip to Hawaii. The passengers are told the goal of this trip is fun in the sun and when you get there, you can do anything under the sun. No rules. It's all about having the money, power, prestige, and personal privilege that goes with being a part of the "in" crowd. The devil used three of his most attractive and successful lures to entice people to sign up for this trip. The lures that he used are called "lust of the flesh", "lust of the eyes" and the "pride of life". As the big airplane powers down the runway and makes a smooth lift off, the plane continues its climb until it reaches a destination of 38,000 feet then it levels off for a smooth 8- hour ride above the clouds.

However, on this trip, the pilots are not really human. On yes, they look and act like they are, but they are demons who have entered the bodies of the Captain and the Co-Captain of this huge aircraft. The passenger's manifesto lists a total of three hundred passengers aboard this air-bus. Halfway through the journey, when all of the passengers have relaxed from several alcoholic beverages, and are sleeping, without any warning, the demons craftily and very skillfully change courses. The demons are taking this plane and all the passengers on board straight to Hell. The big plane now makes a ninety degree nose dive straight down towards the Pacific Ocean. The plane is steady and its speed of 587 miles per hour is unabated. The people now begin to panic, some scream, and many of the "God haters", the non-believers, are heard screaming God's name. They are screaming, "Lord, help us". Other non-believers are calling on God to have mercy and save them. But it's all for naught. In less than ten minutes, this plane will hit the ocean with such force that the explosion can be heard for miles. Moreover, the plane will explode in thousands of pieces. The rest is history. The news media, the airline owners of the air-bus, the Federal Air Traffic Regulatory Agency which oversee all airplane disasters, all seem to agree that something went terribly wrong on Flight 666.

There were a few Christian passengers who were also on vacation and had scheduled their vacations to visit the great state of Hawaii. However, something told them not to ride a plane that had the letters 666 in the flight's manifesto. So these few Christians changed their flight tickets to a different plane on a different day and safely reached their destination. The lesson learned from this short parable is that the Holy Spirit leads and guides in truth. It was the Holy Spirit that gave the Christians the discernment to not board Flight 666. It was the Holy Spirit that protected God's believers from the evil deeds of the devil who only comes but to steal, kill and destroy. This is his mission.

We learn in 2 Corinthians 4:3-4, how the devil blinds the minds of people and make them non-believers. When Satan blinds the mind of people, they become easy targets for his destruction. Please carefully study this verse the Apostle Paul is saying to us, *"But if our gospel be hid, it is hid to them that are lost: In whom the god of this world hath blinded the minds of them which believe not, lest the light of the glorious gospel of Christ, who is the image of God, should shine unto them"*. Do you hear what this great Apostle of God is saying? If you are a non-believer, you have been blinded by the devil. **WAKE UP – WAKE UP – WAKE UP!** Time on this earth is running out.

One of the biggest strategies of the devil is to try and convince people that there is no God. The devil knows that if he can convince men that there is no God, then men won't question the existence of the devil. If you spell the word devil backwards it will say: "L.I.V.E.D". The enemy of our soul is real. He is the main reason for murder, rape, racial hatred, idolatry, mass killings which includes serial murders, wars, same sex marriages, and so many other atrocities that seem to be increasing today. Satan is a master at blinding the minds of people. He's been deceiving people since the dawn of creation, starting with Adam and Eve, and he is still on his job today. He turns mothers against their daughters, fathers against their sons; he destroys families, churches, communities and even nations. One should never under-estimate the tricks and power of the god of this world. Amen.

Despite how bad he is, he is no match for our Lord and Savior Jesus Christ! I will say it again when it comes to Jesus, the devil is already a defeated foe! Yes, he is more than a match for us if we face him in our own strength, but fear not when you have God on your side. In 1 John, 4:4, we are told, *"Ye are of God, little children, and have overcome them: because greater is he that is in you, than he that is in the world".*

Christ is Returning to Gather His People

I have given you what God has given me. My words reflect personal experiences that God Almighty has blessed me to see and to share with you. I have many more personal encounters that I could have added but chose not to. I do not want to be the center or focus of the book. The Goal of this book is to focus the reader's attention on Jesus Christ, the Son of the True and Living God.

As spoken in the Bible in John 3:16-17 *"For God so loved the world, that he gave his only begotten Son, that whosoever believeth in him should not perish, but have everlasting life. For God sent not his Son into the world to condemn the world; but that the world through him might be saved".* If all of us would truly take the time to understand the magnitude and the deep spiritual implications of these two short passages of scripture, we would drop our collective heads in sinful shame.

The point is that God Almighty loved us so much that He sent His only begotten Son to come down from the city of lights (which is paradise) where He was, is, and always will be, a King. He came into His creation, earth (which is like comparing a slum-infested ghetto to Hawaii). He came here to die a shameful and horrible death by crucifixion, at the hands of His chosen people. How could we be so blind? How could we have been so cruel? Jesus, as the firstborn from the dead, rose again on the third day exactly as He said He would. He rose with all power and is now sitting on the right side of His Eternal Father in Heaven.

The people of earth will see Him again. The only question that each of us must be able to answer is: which side of the question of life are you standing on? Which door into eternity will you open? The life you live and your acceptance or rejection of Jesus Christ, will lead you to the door of your choice. There are only two doors of life. One will open into eternal paradise with blessings and acceptance by God saying "well done my good and faithful servant. Welcome home into the kingdom of God". The other door will open into eternal separation from God. All who open this door will immediately fall into eternal damnation and suffering. People will beg for death but it will not come to them, because it (death) will also be thrown into the eternal lake of fire as well.

The last and final book of the Bible is the book of Revelation. John, the Apostle, was allowed to see what God has in store for the last days of all life on this earth. I highly recommend that you read and study the entire book of Revelation for yourself. This book blows my mind each and every time I have tried to read and understand its dark and mysterious secrets. I want to make it clear that I am not and do not claim to be, an intellectual scholar on the book of Revelation. The things that I am going to discuss here were inspired by the Holy Spirit. I am in no way going to attempt to give a doctorial synopsis on the book of Revelation. That would be more than I could accomplish unless inspired by God through His Spirit.

My purpose for ending this short book is that life will end and the final details are described in the book of Revelation. We learn from John that there is a blessing from God to all those who read and hear the words of prophecy that are available in the book of Revelation. (Revelation 2) That alone should speak of the seriousness of studying and taking to heart the message of this book. In the first chapter of Revelation you will meet the Mighty One who says, *"I am Alpha and Omega, the beginning and the end."* Jesus tells the Apostle John to write the things that He is going to bless him to see. He tells John to write the visions that he sees in a book and to send them to the seven churches of Asia (modern day Turkey). Jesus tells John to list the condition of each of the seven churches. If we are completely honest with ourselves, many of these same spiritual faults apply to us individually and to the present day church.

- To the church of <u>Ephesus</u> - They were guilty of losing their first love. They were the loveless church.

- To the church of <u>Smyrna</u> – They were the persecuted church – the church feared suffering.

- To the church of <u>Pergamos</u> – This was the over tolerant church with doctrinal defections. They were the compromising church.

- To the church of <u>Thyatira</u> – This church was the corrupt church. They were guilty of moral departure.

- To the church of <u>Sardis</u> – They were the sleeping church. They were considered to be a dead church.

- To the church of <u>Philadelphia</u> – This was the faithful church. They were the church with opportunity for holding on to the Word of God.

- To the church of <u>Laodicea</u> – This was the lukewarm church. This church was neither hot nor cold, they were complacent.

Jesus talks to us about being an overcomer. In the book of Revelation 3:21-22; He says: *"To him that overcomes will I grant to sit with me in my throne, even as I also overcame, and am set down with my Father in his throne. He that hath an ear let him hear what the Spirit saith unto the churches".*

This same word, "overcomer" is used by Jesus in several passages of scripture. I want to cite 1 John 5:4-5 which says: *"For whatsoever is born of God overcometh the world: and this is the victory that overcometh the world, even our faith. Who is he that overcometh the world, but he that believeth that Jesus is the Son of God?"* If we are to please Jesus Christ, I think we better understand and apply into our lives the need to be an overcomer in our journey in this life. What does it mean to be an overcomer? Answer: A spiritual overcomer is one who has repented of their sins by the grace of God through faith in Jesus Christ. The overcomer does not live by the lust of the flesh, the lust of the eyes, or the pride of life. Even though the overcomer lives in this world, his goal is not to please the world but to do the will of God. The overcomer strives to store his riches in heaven, not the earth. He keeps the commandments of God and tries living peacefully with all men through the love of the Spirit.

God's plan for eternal salvation included the burial, resurrection, and ascension of His Son Jesus Christ. We will be submissive to the will of God through His Son, and we will seek to please Him and not be controlled by the things of this world. What does the love of this world mean? The "world" here is a reference to a system that was developed by man. This system does not recognize the God of the Bible. It is a system that focuses on the competitive nature of man. It is a system that states that man is directly in control of his own destiny. It is a system that challenges the very existence of God. It was this world system, the system of man, who rejected the Lord of Glory. Jesus came into this world to save that which was lost, and the world religious leaders of the time felt threatened by what they called a new religion, "the way", which were the followers of Jesus Christ. When they could not contain the truth, and as more and more people became followers of the way of Jesus Christ, the religious leaders of that time conspired to silence Jesus. Their hatred of Him was so great that they willingly accepted a known insurrectionist in the place of an innocent and sinless Jesus.

The Pharisees and Sadducees ordered the death of Jesus by crucifixion. The Son of God had done no wrong in this world. It is this same world system that continues to reject Jesus to this day. The following two verses show how a Holy God views those who love this world: James 4:4 "You adulterous people! Do you not know that friendship with the world is enmity with God? Therefore whoever wishes to be a friend of the world makes himself an enemy of God".

Romans 12:2 *"Do not be conformed to this world, but be transformed by the renewal of your mind, that by testing you may discern what is the will of God, what is good and acceptable and perfect."*

God warns us not to love this world because the world system of man is under the control or sway of the enemy of our soul, the devil. We learn from the Apostle Paul in his Epistle 2 Corinthians 4:4, *"In whom the god of this world hath blinded the minds of them which believe not, lest the light of the glorious gospel of Christ, who is the image of God, should shine unto them"*. Paul says that the devil has blinded the minds of all unbelievers and this allows the prince of this world, the devil, to easily control them.

Think about it. If something or someone can control what you think, it then can control what you do. Amen. The devil knows this and his attacks are almost always against our minds. Race hatred, sexual perversion, jealousy, and envy are just a few negative thought patterns which always start in the heart of the victim. However, these malicious ideas can become deadly if they are put into actual practice.

The world wants man to distrust the God of the Bible and to put their trust in themselves. For example, the world trusts power, money, political authority, and religions that shape God into the image of man rather than trusts the God of the bible. The world constantly looks for and invents new strategies of luring people away from the Cross. The devil hates the Cross of God because he knows that the Cross is symbolic to his complete destruction.

I believe there is another modern day lure or trick that the world, under the control of the devil, uses against man, and that is Halloween. This ungodly celebration has nothing to do with giving glory or worshipping God. God says all unrighteousness is sin. That said why would adult men and women, some who call themselves Christians, spend their hard-earned money worshipping a pagan holiday? Pagan worship in the Old Testament was an abomination to a Holy God. Since God does not change, any worship of any other deity, false or otherwise, is not pleasing in His sight. The yearly celebration of Halloween gets bigger each year because its underlying foundation is witchcraft and satanic worship which brings into view a whole different view on wickedness. Grown men and women will spend large sums of money to dress up as the dead, with ghoulish costumes and their faces made up hideously dis-figured with fake blood and rotten teeth to make it look as if they are zombies. This is indirectly giving worship to Satan. Many of these same people will argue that Halloween is a harmless holiday. They fail to realize that is what the devil wants them to think. If what I read is correct, the Halloween celebration comes from a dark pagan festival called "Sah-ween". Sah-ween supposedly marked a specific time each year when the human world came within close contact with the spirit world.

Halloween is big business in this country. I read in the newspaper today that the National Retail Federation is predicting the ghoulish holiday spending will peak today at 6.9 billion. They predict that adults will spend 1.22 billion dollars on themselves vs. 1.04 billion dollars for kids. Halloween candy purchases will come in around 2.08 billion dollars, thus making Halloween the biggest ever candy selling day in the country. I have never been a fan of the Halloween celebration. I see Halloween as a sneaky way that the devil has devised to get people to worship him. Make no mistake about it. The devil loves worship. This is why in the book of St. Matthew, we learn how the devil tried to get the Lord of Glory, Jesus Christ, to fall down and to worship him. The devil wants people to worship him and not God.

Again, let's review that passage of scripture: *"Then was Jesus led up of the Spirit into the wilderness to be tempted of the devil. 2And when he had fasted forty days and forty nights, he was afterward an hungred. 3And when the tempter came to him, he said, If thou be the Son of God, command that these stones be made bread. 4But he answered and said, It is written, Man shall not live by bread alone, but by every word that proceedeth out of the mouth of God. 5Then the devil taketh him up into the holy city, and setteth him on a pinnacle of the temple, 6And saith unto him, If thou be the Son of God, cast thyself down: for it is written, He shall give his angels charge concerning thee: and in their hands they shall bear thee up, lest at any time thou dash thy foot against a stone. 7Jesus said unto him, it is written again, Thou shalt not tempt the Lord thy God. 8Again, the devil taketh him up into an exceeding high mountain, and sheweth him all the kingdoms of the world, and the glory of them; 9And saith unto him, All these things will I give thee, if thou wilt fall down and worship me. 10Then saith Jesus unto him, Get thee hence, Satan: for it is written, Thou shalt worship the Lord thy God, and him only shalt thou serve. 11Then the devil leaveth him, and, behold, angels came and ministered unto him"*.

Note: if the devil is bold enough to try and get the Son of God to worship him, what about us? The devil is a spiritual terrorist. He wages spiritual warfare against the people of God every day. He seeks first to blind our minds against the reality of a Risen Savior. If he is successful, then he has control over our life. Unbelief in God, by default, makes you a believer and worshipper of Satan. There is only one faith, one God, one baptism. Any faith other than the Gospel of Jesus Christ is not of God. It is a system that says it is okay for humans to consider alternative forms of marriage. It is a system that tries to make or remake God to fit their image of God. It is the same spirit that Jesus confronted when He walked this earth. It was this spirit of unbelief by His chosen people that led to the rejection and the crucifixion of the Son of God. The world system of man honors the god of money, power, sexual pleasure, immorality, and political politics and so on. The system of man is controlled by the god of this world – Satan.

The world is in need of a spiritual revival. Crime rates have increased to include mass killings, robberies, rapes, and many other deviant crimes. When we combine those crimes with high unemployment, we can see an increase in apostasy away from the Word of God. It is as if the younger generation is walking away from a spiritual awakening with the Almighty. It's seems they are rejecting Christianity as old fashioned. Many are turning to the occult, and some turn to other religions. We are losing our youth to the many tricks of the devil. Yes, we, our families, our communities, our state, our nation, and the world, need a revival. However, a revival can only happen if it comes from God. Man cannot initiate a personal revival. We learn in 2 Chronicles 7:14 that, *"If my people, which are called by my name, shall humble themselves, and pray, and seek my face, and turn from their wicked ways; then will I hear from heaven, and will forgive their sin, and will heal their land"*. When God says "if", He is talking to His people, the people who have professed to believe in Him. He is not talking to the confirmed unbeliever, or to people who have rejected His Son, Those people, if they remain in an unrepentant state, will die in their sins and be eternally judged and forever separated from God. They will suffer eternal damnation and burn forever in hell. That is their fate! Believer, you need to get off the fence and show some sign that you are what you say you are. If you are saved, who are you leading to Christ? Start with your own family and represent Christ in your home. The life you live, your Christian behavior, love, and prayer, start in your own home first. You are the priest of your home; you need to act like it. If you are saved, no one should expect to hear loud vulgar music blasting from your home. Additionally, profane language, arguments, temper tantrums, adultery, fornications, and drug dealings, are not things that a child of God will engage in.

I want to reiterate the wise words of King Solomon from his book of Ecclesiastes 12:13-14. This very wise man is telling all that will listen that when it comes to the finality and judgment of this life, on that day, God will want to know did we fear Him and did we keep His commandments. This is your assigned duty, old man. God is going to bring into judgment all the deeds of your life. Nothing can or will be hidden from Him. All the things, good or bad, that were done in the flesh will be revealed. If you died in a state of unbelief, you will not be able to use this as an excuse by saying: "Lord, I was wrong to be an unbeliever. I now want to repent and change my lifestyle and start to believe in you". The main reason you want to become a believer now is because you can see and smell the reality of Hell staring you in the face. At the Judgment Seat of Christ, it will be too late to apologize for a life lived arrogantly in disrespect and outright denial of the existence of a Holy God. In a real sense, you refused to believe in God; you refused to repent. Therefore, based on the life that you lived, you wanted to go to Hell. That will be where God will send you.

My final appeal is to all unbelievers to repent and seek God. Learn of Him. Have faith in Jesus, and seek to do what is righteous. Don't let the devil blind your mind into thinking there is no God. Our God is a merciful and loving God. He does not wish anyone to go to hell. He wants all to come to Him in repentance. He tells us in Revelation 3:20 that: *"Behold, I stand at the door, and knock: if any man hear my voice, and open the door, I will come in to him, and will sup with him, and he with me"*.

The book of Revelation has 22 chapters and it was not my goal to give a detailed review and discussion on this very profound and complex book. It is my suggestion that you take it upon yourself to read and study this book. I will say if you have never read the Bible before, you might want to start in the book of Genesis. As you progress through the entire Bible with a sincere heart of seeking God, with the help of the Holy Spirit, you will gain some understanding of this complex book, Revelation. I am not suggesting that if you have never serious studied the Bible that you just jump right into Revelation and begin reading it. As I have said before, the book of Revelation is not for beginners.

To the drug dealers, prostitutes, and drug users, stop and repent and ask God to forgive you for your sins. Life is so precious, and you cannot afford to spend any of your short time on this earth under the influence of a controlled substance that the devil uses to destroy us. I do believe that if the drug dealer dies in his sins as a drug dealer, there is a special place in Hell waiting just for him, because, the drugs that he sells have ruined the lives of countless families. Young women and girls have entered into sexual sin (prostitution) and have become trapped by drug use. They end up selling their most precious possession, their bodies, just to purchase drugs to satisfy an out-of-control drug habit. Yes, Mr. Drug Dealer, you have destroyed many people's lives, and you never bothered to care or consider the consequences of your actions as some young child watched in silence as her mother sold her body to get more money to get high. This same child watched you slap her around just because she could not pay you the money that she owed you for buying drugs on credit. This poor child went hungry many nights because her mother was hooked on your drugs. You never cared that the young men that you hired to pimp or sell your crack cocaine and other drugs, risked their very lives or freedom just to sell your product. If they were killed, you just found another young person struggling to make it to take their place. Money is the god of the drug dealer. I have seen drug dealers kill members of their own immediate family over a drug dispute.

Most hardcore drug dealers have disrespect for the God of the Bible. You tell yourself that He is not real. Well, one day you will meet this God; what will you have to say then? Silence, is what you will be told, and you will listen and be judged according to your sins. You will not escape, and your entire drug dealing bravado will not help you.

To the same-sex people who know that this is wrong, yet, you still persist in having your way; my Bible tells me unapologetically, it is wrong for two men to lie together as man and wife. In Leviticus 18:22 it says: *"Thou shalt not lie with mankind, as with womankind: It is an abomination to God".* Moreover, in the book of Romans 1:26-27, in reference to the act of homosexuality between the sexes, scripture states: *"For this reason God gave them up to degrading passions. Their women exchanged natural intercourse for unnatural, and in the same way also the men, giving up natural intercourse with women, were consumed with passion for one another. Men committed shameless acts with men and received in their own persons the due penalty for their error."* This pattern of same sex immorality is on the increase throughout our nation and our world. The Bible says *"woe to those who call evil good and good evil"* God is not mocked. *Whatever a man soweth that shall you also reap".*

I have not always done what was right in my own life. But my God was merciful to me in spite of my iniquities. He has shown me many things. In many ways, I was a lot like Jonah, God was calling me to go in one direction, and I would go in just the opposite direction. When God put it into my mind to write this book, I rebelled. I put it off as long as I could, but God would not let me off the hook that easily. His patience is way beyond our human understanding. Lesson learned: when God wants you to do something, you will do it. Fortunately for me, I was not quite as stubborn as Jonah; I did not have to learn the hard way by spending three nights in the belly of a whale.

To review, some of the past close encounters that I have had with God the Father, Jesus Christ, and the Holy Spirit were:

- The Invisible Hand
- The Mysterious Sign of God
- A Very Large Bird
- The Ice-Cream Truck
- The Night our House Caught on Fire
- The Death of my Grandfather
- The Death of my Brother Tommy – and the Vision at the Grave, and Passing the Truck
- The Death of my Father
- The Death of my Son – and How this Changed my Life.
- The Vision of heaven as I was Driving Home from Work
- The Abortion Vision
- Isaiah 54:14-17 and the Vision of the Letters on the Page
- The Cancerous Years for my Wife and Me
- The Vision of the Moon When I was to Sleepy to Drive
- The Cancerous Years Returned
- The Vision at Barnes Jewish Hospital and the Spirit that Walked In

These are just some of the things that God has blessed me to see; there are others. I did not list everything because as it is, I am of the opinion that many of you will think that I am making these things up. I assure you that I am not.

My Prayer for all who read this book:

"Lord, my prayer is that you open the eyes, hearts, and minds of each and every reader of this book; especially the unbeliever and allow them to see You. Lord, my prayer is that this book will cause people to repent of their sins and focus on Jesus Christ. That they seek Him, by reading and studying the Word of God".

"Lord I pray for all sinners who do not know you in the pardoning of their sins. I also pray that you bless me to reach and plant the seeds of righteousness and belief in Jesus Christ and that many souls are saved".

The Story of Three Little Pigs

I want to end this book with a very old children's fable that we all at some point in our lives have heard. There is a certain ring of truth in this little short story that has profound spiritual implications as to the quality of material that we use to construct our lives.

Think of the big bad wolf as the devil. Think of the devil's desire to kill, steal or destroy each of the little pigs. Think of each little pig as being a human who uses three different kinds of material to build their life. Think of the advice given by the parent (Jesus, the anointed of God) who told Peter that *"on this Rock I will build my church, and the gates of hell will not prevail against it"*.

In case you have forgotten the story of the three little pigs, I will share it here for you:

"Once upon a time there were three little pigs and the time came for them to leave home and seek their fortunes. Before they left, their mother told them "Whatever you do, do it the best that you can because that's the way to get along in the world.

The first little pig built his house out of straw because it was the easiest thing to do. The second little pig built his house out of sticks. This was a little bit stronger than a straw house. The third little pig built his house out of bricks. One night the big bad wolf, who dearly loved to eat fat little piggy's, came along and saw the first little pig in his house of straw. He said "Let me in, let me in little pig, or I'll huff and I'll puff and I'll blow your house in!" "Not by the hair of my chinny-chin-chin", said the little pig. But of course the wolf did blow the house in and ate the first little pig.

The wolf then came to the house of sticks. "Let me in, let me in, little pig or I'll huff and I'll puff and I'll blow your house in." "Not by the hair of my chinny-chin-chin", said the little pig. But the wolf blew that house in too, and ate the second little pig. The wolf then came to the house of bricks. "Let me in, let me in" cried the wolf, "Or I'll huff and I'll puff till I blow your house in" "Not by the hair of my chinny-chin-chin" said the pig.

Well, the wolf huffed and puffed but he could not blow down that brick house. But the wolf was a sly old wolf and he climbed up on the roof to look for a way into the brick house. The little pig saw the wolf climb up on the roof and lit a roaring fire in the fireplace and placed on it a large kettle of water. When the wolf finally found the hole in the chimney he crawled down and "KERSPLASH!" right into that kettle of water and that was the end of his troubles with the big bad wolf.

The next day the little pig invited his mother over. She said "You see it is just as I told you. The way to get along in the world is to do things as well as you can." Fortunately for that little pig, he learned that lesson. And he just lived happily ever after!

The principle to be learned from this very old fable is also a spiritual truth that is taught throughout the Bible. The question that each living soul should ask is "What kind of material am I using to construct and build my life, and will the material that I am using to build my life sustain me through the trials of life? Will my life stand up to the big bad wolf-the devil - and his demons? At the end of my life, will the material that I have invested a lifetime in sustain me in the afterlife called eternity?"

The answer to those personal questions is if you have wrapped yourself up in the Blood of Jesus, you are covered. Any other material will not last or hold up when the big bad wolf (the devil) comes knocking. Only the material of Jesus will last in this life and the life to come. Therefore, I want to say again to all the unbelievers, what factual proof you have on which to base your unbelief? Yes, you might be an intellectual scholar, so what? I promise you that if you study history you will find people a lot smarter than you that were believers. You had better be certain of your beliefs before you reject Jesus Christ, because there is no other way for a man to be saved. If you continue in your rejection of the only way to salvation, you will die in your sins and be eternally separated from God. Make sure; be very sure, that you understand that the position of the unbeliever is "anti-God". To the rich man who sees his money and power as his god, I have one word for you: repent! Use your money to help the poor and put your trust in God. I would advise the rich man to review and take to heart the story of the rich man that is recorded in Luke 16:19-31. Additionally, the unbelieving rich man who sees his money and power as his god should review the story of the rich fool that is found in Luke 12:13-21. When it comes to your time to leave this world, your human wealth, position, and power, will mean nothing to a Holy God at the Judgment Seat of life.

To all people under the control of drugs, lust of the flesh, lust of the eyes, and the pride of life (the world), I say stop! Seek the Son of God- Jesus and His righteousness. He can and will break the cycle of oppression, obsession, and possession in your life. I don't care how long you have been a crack cocaine abuser, a prostitute, drug dealer, hustler, robber, thief, whatever it is in life that Satan has put on you to control your life, the answer is Jesus Christ. You must seek Him with a broken and contrite spirit, and He can and will be found if you want Him. Nothing can separate you from the love of God if you truly want to be saved.

I am reminded of a quote that I once read by a well-known and famous pastor, teacher, writer and a gift to the world, a very spiritual man by the name of T. D. Jakes. I don't know if Mr. Jakes actually coined this particular phrase, but the saying has made a lifelong spiritual impact in my life. He said: ***"I would rather live my life as if there is a God and die to find out there isn't, than to live my life as if there isn't a God and die and find there*** *is."*

This is an example of building a house with the right material. The unbeliever is confident that there is no God, so he is careless in the material that he selects to build his life. Therefore in the day of his calamity, he will live and die in this boastful arrogance that in this life there is no God. Wisdom shouts to all that will listen, it is better to have it and not need it than to need it and not have it. The key word here is to be prepared, choose wisely the material that you will use to construct your life. If the material says "nonbelief", reject it. If the material says "washed in the Blood of the Lamb", buy it, and wrap your life in it.

I feel this was a powerful and wise word from one of most profound deep-thinking pastors in the ministry today. That is just my opinion. Jack Graham is another pastor that I think is placed here on earth to bless us with his prophetic wisdom. There are many more.

Finally, I want to save the best for last. I want to close this book with a warning from our Lord and Savior Jesus Christ. The warning is about what is soon to come upon this world. The warning is found in Revelation from Chapter 1 through Chapter 22.

Revelation–Chapter 22:16-21

16"I Jesus have sent mine angel to testify unto you these things in the churches. I am the root and the offspring of David, and the bright and morning star. 17And the Spirit and the bride say, Come. And let him that heareth say, Come. And let him that is athirst come. And whosoever will, let him take the water of life freely. 18For I testify unto every man that heareth the words of the prophecy of this book, If any man shall add unto these things, God shall add unto him the plagues that are written in this book: 19And if any man shall take away from the words of the book of this prophecy, God shall take away his part out of the book of life, and out of the holy city, and from the things which are written in this book. 20He which testifieth these things saith, surely I come quickly. Amen. Even so, come, Lord Jesus. 21The grace of our Lord Jesus Christ be with you all. Amen". Amen, and to God be the Glory!

Jude 1:24-25

"Now unto him that is able to keep you from falling, and to present you faultless before the presence of his glory with exceeding joy, to the only wise God our Saviour, be glory and majesty, dominion and power, both now and ever. Amen".

Last warning: If you do not know God, get to know Him through His Son Jesus Christ. Do not let the devil deceive and trick you into becoming a non-believer. The sin of "unbelief" as mentioned in John 16:9 is the worst sin which anyone can have on this earth. It is the sin that stamps "rejection" of the Son of God on man's eternally lost soul before a Holy God. The sin of unbelief tells God that you do not need or trust Him. This sin tells God Almighty that you do not appreciate the price that His Son Jesus paid for all on Calvary's Hill.

Proverbs 26:12 says *"Seest thou a man wise in his own conceit? There is more hope of a fool than of him."* Please don't be like this man. Seek and get to know the Lord. He says, *"Take my yoke upon you, and learn of me; for I am meek and lowly in heart: and ye shall find rest. For my yoke is easy, and my burden is light."*

The road of life that each of us are traveling will eventually end up at one of the two doors of life. The life we live will provide a key that will, by default, open the door that corresponds to our life and our beliefs. The path to the one door is wide and full of people who are proud people, boastful and sure of their destination. They have lived a life full of self-pride and self-pleasure. They proudly proclaim they are unbelievers and mock those who are. Many of these people are powerful and rich. Many have rejected marriage as a sacred institution of God. They do not know that the road they are traveling on is leading straight to Hell. Behind the door that their life will open, is eternal separation from God. Therefore to all confessed unbelievers in God, before you die in your unbelief, you had better be sure of your choice. There will not be a second chance to undo or relive your life in the flesh.

The small quiet road is one that not many people look for, but through the help of the Holy Spirit, we find it through faith. This road leads to a special door. Your faith in Jesus Christ is demonstrated by the life that you have lived. You have strived to keep His commandments. Through many trials and tribulations you kept the faith. You were an overcomer of the sins of this world. The life that you lived opens the door to eternal oneness with the Father of Glory. As you walk this small road, you begin to see a beautiful city that sparkles like a diamond in the sun. The closer you get to this beautiful city, you hear angels cheering for you and as you get to the huge pearly gates, the doors open and you hear a mighty voice coming from behind an unapproachable light that says: "well done my good and faithful servant, welcome to the kingdom of God".

REFERENCES

All scriptural references used in this book are from the King James Version of the Holy Bible.

Easton's Illustrated Dictionary

Webster's New Collegiate Dictionary